T0329799

Financial Stability

Financial Stability

Fraud, Confidence, and the Wealth of Nations

FREDERICK L. FELDKAMP
R. CHRISTOPHER WHALEN

WILEY

Published by John Wiley & Sons, Inc., Hoboken, New Jersey.
Published simultaneously in Canada.

For general information on our other products and services or for technical support, please
contact our Customer Care Department within the United States at (800) 762-2974, outside
the United States at (317) 572-3993, or fax (317) 572-4002.

Wiley publishes in a variety of print and electronic formats and by print-on-demand. Some
material included with standard print versions of this book may not be included in e-books or
in print-on-demand. If this book refers to media such as a CD or DVD that is not included in
the version you purchased, you may download this material at http://booksupport.wiley.com.
For more information about Wiley products, visit www.wiley.com.

Library of Congress Cataloging-in-Publication Data:

Feldkamp, Frederick L.
    Financial stability : fraud, confidence and the wealth of nations / Frederick L. Feldkamp
and R. Christopher Whalen.
    1 online resource. — (Wiley finance series)
    Includes index.
    Description based on print version record and CIP data provided by publisher; resource
not viewed.
    ISBN 978-1-118-93581-1 (epdf) — ISBN 978-1-118-93580-4 (epub) —
ISBN 978-1-118-93579-8 (hardback) 1. Financial crises—History. 2. Economic security—
History. 3. Fiscal policy—History. 4. Finance—History. I. Whalen, R. Christopher,
1959– II. Title.
    HB3722
    338.5′42—dc23
                                                                        2014027073

Printed in the United States of America.
10 9 8 7 6 5 4 3 2 1

To Judy
For ever-enduring my folly
—Fred Feldkamp

To Nicole
For making me smile again
—Chris Whalen

$$TRANSPARENCY + \frac{FREEDOM}{EXCHANGE-FRAUD}$$

$$\downarrow$$

$$PERPETUAL\ (RECONCILIATION + PROSPERITY + LIFE)$$

---

*Chinese characters for "crisis".

Contents

Figures, Tables, and Charts

Preface

As He died to make men holy, let us live to make men free,
While God is marching on.

"Battle Hymn of the Republic"
Julia Ward Howe

Christ was crucified in the same city where, in Jewish, Christian, and Islamic tradition, God stopped Abraham from sacrificing his son, Isaac. Christianity holds that God allowed Jesus to be crucified as the grant of universal forgiveness to mankind. The stage for that act of sacrifice was set by Christ's declaration that freedom would overpower both a brutal Roman dictatorship and the economic fraud of a high priest that violated many laws of his own faith. In death Christ made us holy, and, in resurrection, showed the path to freedom, forgiving even His murderers.

Today, technology allows precise calculation of the greater value of freedom over dictatorship and fraud. We are certainly not holy; by combining the ancient laws of Moses and mathematics with modern data (see Charts 9.1, 9.2, and 9.3 and Chapter 9), however, this book shows:

1. In the crisis of 2007–2009, a modern day worldwide money changers' fraud caused investors to lose $67 trillion ($30 trillion in the United States alone).
2. By 2013, the 2009–2012 recovery of free markets was rebuilding wealth at $34 trillion per year ($17 trillion in the United States).

With the United States as the guarantor of freedom following World War II, Germany has chosen almost 70 years of peace and prosperity over the powers of a king and a dictator that led it to pursue the two most widespread wars in history. Germany stood with the United States early in 2014 to challenge a Russian menace over Ukraine. Measured by similar principles, the cost to Russia of Vladimir Putin's pursuit of new dominion in Ukraine was a more than 50 percent devaluation of Russian wealth.

Using rates for 10-year bonds as the metric, the value of each dollar of U.S. cash flow (over 30 years) is now more than twice that of Russian cash flow. Because it can rely on U.S. production for assistance in defense (as Russia did when Germany attacked it in World War II), the value to Germany of its cash flows is now 2.4 times that of Russia's. That's the merit of living "to make men free" versus today's cost of aggression.

Experience is knowledge gained through our blunders; wisdom is knowledge gained by understanding others' blunders. The United States is the world's oldest democratic republic, but also is still a very young nation. We blundered along for nearly 175 years before our Constitution and courts finally granted universal suffrage: one person, one vote. Americans are still trying to understand how free markets operate. We will try not to bore readers as we describe our experiences and repeat the wisdom of others that developed today's U.S. financial markets, the world's best. Few subjects, however, are more likely to induce boredom than the details of finance.

Fraud was defined in the laws of Moses. It was only in response to the 1929 market crash, however, that the United States finally ended some of the off-balance sheet liability frauds of the Gilded Age and the robber barons. Before the United States enacted revolutionary banking and securities laws in 1933 and 1934, speculators used parent company–only financial statements to hide fraudulent schemes under pyramids of subsidiaries and trusts. Mandatory accounting consolidation ended many such practices, but it did not stop the frauds that hid the manipulations and speculations that burst into new financial crises decades later.

This book describes some of the many blunders that are now part of the U.S. financial market experience. The financial crisis of 2007–2009 proved, for example, why we must end the use of all off-balance sheet liabilities. In this book we'll explain why that is and how to do financial transactions properly. Investors now know that by the time the subprime crisis had exploded, gigantic bubbles of unreported liability had grown, over the course of several decades, to $67 trillion worldwide and $30 trillion in the United States alone. In 2007, that accumulated megabubble burst upon an unsuspecting world. That $67 trillion of unreported claims against shareholder equity nearly destroyed all the wealth created since Moses. Some people still wonder how that hidden fraud triggered a massive flight to quality in 2008. It was a bubble hidden in fraudulent off-balance sheet transactions and made viral by accumulated megablunders.

The last time a similar financial crisis occurred, Franklin Roosevelt said: "The only thing we have to fear is fear itself." Because of technology and the disclosure requirements that have been in existence since 2005, the United States now precisely measures the level of U.S. corporate bond investors' fear on a daily basis. Daily disclosure of corporate bond spreads allows leaders to know whether investors deem their daily decisions to be wisdom that will attract new money or blunders that will drive investors away. Before they sit down to dinner, leaders in the United States can now know the actual benefit or cost of their actions with respect to the free market.

The Enron debacle caused the United States to perfect the measures of fear that are contained in bond spreads. These measures are not available at a similar level of precision anywhere else. Except for Ben Bernanke and a few others, however, U.S. leaders largely ignored the new indicators until September 2008. By then the bubble of fraud had burst. It was too late to fine-tune a response. So the United States and its allies were compelled to employ an age-old process: nationalization cum monetization. That expedient saved the financial world by creating a temporary bridge of disclosed liquidity to aid us as we try to convert the experience of our 1998–2008 blunders into wisdom for the future.

Whether other nations elect the path of wisdom over the harder path of experience is up to them. On March 3, 2014, available measures of investor fear warned Vladimir Putin that it was a blunder for Russia to intervene in the free-market development of Ukraine, just as Adam Smith warned King George III that it would be better to trade amicably with Britain's American colonies than to try to dominate them.

To its initial credit, Russia seemed to show wisdom. It backed away from overt threats, but the choice of learning by the experience of repeating its blunders still seems to guide Russia. During the period of perestroika, Mikhail Gorbachev lamented the servile patience of many Russians. Far too many people, there and elsewhere, seem willing to wait, perhaps forever, for personal and economic freedom. While Jesus lived, Hillel the Elder is credited with saying: "If not us, who, and if not now, when?" We hope wisdom, and the peace and prosperity it offers, will prevail in the world and believe now is as good a time as any to cultivate it. When peace wins, as George Marshall showed Russia after World War II, it can redeem all its current losses. We submit that financial stability is vital to that success.

This book began as a way to thank Robert M. Fisher, a lawyer and economist at the SEC who, 11 years ago, listened patiently for five hours as Fred Feldkamp explained a process some clients had perfected to generate stand-alone financial transactions that create risk-free arbitrages for financial assets, such as home mortgages and automotive loans. Done correctly, that private sector innovation, collateralized mortgage obligations (or CMOs), was the process by which the United States finally brought equilibrium to bond markets. Created in 1983 for residential mortgage markets, and spreading to other financial asset markets in 1993, the CMO expanded sources of finance and economic opportunities in an economy that for decades had been dominated by strictly controlled commercial banks. Similar processes to create financial arbitrage were used by central banks to bring financial markets out of crises in 2009–2013. In the hands of private-sector investors, riskless financial arbitrage is the foundation on which investors can sustain financial stability and economic prosperity around the world.

After listening for all those hours, Mr. Fisher looked at Fred and said, "You've just described the solution for financial stability, the last unsolved problem of macroeconomics."

About two years after that meeting, the SEC insisted that pricing, size, and other details of all U.S. corporate bond trades be immediately reported via the TRACE (Trade Reporting and Compliance Engine) system. Soon thereafter, a self-regulatory group called the Financial Industry Regulatory Authority, or FINRA, used that data to begin publishing daily real-time yield indices that allow all investors to see each day's movements in credit spreads, information bankers regularly and carefully hid from competitors in the past.

Credit spreads measure the difference in yield between corporate bonds of different grades. They reflect the precise fear response of investors to daily changes in (1) U.S. market policy and (2) all other events with market implications for investors in corporate bonds. Charts 9.1, 9.2, and 9.3 in Chapter 9 show how credit spreads moved up and down in U.S. markets between 2007 and the writing of this book. Table 9.1 translates that data to reveal the macroeconomic impact of changes in credit spreads.

This book thanks Mr. Fisher for the countless hours of fun—and profit— Fred has enjoyed using credit spread data to anticipate market events and to commend or criticize policy actions since retiring in 2006 from his active law firm partnership.

By noting U.S. bond investors' actual cash trading patterns in response to events each day, and by aggregating that data in a few simple charts, politicians and regulators were able to accurately observe investors' reactions to each step leading to the worldwide financial collapse of 2007–2009. When the dust settled, they were likewise able to track the success and failure of each step to reform U.S. markets and to observe the rise and fall of credit spreads during each of several lesser crises that have affected worldwide investors since 2009.

Each business day, this bond data is published about 90 minutes after the closing bell rings at the New York Stock Exchange. Each evening after the market close, therefore, everyone who is interested in the reaction of the bond market to what transpired that day can learn whether U.S. leaders succeeded or failed. The data allows for instant course corrections, or celebrations, as applicable.

For the first time in the history of finance, everyone has real-time data, generated by actual cash trades, to understand whether policy actions impress or disgust millions of bond investors who vote with trillions of dollars every single day in response to the actions of world leaders. This data provides the facts needed to replace political rhetoric with knowledge, whether acquired by wisdom or blunder.

Everyone can and should vote at elections. Between those events, however, every economist worth hearing or reading understands, generally speaking, that it is only investors' votes that determine the success or failure of leaders' actions. Market indicators like the Dow Jones Industrial Average, the Federal funds rate, and the yield on the 10-year Treasury bond are, after all, the ultimate barometers of political as well as financial success for any U.S. president, Federal Reserve Board chairman, or congressional leader.

As research for this book progressed Fred realized that, when looking at bond spreads, we are not just observing events that impacted the last decade in the United States. Over the centuries, most economic observers had no idea how to generate an accurate and instantaneous daily measure of the fear that drives capital markets. So, this project grew a little bit. As Fred researched the subject further, he began to discuss his findings with Chris Whalen, his friend and coauthor.

Over years of friendship and collaboration, it occurred to the authors that the ebb and flow of confidence and fear in all markets is the essential quality that determines financial and economic stability, and, ultimately, the wealth of nations. The United States is the only nation that has institutionalized the measurement of financial stability by making daily credit spread and other corporate bond market information widely available.

What we observe as daily problems in U.S. corporate bond markets (before, during, and after the Great Recession) has caused crises and wars for perhaps 4,000 years. In *A History of Modern Europe: From the Renaissance to the Present,* John Merriman notes that "Early in the sixteenth century, an Italian exile told the king of France what the monarch would need to attack the duchy of Milan: 'Three things are necessary, money, more money and still more money.'" He was describing the relationship between currency debasement and military conflicts (Merriman 2010).

Until 1776, when Adam Smith won praise for publishing a treatise that differentiated central banking from reserve banking, brave individuals who openly opposed their rulers' use of monetary policy to maintain power and fund wars were regularly executed. In the twentieth century, the expanding use of finance to create new economic opportunities democratized the money game. The fact that investors can vote with their money now empowers individuals to curb bad policy decisions by their leaders.

The solution to financial instability has been sought for at least 2,000 years. We submit that it lies in the public reporting of credit spreads and other bond market data, and in the use of financial structures that contain spreads. Hopefully the financial crisis of 2007–2009 will move us closer to a true democratization of finance and lessen the possibility of future economic dislocations and wars. If we implement the solution correctly, the world can anticipate when the system is beginning to fall out of balance (due to fraud or other sources of instability) and invest whatever it takes to save the world. Once saved, we can sort out a cure that addresses the cause of the crisis.

Central bankers in the United States, United Kingdom, Europe, and Japan have proven that they understood what had to be done in the wake of the financial crisis to raise the value of the economies they guide and restore investor confidence. The question is whether we can institutionalize this knowledge to limit market swings between fear and euphoria and thereby greatly increase the economic well-being of all free people.

Frederick Feldkamp
Christopher Whalen
June 2014

Introduction

This book applies law, logic, and financial history to macroeconomics. Macroeconomics is the branch of economic study that concerns itself with expanding the pie of society. Microeconomics, by far the larger and older branch of economics, concerns itself with expanding the piece of the pie claimed by a particular firm or individual. Microeconomists consider the impact of others' actions on one firm or individual at a particular moment. Macroeconomists look at an aggregate motion picture created by the millions of offsetting actions that firms and individuals generate for their individual economic benefit.

With one major exception, modest changes in macroeconomic variables all produce offsets. Beginning with Adam Smith in the 1700s, every macroeconomist eventually discovered that one variable—the competitive cost of money, represented by credit spread—consistently increases macroeconomic activity when favorable (low) and destroys economic activity when unfavorable (high). Low and stable credit spreads produce, and are indicators of, financial stability. Every credit crisis begins with a sharp decline in confidence and a commensurate increase or upward spike in credit spreads.

Financial stability is the holy grail of macroeconomics, but it is also a very difficult thing to achieve in a free society. Every respectable economist understands that the world's ability to sustain long-term growth has been impaired because we have not, to date, solved the problem of sustaining financial stability in a free market. Each time we observe a period of liquidity-driven growth, we convince ourselves that this problem has been solved. Inevitably, it seems, that's when a new financial crisis or market crash shatters our optimism. The desire for economic prosperity and the freedom to pursue it seemingly ensures acts of fraud and indifference that result in financial instability. Albert M. Wojnilower of Craig Drill Capital wrote in March 2014, "We have booms and depressions not because of lack of economic expertise, but because they are hardwired into human nature."

The first widely reported effort to remedy fraudulent practices that cause financial crises occurred in the time of Jesus of Nazareth. He observed that fellow Jews celebrating Passover were being overcharged to exchange Roman money for Temple money. Since the days of Moses, it has been considered a fraud to use two measures. That's the very essence of the term

1

duplicity. As the week of His crucifixion began, Jesus observed how the high priest profited by the fraud and He famously chased the money changers out of the Temple and into the competition of an open market. His action began a tortured journey that created a new religion but also provides a powerful example of the contrast and conflict between free and transparent markets and markets that are corrupt and fraudulent.

Jesus of Nazareth challenged the fraud of the high priest of His day and was killed. After Jesus' crucifixion, His Jewish backers tried to reform Temple practices, and their next leader was killed as well. That led to a revolt among Jerusalem's peasants, which got redirected at the Romans who supported the Temple priests (it was convenient for collecting taxes). Rome eventually responded to the revolt by the same tactic used in Carthage—it killed everyone in sight, razed the Temple, and destroyed Jerusalem in 70 CE.

Thousands of people have subsequently sought to free financial markets from similar monopoly practices and frauds. Inevitably, those efforts to impose transparency and fair dealing seem only to foster new forms of financial manipulation that, in turn, generate new cycles of crisis that bankrupt guilty and innocent investors alike. Coming out of what may be the worst worldwide financial market collapse ever, it is challenging for us to suggest that anything can change this depressing cycle of human error. Human beings, after all, are constantly seeking new ways to earn a livelihood. Finance has ever been among the most popular avenues to attain this goal, especially in cases in which the markets can be rigged to increase profits.

In 2013, Fred Feldkamp experienced the same currency exchange scam (in a Christian church, no less) that Jesus saw at the Temple in Jerusalem. In Christian theology, Christ's prayer on the cross sought forgiveness even for His killers. He said they did not know what they were doing. In that regard, a great deal has changed. Today, everyone can know and expose a money changer's scam.

We now have data (and means for instant worldwide distribution) that allow victims of fraud to avoid being duped. We have large and liquid markets that provide limitless alternatives to the acceptance of scams. All major equity markets instantly and continuously broadcast the precise level of stock investors' interest worldwide, throughout each trading day. Most governments, however, continue to concentrate (and/or control) credit allocation and pricing within their banking enterprises, but even that is changing.

Through a process that began in 1971 (and may now be approaching completion), the United States has developed the world's largest and most open corporate bond market. The operations of the major U.S. banks and federal housing agencies still effectively control the market for mortgage finance, and that remains a significant problem to be resolved. The market for corporate credit, however, is now so large that it is impractical for

U.S. banks or even the Federal Reserve to control credit pricing and allocation over the long term.

Daily information relating to U.S. bond market activity is now so accurate that regulators have been able to prove manipulation of several private-sector credit pricing procedures (e.g., the Libor—London Interbank Offered Rate—cases, and more recent commodity and swap index investigations).

The United States suffered several major crises as it created this corporate credit market, but the result is the world's best hope for gaining and sustaining financial stability. Privately reported daily indices that reveal the temperature of U.S. corporate bond markets were first published in 1987. A breakthrough, however, occurred in 2005. That's when the U.S. Securities and Exchange Commission (SEC) ordered instant reporting of corporate bond trades. Soon after, FINRA (the Financial Industry Regulatory Authority) began reporting the daily bond indices that were used day by day to monitor the 2007–2009 crisis and to create Charts 9.1, 9.2, and 9.3 in Chapter 9 of this book.

This transparency illustrates how the financial crisis of 2007–2009 became the first worldwide market crash in which every concerned citizen and policy maker could know the precise daily reactions of millions of investors in U.S. corporate bond markets using actual trade information. As we've noted, the resulting data summary is published after each trading day.

The data reveals whether bond investors cheered, yawned, or fled in reaction to that day's policy decisions, eliminating the need to endure the endless speculation over investors' moods voiced by hundreds of talking heads in the financial media. Instead of having to guess, the data lets everyone follow the money. That knowledge furthers our ability to achieve financial stability, because policy makers can read and understand what the data means. They can frame appropriate responses based on facts rather than biased speculation. The data allows each leader to convert today's mistake into tomorrow's opportunity for redemption.

To eliminate crises, moreover, we now know that we must strongly enforce prohibitions on financial fraud by individuals, firms, and nations. Fraud is the force that generates all financial crises. In the first century, Jesus wanted to expose a financial scheme by forcing currency exchange trades into an open market where people could compete and show when a money changer's price was out of line. The idea carried the risk of Roman interference, taxation, or both. It was therefore rejected by those in charge of the Temple.

That too has changed. Rather than confronting a church that quoted him a 67 percent currency mark-up in 2013, Fred joked with the clerk and paid up. Unlike Jewish peasants in the Temple, he knew the exact amount the fraud was contributing to the financing of the church. Everyone present, including the clerk, smiled at the irony. For Fred, the gift for accepting the mark-up was a priceless lesson. We now have an open-market solution for financial stability—the goal of Moses when he outlawed the use of two measures and of Jesus when He confronted the high priest.

Combining the universal ability to expose fraud with data that instantly reveals investors' reactions to every policy change lets us open markets and sustain financial stability forever. Attaining that result only requires patient evaluation of all incoming data and the will to remain open to whatever market change is needed if things go wrong. Former Federal Reserve Chairman Ben Bernanke and his colleagues, it seems, are the foremost modern monetary policy practitioners of this theory.

A Goldilocks economy, which is neither too hot nor too cold, occurs when transactions conducted between informed and confident investors generate and sustain low and stable credit spreads. Low and stable spreads correlate with, and create, what academic economists call equilibrium in financial markets. Financial market equilibrium is elusive, however: so much so that many experts say financial stability is an alchemist's dream. As Ludwig von Mises famously observed, economics is the science of every human action, and is thus impossible to predict (Von Mises 1949).

In 1776, Adam Smith described equilibrium as the state at which the price of a commodity, in all its alternate uses, is equal—that is, determined by one measure. That has been called the most important economic observation in history. It may also be the least understood, and the state itself most difficult to attain. Applied to the role of finance in Smith's seminal economic treatise, *The Wealth of Nations*, equilibrium is the state at which the cost burden financial intermediaries impose on the generation and growth of productive assets (defined by Smith as land, labor, and stock in trade) is minimized. Credit spreads represent that cost burden.

Smith called finance the great wheel of circulation. The wheel facilitates conversion of productive assets (and the goods they produce) into money that is either invested in new productive assets or exchanged for other goods and productive assets (thereby increasing demand for new productive assets). Generating new productive assets expands the wealth of nations. Financial markets keep an economy moving and are, therefore, essential to creating wealth. However, with one exception that is pivotal to maintaining financial stability, finance cannot add value. Finance only allows land, labor, and stock in trade to grow efficiently.

Smith observed that *any* amount by which the cost to maintain finance exceeds the minimum cost of circulating the wheel burdens a nation's ability to generate wealth. Transactions that generate a low-spread Goldilocks, or virtuous, economy in equilibrium minimize that cost of finance. They are, therefore, essential for nations that wish to maximize opportunities for citizens to succeed and to minimize risk that they will be crushed by a great wheel that circulates an overburden of needless (and often fraudulent) cost in the form of high credit spreads.

Despite the thousands of years mankind has been seeking to establish balanced trading rules and to avoid fraud, only the United States has achieved the elusive state of financial market equilibrium—and this only after a terrible world war. Maintaining financial market equilibrium has been as elusive as harnessing nuclear fusion: Each time the United States has achieved equilibrium in finance we have discovered new means by which dishonest financiers have evaded limits on fraud. In each case, a crisis soon follows and destroys earlier accomplishments, most recently in 2007–2009.

After each crisis, lawyers, traders, accountants, economists, politicians, regulators, businessmen, authors, and other professionals announce the cause of our failure from their perspective. In most instances, experts in one silo attribute the cause to an error committed by some other silo. In truth, all (and none) of us are at fault for periodic market failures. When all sides of the relationship between financial stability and financial crises are examined empirically and empathetically, everybody and nobody can be blamed. That's because finance causes, and affects, everything. In financial markets, moreover, all things happen at the same time.

We are all human. Try as we may, even with ample use of technology, we will never understand everything that can go wrong in financial markets. If we pretend to be divine, everyone must be forgiven their errors. As flawed earthly vessels, however, we are all guilty of mistakes. Our real hope lies in the ability to overcome and learn from errors, especially blunders that tend to be repeated. As the great physicist and author Freeman Dyson notes:

> *Mistakes are tolerated, so long as the culprit is willing to correct them when nature proves them wrong. . . . Science is not concerned only with things that we understand. The most exciting and creative parts of science are concerned with things that we are still struggling to understand. Wrong theories are not an impediment to the progress of science. They are a central part of the struggle. (Dyson 2014)*

We submit that it is the lack of good data on the perception of investors operating in the financial markets that has made financial stability a problem that heretofore has escaped resolution. Until 2005, the world lacked reliable, widely disseminated, real-time data on how bond investors price debt purchases and sales in response to policy changes. We understood crises in hindsight when we eventually found good data. That's how Milton Friedman and Anna Schwartz reconstructed the causes of the Great Depression in their seminal 1963 work, *A Monetary History of the United States, 1867–1960.*

The United States used insight gained from this new data to minimize damage from the crisis of 2007–2009, but preventing crises using the theory of financial stability necessitates immediate data to understand what happens to investor sentiment as a crisis develops. Only then can this theory generate new policy directions that address underlying causes before a crisis triggers an economic collapse.

The problem is akin to what medical doctors experienced before they learned how to accurately measure fevers. Thermometers tell doctors when something is wrong. That's when they must probe deeper and treat underlying causation before losing the patient. Without data, deciding when and how to medicate is a stab in the dark that can kill the patient rather than fix the cause of disease.

Obtaining accurate and timely financial market data is not simple. Throughout history, bankers carefully guarded specific price and margin data until it was outdated history. For some of those with insiders' access, having data was a way to control markets or to profit personally. We now know that several markets managed by financial intermediaries (on which investors relied) were manipulated in the years leading up to the Great Depression and the 2008 recession in order to achieve the price results desired by those we trusted to conduct the markets fairly. Until the fall of 2005, a lot of bond market data produced on a daily basis was, in hindsight, nearly worthless for policy planning purposes.

Sometimes we learn from crises. The SEC demanded instant reporting of corporate bond trades as a result of a study it did after the Enron crisis. For those who followed credit spreads using that new data, each and every policy move during the 2007–2009 crisis, good and bad, generated a notable and measurable impact that was revealed by a change in credit spreads. Above equilibrium, each basis point change up (bad) and down (good) in credit spread produces a roughly $10 billion change in the annual wealth-generation capacity of the U.S. economy. When these numbers move too much in one direction or another, policy makers take notice.

Each day, therefore, looking at credit spreads, one could see when mistakes and relief occurred. This new knowledge led to days that were sometimes celebratory and sometimes sickening for investors. For example, credit spreads skyrocketed when the U.S. House of Representatives rejected the Troubled Asset Relief Program, or TARP bill, in September 2008. That meant most U.S. businesses would soon cease to operate. The body blow reversed the instant votes changed and TARP passed. The entire experience of 2007–2013 will be traced later in this book.

Fred began collecting and analyzing available credit spread data in December 1997. He needed a simple way to show Asian finance ministries, using one or two charts, that the Asian contagion of 1996–1997 benignly passed over U.S. credit markets. He was making a speech in February 1998 and needed the audience's attention before explaining how the United States had developed an effective immunity to that serious crisis. By comparing world markets using credit spreads, the U.S. immunity became obvious and eye-opening.

Being curious, Fred next gathered similar data going back to 1987 and began to track whatever data he could find on credit spreads. In the monotony of daily research, he observed thousands of apparent coincidences between policy moves and credit spreads. The coincidences soon fell into patterns. Using the patterns, Fred learned that changes in credit spreads have correctly predicted the impact of financial-market policy changes on the U.S. economy for 27 years.

In September 1998, Fred used the data to show the SEC how a flawed rule it adopted in April 1998 destroyed the U.S. immunity to financial crises that he had demonstrated to Asian finance ministries in February 1998. That SEC rule had caused the hedge fund crisis of 1998 involving Long Term Capital Management. The September presentation resulted in temporary relief that allowed banks and others to safely unwind the crisis. As the data predicted, when the SEC's temporary relief ended, the 1998 rule led to the high-tech bubble/crisis. The same rule also undermined the 2004 period of a Goldilocks economy. This eventually led to creation of unstable bank investments that exploded beginning in August 2007 with the failure of several hedge funds sponsored by Bear, Stearns & Co., and then caused the 2007–2009 crisis.

The 1998 SEC rule is terrible. It represents one of the worst pieces of public policy since the Great Depression. By cutting off market access for good structures generated by nonbanks and creating a way for commercial banks to monopolize access to money market funds, the SEC (1) prevented transactions that balanced an earlier bank monopoly in the market for asset-backed securities, and (2) unwittingly encouraged fraud by bankers who learned to manipulate their way into a new monopoly. In spite of our optimism about changes since 2005, we still fear the impact of the 1998 SEC rule will create further contagion in the financial markets.

These problems were, in our view, muted by the extraordinary policy innovations of Fed Chairman Bernanke after 2008. Over his career, Mr. Bernanke has published articles and given speeches describing the transmission of monetary policy through its impact on credit spreads. He clearly gets it. In identical October 2003 speeches, then-governor Bernanke reported on research that he and Ken Kuttner had done relating monetary policy changes to stock market activity. They found anticipated interest rate changes had little impact on stock prices, but that unanticipated changes had a moderate effect, and they wondered why. They wrote:

> *We come up with a rather surprising answer, at least one that was surprising to us. We find that unanticipated changes in monetary*

*policy affect stock prices not so much by influencing expected divi-
dends or the risk-free real interest rate, but rather by affecting the
perceived riskiness of stocks.*

Soon thereafter, Governor Bernanke became the primary White House
economist and, in 2006, became chairman of the Fed. It also became clear
that Vice Chairman Kohn held similar views—they both got it. Let's hope that
their enlightened thinking on credit spreads and markets continues to guide
U.S. and worldwide banking authorities in the months and years ahead.

Changes in credit spreads exposed the merit and fault of each event
on that awful path to financial Armageddon in November 2008. Whenever Kohn and Bernanke initiated a response, it seemed that the markets
recovered. Until the fall of 2008, however, their efforts were consistently
overwhelmed by the errors of others, particularly Treasury Secretary Hank
Paulson. Changes in credit spreads similarly correlate with each step (and
blunder) during the 2009–2013 recovery.

Understanding what moves credit spreads allows us to construct and
test policies that allow the United States to create and sustain financial stability. The size of U.S. bond markets and the example that the United States
can set will allow the world to do likewise. Through historical data, we
know financial crises start with a spike in the spread, a sudden widening
of the difference between (1) what high risk borrowers pay for credit, and
(2) what high grade borrowers pay. Understanding what generates a spike
permits policy changes that reduce the spike before investors panic. With
proper rules, incentives created by changes in the credit spread affect the
profitability of private-sector transactions that counterbalance the procyclical swings in finance that cause crises. As investors learn to use the theory of
financial stability, credit spreads narrow and the magnitude or volatility of
credit spread movements lessens. That reduction in the variability of credit
spreads generates equilibrium.

Since few economists are active traders, as was John Maynard Keynes,
most economists have yet to realize the opportunity permitted by the SEC's
2005 data disclosure requirements for bond spreads. That's understandable.
Academic economists are renowned for rejecting anything in circulation for
less than a few decades. Many economists seem, only recently, to recognize
that Irving Fisher solved the problem of a debt-contraction depression in
1933. Part of the reason for this systemic failing among economists seems
to be that few of them are truly students of history, especially when it comes
to how finance and law interacts with economies.

Fortunately economic researchers now have 27 years of data (more
than 5,000 daily data points) with various degrees of reliability by which
they can correlate credit spread changes with policy moves and responses

in all areas that affect investors' market behavior. That's sufficient to model policies that will sustain financial stability. The results of that research will surely modify positions espoused in this book. We accept that.

This book includes three motion-picture graphs (Charts 9.1, 9.2, and 9.3 in Chapter 9) that Fred developed to support the many reports he wrote in response to events of the 2007–2009 panic. The charts are updated through May 2014, comparing daily rates for long-term U.S. Treasury notes, investment grade corporate bonds, and high yield corporate bonds. The charts show how financial stability was lost through errors, then regained after 2008 and sustained after 2012 as these errors were corrected. Each chart follows the money of investment decisions affecting trillions of dollars of assets owned by millions of investors.

The theory of financial stability presented here derives from that data and from the transactions described in the 2005 book Fred coauthored. This market-based solution for financial stability is as old as the invention of money, as mathematically demonstrable as physics, as logical (and theological) as the Golden Rule, as current as modern technology, and as futuristic as the quest to eliminate war and the risk of extinction by global warming. Implementation may be difficult, but the problem must be solved.

So, let's briefly review financial market history and see how to improve the future.

A Flight through Financial Market History—Freedom and Fraud

The First Few Millennia

The first five books of the Bible are common to the religious heritage of three monotheistic faiths: Judaism, Christianity, and Islam. For believers, these five books record history from Earth's beginning to the death of Moses. With reliance on one god, monotheism overcame the duplicity of polytheistic faiths where strife was accepted as deceptions of man caused by differences among the various gods.

Deuteronomy is the fifth book of the Bible. Scholars have different theories on the timing and purpose of Deuteronomy. It was written after the Jews escaped slavery in Egypt and before they reached the Promised Land. By the time the book was composed, settlements of anatomically modern humans existed on every continent.

Coming from slavery and having wandered the desert for a considerable time, one can imagine the level of strife and debate within the Jewish tribes over how to treat each other in the face of competition for scarce resources. Deuteronomy seems to be a kind of treaty that lists specific behaviors that followers of Moses required of each other. It let them live in peace while seeking the greater society that was yet to come.

The book is an early statement of the rule of law. Some admonitions (e.g., one requiring that a woman's hand be cut off if she defends her husband by grabbing the genitals of an enemy) seem unique to a tribal community with a need to procreate. The book's definition and preclusion of fraud, however, is enduring.

Deuteronomy mandates that followers apply only *one measure* in their homes and trade. That precludes the use of two measures—that is, duplicity, the core of all fraud. It equally prohibits use of a small measure when a large one is proper (e.g., when selling bread) and use of a large measure when a small one is proper (e.g., when buying wheat).

Deuteronomy dates to somewhere between the twentieth and seventh centuries before the common era denoted by the Gregorian calendar. Precluding the use of two measures is recognition that society has an interest in preventing the threat that fraud poses to peace and prosperity. This side of the rule of law is summed up in the Silver Rule of earliest theology and philosophy: "Do not do to others what you do not want others to do to you."

The Golden Rule, which emerged around the world near the start of the common era, inverts that proposition. It calls for affirmative individual action: "Do to others as you want others to do to you."

The Golden Rule creates an individual obligation to step forward and *make* peace. The Silver Rule creates a collective obligation to *preserve* peace by avoiding specific behavior. All financial crises are founded in fraud. Precluding fraud will not end duplicity, so the law in Deuteronomy cannot assure financial stability. Precluding fraud is essential to financial stability, however, since it provides a standard toward which we can aspire and measure actions. It is only by disclosure and affirmative support for *good* transactions (explained later) that society can identify and undo fraud in a manner that sustains stability.

Punishing fraud is necessary to minimize the gotcha effect, or the sudden ebbing of confidence that surprises markets and triggers financial crises when unsuspected fraud is exposed. Instability begins when confident investors lend money to (or otherwise entrust) intermediaries that prove unworthy of trust. Fraud breaks that trust. It hides speculation until the duplicitous activity generates losses or inquiries that lead to discovery, but that generally occurs only after the entrusted money is gone.

When significant or systemic fraud is discovered, trust is shattered (along with fortunes) and is very hard to regain. Revelations of fraud trigger the spikes in credit spread that create crises. When confidence returns, spreads fall. When the cost of Adam Smith's *great wheel* falls substantially, however, financial intermediaries perceive a need to hide speculation so that smaller margins can be collected on a larger base.

To do this, it is inevitable that some institutions will stoop to using two measures for investment. Speculation will determine that firm's actual investments but will not be disclosed. The duplicity of secret speculation benefits managers at the later expense of investors. The use of off-balance sheet finance, discussed later in this book, is a prime example of this behavior. That is what makes such practices a *moral hazard* problem.

When the fraud fails, investors have no apparent source for repayment, as illustrated by the tiny recoveries in the $7 billion fraud committed by Allen Stanford. As investors rush for the exit, they drag good institutions down because investors lose trust in all institutions and markets contract in synchronicity.

Financial institutions, moreover, can be expected to lose customers when a competitor invades their territory and uses duplicity to permit managers an edge. When fraudulent savings and loans (S&Ls) used accounting gimmicks to hide speculation and undercut the practices of responsible commercial bankers in Texas during the 1980s, the biggest casualties were honest Texas banks that faced the choice of match or die. It is in good times, therefore, that regulators must insist on one measure for all.

Along with preventing fraud, vibrant private markets are also essential to assuring financial stability.

Ancient Rome certainly understood the power of controlling money in the first century. Cicero labeled the unlimited financing of coinage and taxation by a state monopoly "the sinews of war." From ancient Rome to today, governments have used banking schemes (often supported by armies) to create and force acceptance of their currency. The government that exercised this power most carefully, in turn, was the winner of almost all wars in history.

Rome controlled the Mediterranean world by dominating money, through its ability to create currency and collect taxes for its support. Temple priests in Jerusalem used the conversion of Roman money and their control of Temple money to fund their work free of Roman interference. To them it was obvious that their currency exchange and pricing practices would not survive in an open market outside the Temple.

In the United States, disputes over banking started in part because Thomas Jefferson despised central banks as much as he despised the priests and kings who controlled them. The history of money and its control, however, links to just about everything evil *and* good in every society, because banking is the mirror image of the rest of society. The *assets* of banks (loans) are the *liabilities* of the rest of society and the *liabilities* of banks (deposits) are the *assets* of the rest of society. Because production and finance are intertwined in this manner, banking is both supremely important and utterly frustrating. As we discuss later, the world of finance can be explained using the image of a large water balloon. Whenever the balloon is pushed from one or more sides, an equal and opposite reaction must occur somewhere else. The key to financial stability is understanding the precise places where each push will generate a response.

In the four millennia between Deuteronomy and the eighteenth century, death was a likely end for anyone who dared to challenge those who controlled people by controlling money. Chinese emperors, the Incas of Peru, European despots, and religious tyrants all monopolized the processes of finance to control the money and thoughts of their subjects.

There is little evidence that these despots had much regard for the well-being of individual subjects. It is only as independent central banks emerged after the Dark Ages that we begin to see free and open debate between the critics and proponents of banking. Only then do we begin to see suggestions for how to use money and banking for the general welfare of citizens.

Erica was virtually allowed to say just about anything she

CHAPTER 2

The Bank of England and the Scottish Enlightenment

Under the rule of English monarchs, before the seventeenth century British civil war, anyone who sought to open finance and interfere with the ability of the crown to fund its whims faced the possibility of horrific punishment and death. It was treason to undermine supreme rulers. In England, treason could be punished by public hanging, disembowelment, decapitation, and just about every other torture conceived by man.

Then came the Glorious Revolution and the Scottish Enlightenment.

By a confluence of unusual events, as the middle of the eighteenth century approached, a small group of gifted thinkers in the Scottish capital of Edinburgh (theretofore a rather dreary regional capital dominated by a hilltop castle) was suddenly allowed to say just about anything that was well-reasoned in regard to the rule of recently crowned Hanoverian kings in London.

In the seventeenth century, Charles I, a Stuart and a Scot, became the king of England. His assassination led to a civil war. After the dictatorial rule of Oliver Cromwell, Charles II was for a time the king of England, Scotland, and Ireland. Then came the Glorious Revolution. In 1688, William of Orange and his wife, Mary (both Stuarts, descended from Charles I), came to England from Holland. William deposed James II and became King William III of England.

Parliament refused to tax citizens to allow William to make war with France. In 1694, however, it borrowed a concept from Sweden and Holland. Parliament created the Bank of England. The BOE allowed William to take in deposits, which were borrowed by the government to make war with France. This was rather like the United States using war bonds to finance World Wars I and II and the later deficit funding of wars in Vietnam, Afghanistan, and Iraq.

In Holland, having a central bank enabled the government to control lending and lower the cost of long-term government borrowing. That allowed Holland to build dikes and fund the land recovery needed to convert the bottom of the North Sea to farmland.

The process of turning salty sea beds into arable land can take decades or even a century. Using a central bank allowed for development of a farm infrastructure with limited risk (aside from a tulip mania) of disrupting the means of funding normal commerce. The same process, in the hands of militarist rulers, permits high-risk gambles on the success of war.

In England's case, William's war with France and a series of conflicts with Spain proved economically imprudent (as is usually the case). The lesson of history is that no nation can afford war. William died in 1702 and was succeeded by Anne, the last of the Stuarts. When she died in 1714 with no surviving offspring, the Stuart reign ended as its other potential successors were barred from ascending to the throne as Roman Catholics.

George I, the elector of Hanover, Germany, succeeded to the British throne in 1714. The Hanover family (who later changed their name to Windsor when Germans became notably unpopular) has reigned in England since 1714.

Rather than tax their subjects to pay for past errors, Parliament embarked on a series of schemes by which they sought to hide incurred losses. These gambles backfired.

One idea created the infamous South Sea Bubble. In 1711, Parliament approved the creation of a company with a monopoly on British trade with South America. It was capitalized with British government liabilities, and shares were sold to citizens based on expected returns from the bonds and prospects for favorable trading. It was a Ponzi scheme.

Investors, lured in by the promise of quick returns, rarely stopped to ponder the problem Spanish and Portuguese control of South America posed to the firm's trading prospects. England was often at war with Spain. The company failed, of course, and a decimating financial crisis followed.

In addition to destroying firms in London by its perceived need to increase revenues, the Bank of England felt compelled to charge high rates on advances made to Scottish banks that used the money for investments in and around Edinburgh. At least one of the Scottish banks was owned by friends of Adam Smith. With no means to collect more interest from customers, the Scottish banks and their owners went broke.

In short, the first 50 years of British central banking were grim for English and Scottish investors alike. One benefit of this debacle, however, was the thinking generated in the mind of Adam Smith by his friends' losses. The result was an analysis of how banking should be conducted that remains as relevant today as when Smith wrote it in 1776.

In 1745, despite financial losses and the city's capture by an army supporting a Scottish claimant to the throne of England (Bonnie Prince Charles),

Smith and other intellectuals in Edinburgh remained loyal to the Hanoverian King of England, then George II. These intellectuals did not challenge the Scottish Highland clans that joined forces with Prince Charles to seize Edinburgh and fight the English army (which soundly defeated them) but neither did they join the clans.

Perhaps the English saw a need to encourage loyal Scots who could serve as a buffer while they resolved issues with the clans that fought to enthrone Charles. The intellectuals of Edinburgh, in any event, became a loyal opposition recognized for enlightened thought, even in dissent.

The Scottish Highlands suffered as British policy gave the land to clan heads that proceeded to depopulate tribal areas, replacing tenants with sheep. The chiefs were encouraged to gain wealth by the same policies of austerity that some people profess today as the means for recovering from the bubbles and crises of 1998–2008. The insanity of seeking to create wealth by starvation can still be seen in the clan country of Scotland, which remains beautiful, desolate, lacking in infrastructure, and notably poor.

In Edinburgh, however, the group of loyal intellectuals guided the city in building infrastructure, education, housing, health care systems, bridges, roads, ports, and centers of production. Blessed by the freedom of thought and action that their loyalty to the crown gave them, they created a vibrant and beautiful city, along with a body of independent thought comparable to what is found in the world's much larger population centers.

The Scottish Enlightenment produced great thinkers that became a powerful influence on the American colonists. The books they wrote in Edinburgh were read by America's founding fathers. The interplay of religions in and around Edinburgh supported the American concept of absolute separation between church and state—that is, no government support and no government interference with a citizen's right to worship as he or she chooses. Roger Williams first applied the concept to government in Rhode Island, then had it ratified by the British Parliament.

In 1776, Adam Smith set forth an outline of reserve banking on which the U.S. Federal Reserve System is likely based. Smith not only outlined how—and how not—to conduct banking and commerce within and between nations, he showed the British, by undeniable logic, that trading with the former colonies was economically better for England than seeking to tax them by force. When colonial American separatists faced execution for treason by revolting against the throne, Smith led a commission that advised the king to give up the fight.

Smith's last revision (in 1790) of a philosophical treatise he first published before *The Wealth of Nations* includes a demonstration that benevolence is the sole driving force by which the invisible hand of economics can produce optimal benefits. His work supports the approach of the post-World

War II Marshall Plan and explains the illogic and necessary failure of nations that seek to punish actual and potential trading partners by reparations, like those applied to Germany under the Versailles Treaty after World War I.

Smith also lays a foundation that explains how international imbalances, which were the driving force behind the bubble of the first decade of the twenty-first century, led to the subprime collapse that started in 2007. Though often cited as an inspiration for conservative and even libertarian policies, taken as a whole Smith's economic and moral philosophy is consistent with a broad range of thoughtful modern economics that is the essence of classical liberalism.

Answers for most economic questions are far more consistent than the experiences that create the questions. As discussed throughout this book, almost anyone unrestrained by loyalty to a particular line of thought or other bias sees the formula for financial stability. It was as consistently espoused in eighteenth century Edinburgh as in the twenty-first century United States. It is learning the factors that cause stability and instability that has presented difficulty, not recognizing the solution.

Once the problem of financial crises was understood in the eighteenth century, the solutions were first applied in London shortly after the U.S. Civil War. But first let's consider the early development of banking in the United States.

CHAPTER 3

U.S. Banking from the Colonial Period to 1865

When they were created, courts in the several colonies that eventually became the United States adopted judicial precedents of English common law. U.S. constitutional and statutory law, however, is based on a fundamentally different concept of government. Under the English constitutional model, kings (and later parliaments) hold absolute authority, tempered by common-law principles of interpretation and a rather muddled early Anglo-Saxon concept of voting rights whereby the people (through representatives) elect kings as the need arises.

European feudal law, with its foundations in the civil codes of ancient Rome (adopted in France and through Charlemagne's Holy Roman Empire), was introduced into English law when William the Conqueror invaded the British Isles and seized control in 1066. While he sought to ensure his own family's succession to the British throne, William also embraced the Anglo-Saxon approach of electing officials as the means by which he could free himself from obligations owed under feudal law to the Norman lords who helped him conquer England. The interplay created by this bifurcated thinking generated constitutional debates in England that make for an entertaining and wonderful history, but one far too long and complex to repeat here.

The principle of rule by vote of the people of England was finally and firmly established when William III became king at the conclusion of the Glorious Revolution in 1688. The comparative voting powers of lords and commoners continued to evolve, but rule by the people prevailed.

At its inception in 1789, the United States created a new concept from that outcome of England's constitutional debates. Under the U.S. Constitution, we are a nation of sovereign states. Each state and the federal government directly and indirectly derive all powers solely from the people. The U.S. Constitution includes (1) powers granted by the people that the government of the United States can exercise unless a supermajority of the people change the document, (2) rights the people have that cannot be denied without a supermajority vote, and (3) a declaration that the states get what's left.

From the beginning there was debate in the United States about the meaning of the terms within each category. That debate will continue as long as the nation survives. Americans have amended the Constitution only 27 times, and 9 of those alterations relate to election procedures and timing, and other voting matters.

Within the listed powers of the federal government, a bifurcated elected Congress holds all legislative authority. A president, elected by a deliberately obscure and oft-changed electoral college process with origins in the Anglo-Saxon approach William I found useful after 1066, holds the nation's executive powers. The Constitution offers little definition, however, of what executive power means. The judiciary is headed by judges who hold guaranteed life appointments with no reduction in pay—a system that remains unique in the world.

The United States has come to recognize its judiciary as the arbiters of when government can and cannot exercise power. That is important to finance because debt only has value to the extent that people can enforce its repayment in courts. Under the Constitution, only Congress can enact bankruptcy laws with uniform application throughout the nation. The United States is both a tariff-free trade area, wherein Congress ultimately determines rules of interstate trade, and a monetary union. Only Congress can authorize that U.S. currency be issued and U.S. debt incurred.

For better or worse, therefore, debt and its value in U.S. commerce are largely functions of federal law. While maddening for writers, businessmen, economists, accountants, and financiers, it is a good thing that Americans have proven to be a litigious people. The result is thousands of cases and opinions, many by the U.S. Supreme Court, that define rights relating to finance and the trading of financial instruments. That body of law is truly incomparable.

Finance during the period before the American Revolutionary War reflected a tumult of shifting issues mirroring the civil war in England and economic problems encountered during the first century of British experiments with a central bank. When the Bank of England got a cold, American colonists suffered pneumonia, and more emigrants arrived in the colonies whenever economic prospects in Britain (or in continental Europe) deteriorated.

It is an axiom of finance that the sale of a note or draft is economically identical to creating a loan secured by the note or draft. Rather than borrow at high rates from the king's banks, therefore, Colonial merchants tried to finance trade by exchanging bills of lading and the like among themselves. The British government imposed stamp taxes on such exchanges. The tax could be viewed as replacing the interest British banks would otherwise have received on loans, achieving the same result. Southern landowners in need of cash for operations mortgaged land to the monopoly of British banks and suffered along with Adam Smith's friends when the king's follies forced the Bank of England to raise loan rates

As Adam Smith showed, colonialism became a fool's game on both sides of the Atlantic. The United States would have been better off on its own (and better for Britain as a trading partner) than as a bunch of unruly colonies. It took time, but U.S. backing of the United Kingdom in World Wars I and II finally settled (or should have settled) arguments over whether England should have continued to oppress and fight its former American colonies. Indeed, between World Wars I and II the United States and Britain literally changed places, with the global hegemon of the nineteenth century becoming dependent upon its former colonies for economic and military support in the twentieth century.

The model of the U.S. Constitution of government by one sovereign state over an amalgam of separate state sovereigns remains the world's only long-proven method of achieving that goal in a balanced manner that respects shared rights of sovereignty and individual freedom. Try as we may, however, the United States has still not resolved the problem of sustained financial stability. Indeed, the ebb and flow of economic fortunes seems to be one of the unfortunate attributes of a free society where fraud and righteousness exist side by side.

Many of the first constitutional arguments over the relationship between the states and the U.S. government involved banking. Courts had to decide if silence on the issue of creating a bank allowed the federal government to organize one. The answer to that was yes, because it was deemed appropriate and helpful to the power to regulate interstate commerce and international trade (among other things).

Next, if a federal bank decided to speculate in a manner that disrupted established state banks, could a state protect its own banks by restraining a federally chartered bank? The answer to that was no. If the federal government exercises its power to establish and regulate a bank, states cannot interfere with that exercise of federal supremacy under the U.S. Constitution.

It remained, however, a political question whether federal powers of banking would or would not be exercised. Experiments with versions of the British central bank model led the United States to twice eliminate a central bank. Experience with so-called wildcat banks in the 1800s, however, proved disastrous. They raised fortunes and then ruined many businesses. The United States came to learn that neither the British central bank model nor an entirely free banking model could solve problems with speculative fraud and the demise of wealth generated by bank failures.

During the Civil War, Lincoln discovered that state-chartered banks were only willing to lend to the Union at market rates (which the bankers set high) for war funding. Rather than refighting the central-bank battle a third time, Lincoln convinced Congress to create the system of private national banks (which were chartered in Washington, DC, but owned and operated throughout the nation) that endures today.

Some argue that the Union's success in the Civil War arose as much from superior finance as from more and better manufacturing processes. With the creation of national banks to support the financial needs of the Union, Lincoln gained access to depositors who had previously funded state-chartered banks. He also issued massive amounts of paper currency—greenbacks—to further increase the pool of liquidity to finance the conflict. State banks, which at first had opposed the war, soon found greater merit in accommodating the nation's war needs. The relative cost of funding the war fell, and the United States has operated a dual charter (state and federal) banking model ever since.

Dual bank chartering has, at times, led to competition over which authority will provide the least regulation. At other times each group has correctly noted defects in the other's regulations and generated better governance.

Before 1933, when the Federal Deposit Insurance Corporation (FDIC) became the insurer of U.S. bank deposits and the designated receiver of failed insured banks, another form of legal competition greatly informed the history of U.S. banking. That unfortunate competition occurred via litigation between receivers of banks driven to insolvency by managers' speculations and borrowers to whom managers chose to loan the bank's money.

Perhaps by virtue of the balance of funds available for such suits, lawyers representing bank receivers convinced the courts (both state and federal) that appointed their clients that receivers were entitled to exercise remarkable powers when seeking to collect money needed to repay an insolvent bank's innocent depositors. Case law from the nineteenth century deemed banks "instruments of monetary policy" for the governments that chartered them, in part because all currency in the United States at the time was issued by private banks. Bank receivers, therefore, can still collect bank assets, such as loans, free from any defense arising by actions of the defunct bank—unless those actions are set forth in duly enacted written bank records approved by the bank's directors.

In a famous 1942 U.S. Supreme Court case relying on those precedents, a note guarantor offered proof that he had, in fact, paid the guaranteed loan before receivership occurred. Since he failed to take possession (or cause cancellation) of the note he guaranteed, however, the receiver was allowed to collect on the guaranty. Because the accuracy of the bank's records with respect to the loan was the guarantor's responsibility, as opposed to the receiver representing "innocent depositors," the guarantor had to pay twice for the same debt.

Thus, none of the normal defenses against repayment that borrowers assert when a bank seeks collection are available against a receiver if the bank goes bust. To this day, when the FDIC considers hiring attorneys to advise bank receivers, the first (and sometimes only) question relates to that 1942 case and whether the attorney really understands what it means.

If the prospective attorney fails to see the ironic humor in receivers' rights, he or she may not gain appointment from the FDIC. By the time they go broke, large banks often face hundreds of lender liability claims asserted to delay payment by defaulting borrowers. The cases occupy a large share of senior management's time and generate huge legal bills. When a receiver is appointed, however, these claims are all generally dismissed on the basis of a standard motion and a brief the FDIC provides to the receiver's counsel.

Before getting to the post–Civil War legal and economic matters that gave the United States robber barons, reenslavement by outrageous abuses of legal process, and periodic financial crises that ultimately led the United States to create the Federal Reserve System and the FDIC, let's first return to London in 1866.

CHAPTER 4

Bagehot's Dictum
(a.k.a. the Greenspan Put)

Henry Wadsworth Longfellow probably did not have financial markets in mind when he wrote

---

There was a little girl,
Who had a little curl,
Right in the middle of her forehead.
When she was good,
She was very good indeed,
But when she was bad she was horrid.

Banking is a business of leverage. Potential return on a bank's shareholder equity is magnified and multiplied by issuing debt (such as deposits and bonds) to multiply the amount of assets (loans to customers) that the bank can own. Leverage, however, is a "little girl" with a "little curl . . . in the middle of her forehead." When leverage is "good," banking is "very good indeed," and when "she" is "bad," banking is "horrid."

Credit is built on trust and the legal capacity to enforce contracts of trust. Disclosed leverage (e.g., today's central bank investments in the debt of nations) openly portrays the trust that we place in each other. It is disclosed so that the world can see whom the bank trusts and for how much. Hidden leverage is used when bank managers bully investors (in debt and equity), accountants, lawyers, and regulators to let them hide leverage (e.g., using off-balance sheet liabilities and shadow banks) without earning trust by open disclosure. When hidden leverage generates a positive return, it generates magical profits out of thin air. When it generates loss, however, the magic becomes a monster that devours shareholder value, and leads to insolvency and losses for uninsured bank depositors. When such losses are widespread, a debt-contraction crisis—a panic—soon follows.

The history of banking is dominated by great institutions that have been randomly picked off by the lunacy (or self-aggrandizing arrogance) of financial geniuses who gain control of credit decisions and undertake large investment schemes that are hidden from scrutiny and later prove fatal to the institution and its investors. The classic nineteenth century novel *The Way We Live Now* by Anthony Trollope is the tale of a railway bond fraud, mad speculation, and, finally, the bursting of the bubble in a crash that utterly disgraces the deluded promoters. The city of London is a place that seems to attract an inordinate share of such schemes.

By the mid-nineteenth century the thinking of Adam Smith had penetrated London's banks. The patterns of war and speculation that plagued the United Kingdom in the eighteenth century receded after Napoleon finally was defeated at Waterloo. After a crisis in 1857 relative prosperity took hold in London, until a wholesale note discounting firm—Overend, Gurney & Company—failed. A panic began on May 11, 1866. This time, however, it ended almost immediately, because the U.K. central bank, the Bank of England, quickly acted as a lender of last resort.

Walter Bagehot was the editor (and son-in-law of the owner) of London's *Economist* newspaper. As loss of confidence generated by Overend's failure spread, banks refused to lend even to other banks with good collateral. As a result banks began to demand repayment of loans to meet the withdrawal demands of depositors. Bagehot observed as authorities stopped the panic by lending freely and openly to anyone with sound collateral.

Bagehot enumerated the terms of those loans in the form of a dictum, or principle, which began by noting:

> *First. That these loans should only be made at a very high rate of interest. This will operate as a heavy fine on unreasonable timidity, and will prevent the greatest number of applications by persons who do not require it. The rate should be raised early in the panic, so that the fine may be paid early; that no one may borrow out of idle precaution without paying well for it; that the Banking reserve may be protected as far as possible.*
>
> *Walter Bagehot,* Lombard Street: A Description of the Money Market, *p. 199*

When he talked about "a heavy fine on unreasonable timidity," Bagehot had in mind the commodity money regime of that era in which the amount of reserves available was limited. Thus, keeping rates high was not only a penalty for the borrower, but also a way to draw liquidity, that is to say gold, back into the markets. Bagehot also understood that low interest rates fuel bad asset allocation decisions—what we call moral hazard. In the age of fiat money, however, economists have taken the opposite view, namely that an unlimited supply of reserves obviates the need to attract money back into the financial markets.

Today we see that the "heavy fine" part of the dictum was inappropriate. There is no room in Adam Smith's great wheel of circulation for avarice or retribution. Whatever the cause, it always burdens society for the cost of finance to exceed the minimum rate required to keep the wheel circulating. We now know that the cost of the wheel rises when investors panic. Charging that raised rate only reflects the market rate. For a bank to charge even one penny more than market rate, however, signifies monopoly power that cannot be allowed if we wish ever to achieve enduring financial stability.

In 1866, the monopoly granted by Parliament to the Bank of England apparently allowed it to charge punitive rates for such loans. It would take 127 years to reach a point in the United States where corporate bond markets successfully overcame the bank monopoly imputed by the "fine" of Bagehot's dictum. That resulted from what economists have called the *democratization of credit*.

The dictum that authorities should lend whatever is needed until a crisis eases, but only on good collateral, became known as the *Greenspan put* after the stock market crash of 1987 and the subsequent bailout of Long Term Capital Management in 1998. Mr. Greenspan made commitments that proved he would follow Bagehot's dictum whenever a crisis loomed, namely to effect a bailout in the event of trouble, even though many believe his put exacerbated subsequent moral hazard behavior.

Kevin Villani notes that "banks began making loans in reliance on Greenspan's commitment to flood markets with money in response to any crisis" (Villani 2013). By 2008, accumulated fraud in the system pushed the Wall Street investment banking firm, Bear, Stearns & Co., to equitable insolvency.[1] Application of the Greenspan put to resolve the Bear Stearns situation revealed flaws in the U.S. financial model that made a rescue of Lehman Brothers by the Fed impossible, precipitating the largest financial crisis ever.

After several decades, fear of fraud became the casualty of the conversion of Bagehot's dictum into the Greenspan put. If one studies the penalties for fraud one finds that the remedies are effective, but only in falling

---

[1] *Equitable insolvency* arises when a debtor is unable to pay debts as they mature (as opposed to *legal insolvency*, which occurs when liabilities are greater than assets, but the debtor can still raise money to pay maturing debt). Equitable insolvency is the primary reason by far that banks are placed in receivership and that other financial firms file bankruptcy. In good times the terror of equitable insolvency is an oft-forgotten nightmare about which the FDIC finds it must regularly remind bank managers, lawyers, and judges when a new crisis looms.

markets. Any fraud, even an innocent misrepresentation, can be grounds for rescission of a sale of securities or other assets. Courts will not let a liar profit by forcing misrepresented assets on an innocent purchaser when the assets fall in value. In a falling market, rescission is a complete remedy for almost all fraud.

As long as the Greenspan put assured markets would not fall, fraud committed in the trading of financial assets seemed harmless. Courts don't rescind transfers in order to give assets that rise in value back to a lying seller. As a buyer, moreover, if assets rise in value despite fraud, where's the damage? Proving that an asset's value would have been even higher is notably difficult.

By creating an expectation that markets will be saved in any crisis, the Greenspan put contributed to generating the enormous bubble that burst in 2007–2008. While Greenspan chaired the Fed, more and more managers came to believe that fraud was an inconsequential issue. This delusion became even worse when Greenspan's misconception about fraud (he said it was self-correcting) helped convince regulators to waive many fraud claims during the years preceding the 2007–2009 crisis.

In view of the enormity of the $67 trillion worldwide bubble generated by these blunders, what the Federal Reserve achieved between 2008 and 2013 is even more impressive. We must, however, end fraud and unwind expectations for a continued Greenspan put to truly sustain financial stability.

With that diversion, let's return to the United States in the late 1800s.

CHAPTER 5

U.S. Financial Markets from 1865 to the Great Depression

Wars tend to generate a temporary increase in demand for goods and services. Funding for reconstruction following the Civil War generated some banking demand, but not at a level that overcame the usual problems of shrinking employment and adjustment from wartime production to peacetime demand. Many people became dislocated due to a lack of jobs. Thousands of soldiers who were hardened by war and not trained to perform available civilian jobs stood idle. The inability of former Confederate supporters to change their thinking, animosity from retribution at the time of the North's occupation during Reconstruction, and other limitations combined to enflame race relations. This led, eventually, to a shameful period during which the federal government averted its eyes and allowed reenslavement to run rampant in the South. A century passed before the nation forcefully addressed many of the racial issues that were generated during the late 1800s.

During the period between the Civil War and the Great Depression, the United States became the world's leading economic power. The Gilded Age brought personal fortunes to railroad and industrial pioneers, and to the bankers and speculators who financed them. Many were built on a foundation of squandered natural resources, labor and safety abuses, and by the abuse of legal process. There were outrageous legal precedents whereby states wrote laws that excused bribery of officials, eliminated voting rights for former slaves, and replaced slavery with forms of peonage that proved even more onerous. Most who sought to challenge these developments were intimidated or murdered, as courts blinked when confronted with harsh realities.

In finance, robber barons speculated under cover of pyramidal trust and corporate structures. They borrowed off-balance sheet using subsidiaries and reported only their net positions as holding company assets when selling shares to investors. Lawrence Mitchell argues that "the stock market became the driving force of the American economy in the first decade of the twentieth century as a result of the birth of the giant modern corporation" (Mitchell 2007). He contends that the legal, financial, economic, and social transformations precipitated by the emergence of the public stock corporation

> *allowed financiers to collect companies and combine them together into huge new corporations for the main purpose of manufacturing stock and dumping it on the market. Businessmen started to make more money from legal and financial manipulation than from practical business improvements like innovations in technology, management, distribution, and marketing.*

It was only through Depression-era securities laws that most firms were finally required to account to owners on a consolidated basis, disclosing the leverage incurred at subsidiaries. An important point discussed later in this book is that in the 1930s consolidated reporting became required for financial firms and industrial firms, but not for industrial firms and the finance subsidiaries they owned. As a result, General Motors (GM), Ford, and General Electric (GE) did not consolidate General Motors Acceptance Corporation (GMAC), Ford Motor Credit, and GE Capital Corporation, respectively, into their financial reporting until the early 1990s.

Bankers followed the pattern of hiding leverage in subsidiaries before the Depression by creating holding companies for their banks. The holding companies created nonbank subsidiaries to issue guarantees of loans made by affiliated banks. This device allowed double-dipping into holding company equity in order to prevent subsidiary bank losses due to defaulting borrowers from being recognized. Many banks, of course, failed as these abuses came to light.

Probably the most important financier of that time was J. Pierpont Morgan. When a panic threatened New York banks in 1907, he famously gathered bankers together and "persuaded" them to invest enough to prevent the panic from spreading. The House of Morgan was the de facto central bank of the United States in that day, a role exemplified by the fact that it did not belong to the New York Clearinghouse. Instead it made other banks stand in the lobby along with retail customers. Less noted is that it appears the largest loan funded by the money Morgan raised in 1907 allowed U.S. Steel to buy its only significant competitor, Tennessee Coal, Iron and Railroad Co. (TC&I), at perhaps five cents on the dollar. TC&I also appears to have been the South's largest employer of reenslaved African Americans. Its labor practices did not change for decades thereafter.

A few years later, Morgan hosted a meeting that produced the draft legislation creating the U.S. Federal Reserve System. The new entity was ostensibly to take up the role Morgan had played in 1907 as lender of last resort. Unnoticed for the most part before 2000 was a clause that made it difficult for the new Fed to undertake that role.

When a panic hits, money withdrawn from the banks being squeezed has to go somewhere. Even if that somewhere is into a pillowcase under a bed, any responsible entity that serves as a lender of last resort needs to attract the frozen money over time. The Federal Reserve Act, however, precluded the Fed from paying interest on the reserves that banks deposited at the Fed. But money center banks (e.g., Morgan's bank) were permitted to pay interest on various interbank funding mechanisms, giving them an advantage in the markets in times of financial stress. As a consequence, excess reserves that ran to banks that continued to be considered safe flowed to banks like Morgan's but not to the Fed, an illustration of Bagehot's dictum about keeping interest rates high to attract liquidity back into the markets. In the days of Bagehot, however, the money he wanted to attract back into circulation was gold, which was attracted by the high deposit rates paid by banks. Banks could then expand their lending based on the higher levels of reserves on deposit, an illustration of the rigidity of the central banking model of England in the 1800s.

A century ago, the Fed could only stimulate business lending by banks that were short of funds by acquiring assets suitable for *repurchase agreements* (or *repos*). Prior to 2008, to further stabilize the overall money supply, the Fed found itself limited to demanding a higher level of mandatory reserves (at 0 percent interest to depositing banks) from all banks in order to obtain funds to help weaker institutions.

Demanding larger mandatory reserves in that way both unfairly reduced the earnings of safe banks and increased the liquidity needs of marginal banks, generating a need for even more liquidity. Preventing the Fed from paying interest on deposits, therefore, had the effect of (1) limiting its ability to stabilize banks in a crisis, and (2) increasing the potential for Morgan's bank (and his friends) to profit in a crisis. Yet resistance to the idea of the Fed paying banks interest on reserves prevented this meaningful reform for almost a century. Even today, many observers bristle at the idea of the Fed paying banks for deposits, even though the systemic benefits of such an arrangement are obvious to those that understand the processes used to resolve the 2007–2009 crisis.

Milton Friedman recognized the need to permit the Fed to pay interest on reserves more than 40 years ago. The Fed finally convinced Congress to let it pay interest on reserves in 2006, effective in 2011. Thankfully, the TARP law (Troubled Asset Relief Program) advanced the effective date from

2011 to the fall of 2008. Doing so allowed the Fed to attract (and retain, as needed) reserves to purchase and hold Treasury debt and mortgage securities. It can thereby affect market rates (and to some extent credit spreads) on longer term assets as part of a low interest rate regime using quantitative easing, or QE.

On the first day in 2008 that the Fed could attract excess reserves by paying interest, some money center banks apparently had underestimated the amount of reserves the Fed would attract. As a result, that day is commemorated by a large spike in the rate banks paid for overnight funds as trading ended. That spike meant some banks found themselves short as the funding window was shutting for the day.

That situation corrected itself the next day, however, as banks that now had to compete with the Fed for funds took its presence (and published rate) into account.

It was the Fed's unconstrained ability to raise funds in competition with money center banks that made its role as lender of last resort rather seamless after 2008. The authority to pay interest on reserves also makes it comparatively easy for the Fed to wind back liabilities as its several-trillion-dollar asset portfolio shrinks through sales, or, if it chooses, by letting the portfolio mature. Via QE, the Fed purchased risk-free financial assets while giving cash to banks that used the funds to stabilize prices for other securities.

As the Fed becomes able to unwind its portfolio, it provides a good indication that investor sentiment is improving. With the ability to change rates paid on reserves, the Fed can manage daily funding needs simply by adjusting its own deposit and overnight repurchase agreement rates (as all banks do). Without the ability to pay interest on reserves, conducting similar operations on the scale needed to stem a nationwide run before TARP would have raised many extraordinary and unpredictable issues.

This former limitation on the Fed's authority is one of many examples in finance where what seems to be a legal technicality has great consequence for the economy as a whole. When the Fed acts as a lender of last resort, all normal market responses have ceased. The Fed must engage in an activity of enormous magnitude, therefore, to change market perceptions and perform its stabilizing role.

That's why, for example, the problem of shorts (short sellers) taking swipes at the bonds of European nations in the period between 2009 and 2012 (and the United States during its 2011 and 2013 budget battles) only subsided when central bankers credibly announced they would do whatever was needed to stabilize markets. Facing a monetary authority with an infinite capacity to print money and the determination to prevent a short seller's squeeze tactic from succeeding, all shorts eventually resort to intimidation through media hype for a while, but only while they're unwinding positions.

In the nineteenth century, robber barons who specialized in watered stock taught the world about the need for a central bank to provide liquidity when confidence fails. Financier Daniel Drew summed up the problem for a short seller in that circumstance: "He who sells what isn't his'n, must buy it back or go to pris'n." In a small transaction, it is unlikely the perpetrator will actually get "pris'n," so investors will proceed in the face of illegality. When there is even a tiny legal problem with a trillion-dollar trade, however, that small problem can trigger a catastrophe for investors and society as a whole.

When viewing the role of the Fed before and throughout the Great Depression, a 1925 decision by the U.S. Supreme Court also greatly complicated the Fed's ability to follow Bagehot's dictum. Louis Brandeis, perhaps the most respected scholar then on the court, opined that a common law pledge of collateral "imputes fraud conclusively." The decision meant that a receiver could challenge any pledge of collateral made to the Fed before receivership if the pledging bank continued to collect on the loan. The case caused enormous debate in the legal profession and slammed shut the door on fraudulent *incomplete sales* and *pledges of assets*. It stifled private credit creation in the United States for more than three decades. The relevant part of the Brandeis decision said:

> But it is not true that the rule stated above and invoked by the re-
> ceiver is either based upon or delimited by the doctrine of ostensible
> ownership. It rests not upon seeming ownership because of posses-
> sion retained, but upon a lack of ownership because of dominion
> reserved. It does not raise a presumption of fraud. It imputes fraud
> conclusively because of the reservation of dominion inconsistent
> with the effective disposition of title and creation of a lien.

Brandeis took a squarely Progressive stance against the prevailing business practices of the day and literally shook the ground of commercial finance. In the *Benedict v. Ratner* opinion, he considered the many ways in which a purported pledge of collateral could be hidden from creditors. He found the process so entirely opaque that he could not justify allowing unsecured creditors to lose rights while creditors favored by the borrower took all the entity's liquid assets. In many cases, such pledges precluded effective reorganization of the debtor and the consequent preservation of jobs.

Importantly for the problems of today, Brandeis also noted that an incomplete sale of assets likewise "imputes fraud conclusively." This failure to perfect a true sale of assets to another party would play a significant role in the S&L crisis of the 1980s and the subprime debacle that started in 2007. Just as the Securities Act of 1933 embodied Brandeis's vision of public disclosure of financial information, the decision in *Benedict* was another piece of a larger puzzle for the justice known as "the People's Lawyer." We will come back to that point, however, later in the book.

At this point, we will only note that a mere four years before the 1929 stock market crash the highest judicial panel in America, in an opinion written by its most respected and militant jurist, declared that accepting a common law pledge of collateral (as Bagehot directs when making loans of last resort) "imputes fraud conclusively." Anyone sitting on the Federal Reserve Board at that time, before proceeding with a program to loan more money than anyone had ever done in history, would demand an unqualified "full faith and credit" opinion that every step required by Justice Brandeis was fulfilled. As a result of Brandeis's passion for financial accountability, the Fed and private lenders were hamstrung in terms of providing credit to the U.S. economy for decades after the decision.

Indeed, it would take a combination of three then-nonexistent laws, the Uniform Commercial Code (UCC), the U.S. Bankruptcy Code (USBC), and the Uniform Fraudulent Transfer Act (UFTA), all of which were adopted between the mid-1950s and 1990s, to address the concerns of Justice Brandeis and assure that pledges for secured lending by banks and other true creditors would be upheld in U.S. bankruptcy and receivership proceedings. Thankfully, by 2008 all of those ducks were finally in order. That fact allowed the Fed to accept pledges and apply Bagehot's dictum in service as the U.S. lender of last resort without any limitations.

The resolution of the 1925 Brandeis decision and the ability to draw excess bank reserves by paying interest are why the Fed under Chairman Bernanke was able to avoid the mistakes of the 1930s, when the Fed was a relatively minor player. In that era, the Fed could not act with the necessary timing and assurance of sufficient continued funding. Outright expenditures, using bonds to fund other government agencies such as the Reconstruction Finance Corporation, were needed while the FDIC undertook the long process of restructuring banks with insured deposits and federally backed bonds.

The Roaring Twenties, built on speculation hidden from investors and constrained by the inability of lenders to secure advances, therefore, came to a screeching halt after the stock market crash of 1929. By law, the Fed could not act to stabilize the system by paying interest to attract money hoarded by banks that stopped making loans or by accepting general pledges of loans from banks that continued to make and manage them (as prescribed by Bagehot's dictum). It was not until 1940, and then only to address the financing needs of the manufacturing sector for what would soon become World War II, that Congress finally passed a law that allowed banks to rely on payments due from the U.S. government as collateral for loans to wartime manufacturers. That process, moreover, proved so complicated that it was used only for very large projects.

Some prescient managers were able to change course in time to avoid the worst of the Great Crash of 1929. General Motors, for example, dismissed its founder, William Durant, in 1920. He was replaced in 1923 by Alfred Sloan, who structured the company as a fortress within what became the nation's "fortress of democracy" during World War II. Unlike Ford Motor Company, which almost failed during those terrible years, Sloan's GM lost money in only one year during the Great Depression, and produced some 10 percent of all goods used in the war effort.

GM made dealers pay the wholesale price of cars immediately on delivery, then financed the dealers' purchases through its AAA-rated finance subsidiary, GMAC. Moreover, by paying suppliers more than 180 days after their delivery of parts, GM was able to construct plants and meet short-term capital needs on its accumulated float. Indeed, the genius of Sloan was that he understood the power of leverage, properly used, while Ford was still operating on a cash basis and did not offer credit to customers until it was forced to imitate GM in 1927. By then GM was so much larger than Ford that the latter was often compared to a single division—Chevrolet—of the former.

GM and its major suppliers were financially sound enough that banks justifiably relied on GM payables as collateral for loans to suppliers even after the Supreme Court ruled that a pledge "imputes fraud conclusively." But all things change. Following the recession caused by the S&L debacle of the 1980s, in 1993 GM came within a few weeks of declaring bankruptcy. As a result of the market debacle of 2008, GM was finally forced to reorganize in bankruptcy, a result made feasible by investments the government made in major banks under the TARP law.

The banking collapse of the Great Depression started in Detroit early in 1933. When Henry Ford defied President Hoover and threatened to withdraw his money from the Union Guardian Trust Company and other banks, Michigan Governor William Comstock ordered a bank holiday on February 14, 1933. In the two weeks between Comstock's action and the inauguration of FDR, more than thirty states followed suit and closed their banks. The banks remained closed for months. That is when President Roosevelt said, "We have nothing to fear but fear itself."

The Great Crash had such an enormous impact on Detroit that its effect can still be seen. While not a direct cause of Detroit's 2013 bankruptcy filing, seldom-told consequences of the Depression will be referenced as we move to the next topic.

CHAPTER 6

Depression, War, and the Aftermath—Reflecting on Finance from 1929 to 1973

In April of 1929, a yellow taxicab turned into the White House grounds carrying the great Wall Street speculator William Durant, Earl Sparling recounts (Sparling 1930). It was after 9:30 P.M. and the visitor had no appointment. After convincing the staff and the private secretary to President Hoover that the matter was urgent and, indeed, secret, the visitor was shown up to the second floor study. After a while the president appeared and listened to one of Wall Street's greatest investors warn that the worst financial panic in the history of the republic impended. He cautioned the president that unless the Federal Reserve Board was forced to cease its attempts to curtail brokerage loans and security credit, a crisis was inevitable.

Of course, the Federal Reserve Board did not end its attempts to restrict the use of credit on Wall Street in the early part of 1929. Applying a gold standard model, the Fed felt compelled to continue to restrict credit. By May, the crisis of which Durant warned was already visible and would increase like a massive storm, reaching its peak in October and November of that year.

Durant, being a sensible man, sailed to Europe the month following his meeting with President Hoover for a lengthy holiday. The master of the market knew what would happen and even predicted it in his audience with the Great Engineer. Though ruined in the 1920s after he lost control of GM for good, this pauper managed to trade stocks and ride the last desperate wave of speculation on Wall Street before the final collapse into the Great Crash.

As noted, the stock market crash of 1929 occurred just four years after the U.S. Supreme Court ruled in the *Benedict* case that an incomplete transfer of assets, whether by pledge as collateral on a loan or outright sale, "imputes fraud conclusively." This meant, among other things, that lenders like the Fed would be very reluctant to make loans to troubled banks. It would take four more years for Congress to create the FDIC to be the insurer of deposits and receiver for any federally insured bank that went bankrupt after the 1933 bank holiday.

When Roosevelt took office in March 1933 (the presidential inauguration date was later moved to January due to events in early 1933) bank holidays had been declared in most states. On inauguration morning, the head of the Detroit bank holding company that owned the banks serving Ford Motor Company (and many of its suppliers and employees) advised Roosevelt that it would file for receivership and close those banks. The holding company for the banks that similarly served GM filed for receivership within weeks thereafter.

The auto firms were America's largest employers, with supply chains and facilities around the world. Within two weeks, 90 percent of the banking assets of Michigan were in receivership. Workers' paychecks could not be cashed. Supplier payments could not be processed. The center of U.S. manufacturing was falling into a financial wastebasket because of the speculations of the Gilded Age and of the 1920s, and the failure of U.S. legislators (state and federal) to understand and resolve the effects of the downturn that began in the mid-1920s with the implosion of the Florida real estate market.

By 1933, automobile production was about 30 percent of the highs achieved in the late 1920s. Pre-Depression levels of auto sales would not be restored until 1949. To support the war effort, domestic automotive manufacturing was stopped from 1942–1945. When production resumed, trucks (built first for the war and later for personal use) replaced a lot of cars.

In the 1950s, Detroit's Big Three controlled 93 percent of domestic automobile production (and 48 percent of worldwide production). In the early 1970s, domestic production peaked at levels nearly twice as high as those of 1929. Soon, however, imports took an ever-larger share of the market and U.S. affiliates of foreign manufacturers began to build new and more efficient assembly plants in the United States.

Before the Great Depression, Detroit was a place of industrial growth unlike any seen before or since. In 1910, some 10,000 automobiles were produced there. By the late 1920s, total automotive assembly exceeded 4 million. Putting $50 into the right Detroit business in 1910 netted an investor millions by 1929. From the 1920s through the 1950s, GM actually sent buses to scour America's countryside for employees to fill its plants.

In 1933, the Ford family and GM each established new national banks in Detroit to serve their respective firms' check-clearing needs and the other banking needs of the firms, their employees, dealers, and suppliers. It would take years to work out the colossal muddles left by the failure of Michigan's major banking empires after the end of the Roaring Twenties.

Six months after FDR was inaugurated Michigan passed a law that precluded the operation of bank holding companies and their subsidiary banks in Michigan. That law prevented any corporation authorized to do business in Michigan from owning even one share of bank stock—a restriction that remained in place until the 1970s. General Motors, therefore, spun off its National Bank of Detroit subsidiary to shareholders. Through a 1996 acquisition it eventually became Chicago's largest bank. After merging with Banc One, the combined bank became part of JPMorgan Chase Bank, N.A. The successor to the Fords' bank, Comerica, is now headquartered in Texas.

If holders of GM stock in 1933 were corporations that did business in Michigan, of course, they also were forced to sell or spin off their bank shares. Since there were many suppliers and customers of the auto giants around the country, Michigan's law was the primary source of the widely held belief that federal banking law required the separation of banking and commerce. After Michigan ended that prohibition, Sears, Roebuck & Co. entered the lending business and thereby proved that the principle of separation had never been part of federal law.

Between the stock market crash of 1929 and creation of the FDIC in 1933, there was no intervention similar to what Walter Bagehot saw the Bank of England doing in the crisis of May 1866. Although the 1913 law creating the Fed had been enacted to address the nation's need for an agency that could provide a flexible currency to stabilize finance and end periodic financial crises, there was, as yet, no federal receivership for state banks. Failed state banks were placed into the hands of state receivers.

Thousands of writings on the Great Depression cast blame on everything from mistaken economic theories of the time to the untimely 1928 death of Benjamin Strong, the man who led the Federal Reserve Bank of New York throughout World War I. Consider, however, the enormous practical and legal hurdles the Fed faced if it had chosen to conduct operations like those performed on London's Lombard Street in 1866. Agents of the Bank of England (BOE) had gone out searching for notes on which the bank could lend, which were secured only by a common law pledge and possession of the notes themselves. The pledged loans continued to be collected by the banks that pledged them to the BOE. The BOE, moreover, could attract any money it needed by offering to pay whatever interest rate was required to get sound banks to lend it the funds required to introduce liquidity into the system.

By the early 1930s the U.S. crisis that began in 1929 affected banks all over the nation, not just those located on Wall Street in New York. While there were district Federal Reserve banks in other cities, banks everywhere were in need of funds. A few affected banks were subject to national regulation, but most were regulated by the states and could employ the powers of state-appointed receivers in the event advances against collateral proved insufficient to prevent insolvency and failure. Not only did Bagehot's dictum require that a bank of last resort take only good collateral as security for an advance, but Bagehot also said a punitive rate of interest should be charged so as to ensure that money hidden outside of the markets would return. In those days, because of the gold standard, central banks could not expand their balance sheets at will.

Could state-appointed receivers for a U.S. bank that became insolvent, despite the Fed's best efforts to revive it, successfully challenge a pledge of loans that the bank continued to manage if the borrowing bank did not survive? If so, the Fed would become just another unsecured creditor of the insolvent bank—and one charging a punitive rate, no less. If you think of the views that applied to the Fed and all of government finance in the early twentieth century, the problems created by the powers of state receivers were immense.

As is the case today, it was not uncommon a century ago for state laws to give a preference favoring depositors over other bank creditors in insolvency. Indeed, a depositor preference rule is now part of U.S. law, and has been recommended for adoption as part of planned banking reform in Europe. The purpose is to prevent depositors' rights (to which a receiver succeeds) from being diluted by the need to pay other creditors. In the United States, for example, after 1989 the depositors of a failed bank became senior to all other unsecured creditors.

Until 1933, if a state bank's receiver challenged the Fed's acceptance of pledged collateral as "conclusively" fraudulent (under the 1925 U.S. Supreme Court ruling), the case would be heard by the same elected state court judge that appointed the receiver. If the receiver's argument was accepted, the court's decision would shift much-needed federal money to depositors in the insolvent bank's state and result in a loss to the Fed.

All told, speaking as a lender's counsel prior to 1933, it would be hard in those circumstances to opine that a pledge of collateral was free of receivership risk. The problems of pledging raised in the *Benedict* opinion, moreover, had to be addressed state by state.

The Supreme Court opinion declaring that a common law pledge of collateral "imputes fraud conclusively" was just a few years old when the Great Crash occurred in 1929. Every finance lawyer debated it (and lawyers still do). Even when collateral is pledged correctly, a matter of considerable difficulty to assure when pledged notes are being gathered by agents around the nation, the pledging bank continues to act as lender and collects for the secured party. Only the 1978 U.S. Bankruptcy Code and adoption of the Uniform Fraudulent Transfer Act resolved that issue. Today the UFTA deems any creditor (or buyer) that advances funds without knowing that it is receiving a fraudulent transfer to be a secured creditor with a lien on the assets it receives for the amount of its advance.

In 1929, however, it could be argued forcefully that if the Fed allowed a bank leeway to collect pledged assets, a lien granted to the Fed for last resort advances was entirely fraudulent with respect to bank depositors. In short, the Fed could face a total loss on a loan to a troubled bank.

Ask yourself if you, as a Federal Reserve official in the 1930s, would be willing to advance what would likely be the equivalent of the Fed's current $4 trillion portfolio in those circumstances. Moreover, even if the Fed could have overcome the legal hurdles to receiving proper collateral, where would it have gotten the funds? Until 2008, the Fed was denied the right to pay interest to draw reserves from banks that held excess funds.

This fact may explain why Eugene Meyer, the conservative chairman of the Fed during the early 1930s (who went on to buy the then-bankrupt *Washington Post* in 1933 and restored the paper to health) supported expansive use of fiscal policy (deficit spending) during the Depression, but not the use of the Fed to create a similar result. If there was a lot of government borrowing and spending, the Fed could provide liquidity by printing money to buy new government debt and fund those expenditures without the risk of losing money to a bank receiver.

Without an expansive fiscal policy, the Depression-era Fed was powerless, by law, to perform the lender of last resort duty for which it had been created in 1913.

Roosevelt voiced clear opposition to deficit spending and any federal guaranty of deposits during the presidential campaign of 1932. He had changed course entirely by the time of his inauguration, after spending months ignoring pleas from President Hoover to act jointly to stem the mounting banking crisis.

Early in 1932, FDR had been contacted by Jesse Jones at the Reconstruction Finance Corporation and so was fully aware of the scope of the banking crisis before the election. He waited for inauguration, however, before presenting new laws to Congress and, through his famous fireside chat regarding the bank holiday, assured a worried nation that only sound banks would reopen after the holiday and that consumer deposits would be insured.

To their credit, Presidents Bush and Obama chose a different path in 2008. They immediately and fully cooperated to resolve the financial crisis.

We will never know if the legal obstacles to secured lending persuaded FDR to change course and support an aggressive fiscal policy in 1933. The package of laws Congress adopted in the first few months of Roosevelt's first term changed everything. Along with suspension of the gold standard, New Deal spending allowed the Fed to expand money by purchasing federal debt. In addition, new banking laws ended the legal risks associated with the Fed accepting a pledge of collateral from insured banks.

The Fed could safely make advances to troubled banks before or after they were in receivership, because along with guaranteeing deposits, the 1933 laws made the Federal Deposit Insurance Corporation—an agency of the federal government—the sole receiver for any insolvent insured bank. As a result, any Fed decision to advance against a pledge of sound assets became easy because the central bank no longer had to deal with state-appointed bank receivers.

With the FDIC as sole receiver for federally insured state and national banks, the Fed was assured consistent national standards for receiverships. Since people appointed to act as receivers for the FDIC are indemnified for their actions (but only if approved by the FDIC) it became inconceivable that any receiver would challenge a pledge of collateral to the Fed. Using solvency tests, sound banks were allowed to reopen with FDIC-insured deposits. Banks that could not qualify for FDIC insurance were restructured by the Reconstruction Finance Corporation.

By means of these changes, the United States effectively nationalized all banks in 1933. For the next 20 years, American banks became risk averse to a degree that is little noted in much of the economic literature on the Great Depression. Public records of banks that became regional banks of last resort by being placed in conservatorship (so they could fund, as federal agents, local banks that did not survive the bank crisis that followed the 1929 crash) show a pattern of limiting extensions of credit, which choked the nation.

As an example, a national bank in the Midwest that had restored hundreds of local banks to local ownership while in FDIC conservatorship had invested about 80 percent of its assets in commercial loans before 1929. When the conservator finally returned control of the bank to its owners in the 1950s, 50 percent of the bank's assets were cash in vault; roughly 40 percent were invested in federal, state, and local bonds; and only about 10 percent were in commercial and consumer loans. That's an 87 percent decline in business and community lending, and the direction of the contraction in credit didn't reverse itself for another 20 years. It took two decades to train enough loan officers for the bank to successfully revert to a true commercial bank that provided credit to the community it served by taking deposits. This is just one example of why the credit expansion by the U.S. government to cover the expense of fighting World War II and the post-war rebuilding of Europe and Japan was the only thing that saved the nation from the Great Depression.

While Justice Brandeis was certainly correct in his thinking about disclosure and transparency, his 1925 opinion in *Benedict* cast a long shadow over the markets of that day. Only enactment of the U.S. Assignment of Claims Act of 1940 made it safe for banks to lend on the collateral of

U.S. government contract obligations. The law anticipated a build-up of contracts for FDR's lend-lease program. However, 1941 letters from the agency charged with resolving questions about the law continue to indicate reluctance in accepting anything short of the strictest compliance with every detail before a lender could be assured that the government would pay the assignee bank. Small wonder, then, that it took four years before the United States could manufacture the supplies needed to successfully invade Normandy and save Europe from German control. There was little or no private credit available to American industry.

Even during World War II, the federal government was concerned that it would lose money if any other government agency had claims against a contractor (or a lender). Those claims would have needed to be resolved before sending money to a secured creditor of the contractor. In private contracts, this issue was contested until the Uniform Commercial Code, which was first approved for adoption in 1951, created a workable compromise that was eventually implemented throughout the United States.

From 1933 on, conservators, receivers, and bankers became entirely dependent on U.S. government support for their existence. They were not about to take risk. Likewise, borrowers were reluctant to get loans. Some 35 percent of all residences mortgaged in the 1920s had been foreclosed by the 1950s; estimates range as high as 50 percent for the Detroit area. During the 1950s and 1960s in Detroit it was so uncommon for homeowners to seek mortgages that as late as the 1970s Detroiters had a hard time adjusting to the more liberal mortgage lending practices they found in other American cities.

Disasters that struck mortgage insurers during the Great Depression caused regulators to shut the business down entirely until the late 1950s. Finally, a very wise and foresighted individual, Max Karl, created a reserve/investment structure that allowed reopening of the mortgage insurance business in the post-war era.

As the Uniform Commercial Code made it feasible for private banks to re-enter the business of secured commercial lending, the absurdity of Depression-era rate controls required by Regulation Q (which set a ceiling on the rate banks paid on deposits—preventing banks from raising deposit rates to seek funds when liquidity needs rose) was soon apparent. How can a bank expand its lending safely if it cannot increase deposits by paying higher interest rates when liquidity is needed? What business, moreover, would borrow when banks can be cut off from funding at the whim of the federal government?

While many abuses arose following deregulation, a 1971 report by a bipartisan presidential commission was correct when it declared that Depression-era banking controls had to end if the U.S. economy was going to expand significantly. The trick is to establish a balance among leverage, growth, transparency, and disclosure that will endure and support a free society. That presidential commission cited as its primary recommendation the establishment of a level playing field where barriers to competition in finance are lifted.

Creating a level playing field meant eliminating the curbs on credit and monopoly practices created by depression-era restraints and the generation of new investment processes that could attract investors without federal guarantees or the payment of excessively high rates. The monopoly practices could be summed up by the Rule of 3-6-3: bankers of the 1950s and 1960s were said to take deposits at 3 percent, make loans at 6 percent (but only to customers that did not need them), and start a round of golf (with customers) by 3:00 P.M.

Blunders have occurred during 40 years of deregulation. Removing barriers to competition in finance led to mistakes and outright frauds that are hard for all honest people to tolerate. It took until 1983 for market participants to invent a structure (the stand-alone Collateralized Mortgage Obligation or "CMO") that was sufficiently sound to attract funds at risk spreads that allowed homebuilders to fund mortgages without relying on the thrift industry. It took another decade to open other consumer credit markets to that innovation. The entire process was complex and fraught with risk, yet none of us would want to return the United States to the tightly constrained, slow-growth banking world of the 1950s and 1960s.

CHAPTER 7

Early Deregulation: The Transactions That Replaced Depression-Era Thrifts

By the early 1970s, the Uniform Commercial Code (UCC) had been adopted in just about every state. Louisiana based many of its laws on the Napoleonic Code and was reluctant to change. In 1990 it became the last state to adopt the UCC. Until 1990, Louisiana only recognized real estate and chattel mortgages, entirely precluding pledges of incorporeal hereditaments (a fancy way of saying financial collateral, such as accounts, loans, or contract rights).

Article 9 of the Uniform Commercial Code resolved most problems caused by the Supreme Court's 1925 *Benedict* opinion precluding a pledge of assets because it "imputes fraud conclusively." In 1971 the Government National Mortgage Association (GNMA; Ginny Mae) successfully launched the first post-Depression mortgage-backed security, relying on the supremacy of a federal law that protected holders of GNMA pass-through certificates. Moreover, since GNMA only issued securities backed by mortgages that other federal agencies guaranteed, its full faith and credit guarantee of repaying investors ended debate on the security it offered investors.

GNMA constructed its program with great attention to legal details. Mortgage seller-servicers had to deliver duly endorsed mortgage notes and related papers to a specified custodian who carefully reviewed everything (and retained custody) before countersigning the guaranteed certificates for GNMA. Sellers made, and auditors confirmed, representations that assured GNMA it would not acquire defectively underwritten loans. Loan servicers were tightly controlled.

The new GNMA security created a preference for mortgages and mortgage originators that conformed to standards established by the Veterans Administration and the Federal Housing Administration.

Soon thereafter, Fannie Mae (Federal National Mortgage Association) and Freddie Mac (Federal Home Loan Mortgage Corporation; today's primary mortgage government-sponsored enterprises, or GSEs) copied the GNMA program, with minor changes. Their securities created a similar preference for conforming mortgages that the GSEs bought from banks, mortgage bankers, and S&Ls. By 1973 it was clear that nonconforming mortgages could be priced out of the market unless a similar product opened new sources of funding for private originators of those loans.

When a major firm in the nonconforming loan business decided to attempt issuance of securities backed by the mortgages it owned, rating agencies and investment bankers (and the lawyers they consulted) recited a plethora of problems that precluded competition with Fannie Mae, Ginnie Mae, and Freddie Mac. All those problems related to the 1925 *Benedict* decision imputing fraud conclusively to incomplete pledges and sales of assets.

When a group of attorneys gathered to see if there was a resolution for the client, a young lawyer named Fred Feldkamp naively raised his hand and said he believed Article 9 of the Uniform Commercial Code offered a way to resolve the matter regarding pledges of mortgage notes. As a reward for his optimism he received a six-month sentence in his law firm's library, researching each and every counterargument to the client's concept for a nonconforming mortgage security.

The UCC had, in fact, resolved most concerns, except the issue of whether parties granted secured status could be said to have negligently entrusted an issuer of nonconforming mortgage bonds by letting it continue to collect (service) pledged mortgages. Since a mortgagor could pay the servicer and the servicer could fraudulently discharge the mortgage (and let the mortgagor sell the property) without paying the mortgage pledgees, Fred's opinion had to exclude that possibility. The U.S. Bankruptcy Code later resolved this by specifying that servicers are permitted to hold title to a mortgage for collection purposes without conferring rights on other creditors of the servicer-pledger.

The client's transaction closed, however, only when rating agencies noted that the exception taken involved an intentional fraudulent conspiracy between the underlying mortgagor and the servicer, and rated the transaction despite that exception. All of the parties understood that rating opinions exclude intentional fraud and trusted the particular seller-servicer in that regard.

The year of the transaction was 1973. That was when shadows of the Great Depression finally faded and nonbank finance began to blossom. From then on, the United States was on a path to a system that now, finally, supports private extensions of credit and transactions that allow sustained financial stability.

Fraud will always be a problem in a free society. By creating truly sound universal funding processes that eliminate the threat posed when fraud is combined with monopoly power (financial, political, or religious) in financial markets, however, U.S. law forces fraudulent moneychangers into an open market. With market transparency of the type sought by a revolutionary such as Justice Brandeis, good structures eventually override the threat of fraud. In a state of sustained financial stability and relative market equilibrium, loss by rescission of deceptive transfers (sale or pledge) eventually weeds out defrauders—they are driven broke.

During the decades after 1973, adoption of the U.S. Bankruptcy Code and Uniform Fraudulent Transfer Act affirmed that servicing does not preclude a valid pledge and that an unknowing fraudulent transfer is, by law, deemed a secured loan, thereby protecting innocent transferees. The 1925 Supreme Court decision continues to preclude incomplete sales as conclusively fraudulent, but that helps to support transparent accounting by requiring that incomplete transfers be reported as the secured debts (with or without recourse) that they are.

Consequently, incomplete sales cannot honestly be disguised as off–balance sheet liabilities. This would become crucially important in the 1980s and thereafter, as the distinction between a true sale and a secured borrowing became deliberately blurred to evade accounting and regulatory capital rules. This blurring of the line between sales and borrowing would lead to the 2008 failure of some of the largest financial institutions in the United States.

CHAPTER 8

Riskless Arbitrage— Stand-Alone Collateralized Mortgage Obligations (CMOs)

As deregulation progressed, the effects of the monopolies created to overcome the Great Depression and Axis nations finally faded. The first sprouts of a level playing field in finance began to emerge within U.S. trading markets and among our trading partners. Without new risk averse transaction structures to support new entrants, however, the advantages of deposit insurance prevented the sprouts from growing enough to support U.S. capital market needs.

In all trade, riskless arbitrage is the process that moves markets from monopoly to competition. If a local monopolist raises prices or rates, its profits are restricted when outsiders find ways to use lower prices elsewhere to bring goods (or money) into the monopolist's market, risk free, to sell at a price lower than what the monopolist charges. The key to creating a true level playing field in finance, therefore, is to generate true riskless arbitrages that are indubitably safe and allow the new sources of money to grow and compete with former monopolists.

Many people are shocked when we say that the hangover of the Great Depression lasted nearly half a century, but this is the reality in terms of credit creation and private-sector growth. "Contrary to conventional wisdom, FDR's New Deal did not rescue the economy from The Great Depression," notes author and columnist Sol Sanders. "That took the unprecedented World War II mobilization which revamped the American economy's entire nature, producing the great postwar prosperity" (Sanders 2014).

Such is the power of the mythology of the World War II and Cold War eras created by the media that few of the citizens of the victor nations realized that the government expenditures needed to fuel the conflicts (and rebuilding thereafter) are what drove the recovery of jobs and economic growth for three decades after V-E Day. War itself wastes a great deal of manpower and materials, but the vast government outlays needed to rebuild postwar Europe and Japan, combined with the military and technological buildup involved with the Cold War, provided ample liquidity and economic stimulus to the United States and its allies. Another decade of work remained, however, before financial market alchemists created arbitrage transactions that were sufficiently risk free to reintroduce financial intermediation structures that existed prior to the 1929 crash.

In 1983, a riskless arbitrage innovation emerged that changed everything: the stand-alone collateralized mortgage obligation, or CMO. The stand-alone CMO is the only financial innovation of the past several centuries that, when properly implemented, generates profit merely by altering the intermediation process. We discuss later how these instruments came to be debased in the period from 1998 to 2008. For now we focus on the process and forces that led to and were unleashed by its creation.

The CMO is an advanced form of mortgage-backed security built on the new foundations for secured borrowing discussed in the previous chapters. The process pairs investors that have similar prepayment preferences to structurally segregated mortgage cash flows that remarkably improve the likelihood of attaining each investor's preference. It allows intermediaries to "buy" mortgages at low prices (reflecting high prepayment risk) and to "sell" securities with lower prepayment risk (at higher prices)—a "perfect" riskless arbitrage.

CMOs used cash flows from mortgage-backed securities guaranteed by the federal housing finance agencies Ginnie Mae, Freddie Mac, and Fannie Mae. These agency securities merely pass-through payments on underlying mortgages to the owner of the security as mortgage payments are due or prepaid, even when the underlying mortgages default. Thus, they give no "prepayment" protection.

CMOs then use the guaranteed cash flows to pay bonds issued by an intermediary owner in a very strictly prescribed order of payment. The intermediary company buys the mortgage-backed securities and funds that purchase by selling bonds with maturities based on the specified payment order to investors that are paid in order, with mortgage proceeds going first to some investors and later to others.

Although eventual payment of all interest and principal payments on the mortgages is guaranteed, for true stand-alone CMOs, the timing of payment was not guaranteed.

Underlying mortgages and normal pass-through securities prepay more rapidly (1) when defaults rise, and (2) when low mortgage interest rates cause performing mortgages to be refinanced. Conversely, when rapid prepayment is expected and then gets delayed (e.g., because rising interest rates slows the refinancing of performing mortgages), the mortgages and pass-through securities will be paid more slowly. Since CMOs pay investors in a preset order, the security creates a sharing of prepayment risk by allowing investors to choose bonds based on order of payment. Actual payment timing as the mortgages are paid, however, will depend on market factors.

In finance, bond investors love prepayments when interest rates rise and hate them when interest rates fall, in the latter case because the reinvestment rate is lower. A bond that performs well by those tests is said to have positive convexity. Because mortgages generally prepay more rapidly when rates fall and more slowly when rates rise, mortgage investments are said to have negative convexity. The Federal Home Loan Mortgage Corporation, or Freddie Mac, takes credit for introducing the first CMO in early 1983. It created a highly efficient security structure for distributing mortgage cash flows from homeowners to investors. In fact, the structure was overly efficient, because Freddie Mac actually guaranteed the timing of repayment on the CMOs, a guarantee that over time could only be supported by a government agency. Freddie Mac's CMO structure, therefore, created a monopoly to benefit only the largest banks and federal housing finance agencies because no private issuer could finance the guarantee of the timing of repayment on similar terms.

The first stand-alone CMOs were designed to reduce the negative convexity risk of mortgage investment for investors but not to eliminate the risk. The intermediary that creates a CMO can therefore profit by creating securities that generate more cash than is needed to purchase the underlying pass-through securities. We will explain later how that advantage of CMOs came to be monopolized by the large banks and housing GSEs after 1998 and was manipulated to the detriment of investors. This was a major cause of the 2007–2009 crisis and the Great Recession.

The changes in laws that made the CMO (and its various permutations) possible include the Uniform Commercial Code, the U.S. Bankruptcy Code, and the Uniform Fraudulent Transfer Act—each of which responded to court decisions and regulations imposed from the 1920s onward. Over the decades since its 1983 creation, the CMO has changed everything in finance—both for good, and, at times, for bad.

The first stand-alone CMO was issued in June 1983. An affiliate of Pulte Home Corporation broke the Freddie Mac monopoly by creating CMOs that only paid as their underlying mortgages paid or prepaid. That allowed the Pulte CMO to be a true riskless arbitrage and go viral. Anyone who understood the process could enjoy arbitrage profits, risk free, by buying guaranteed pass-through securities and selling CMOs. By 1987, more than $60 billion of stand-alone CMOs had been issued by a variety of institutions and entrepreneurs.

Investment bankers, homebuilders, thrifts, mortgage bankers, insurance companies, and real estate investment trusts (REITs) issued these CMOs for a variety of reasons. The advent of the stand-alone CMO revolutionized housing finance and in particular expanded the possible investment pool for housing beyond the monopoly of bank, thrift, and agency balance sheets. CMOs raised new funds that allowed builders to build more homes that were collateralized by the mortgage payments made on homes that had previously been sold.

In a pattern that is all too familiar, the CMO's success quickly drew pretenders. Its proper use as a risk-free arbitrage soon lost its magic as the CMO concept spread to credit risk trades. The strategy adopted by one firm, U.S. Home, to expand into manufactured housing in rural areas was less than astute. Manufactured housing in the United States was an outgrowth of World War II, when millions of semi-permanent dwellings were required to house troops and refugees.

U.S. Home acquired Brigadier Industries, one of the nation's largest producers of manufactured (that is, mobile) homes. The acquisition was intended to allow U.S. Home to operate more efficiently and better leverage the new financing technique. But the firm did not anticipate the collapse of the oil sector and the resulting decrease in the demand for such homes. The oil patch bust left U.S. Home with a chronic overcapacity for many years and nearly bankrupted the firm. But the problems being experienced by U.S. Home in the mid-1980s in the so-called oil patch states of Texas, Oklahoma, and Louisiana were just one part of a broader debacle in the housing sector.

The stand-alone CMO that Pulte invented was a very positive development, which helped millions of Americans achieve their dream of home-ownership. As the operating problems experienced by U.S. Homes proved, however, every financial innovation can be destroyed by misuse. Thus, finance will always be a business with positive and negative aspects.

The virtues of stand-alone CMOs were soon tarnished by abuses and acts of fraud—acts not unlike those committed a century before in the decades leading up to the Great Crash. These bad acts hid the merits of very useful vehicles under a mountain of problems. A free society disperses and reduces the damage of fraud by equally permitting success and failure. History teaches that precluding freedom in order to end fraud merely centralizes corruption and increases the damage caused.

At about the same time that U.S. Home was jumping into the deep end of the pool with respect to manufactured housing, a series of failed experiments in deregulation began generating a huge off-balance sheet financial bubble, primarily in the Southwest region of the United States—the very area that U.S. Home saw as being ripe for expansion.

The financial bubble that burst in 1987 to become the S&L Crisis was the first serious financial crisis since the real estate bust of the late 1920s and the subsequent Great Depression of the 1930s. This calamity may not seem as serious as the subprime bust that occurred 20 years later, but the S&L crisis nearly bankrupted the United States in 1988.

After 1992, as effects of the S&L crisis receded, virtues of the stand-alone CMO resurfaced. The structure was expanded to financial assets other than home mortgages. It was used to revolutionize the automotive finance industry just in time to save GM after it suffered enormous losses in 1992. Another bout with mortgage abuse, however, also emerged from the obscurity of a few private placements to become a dominant part of the government sponsored mortgage market: the companion class CMO. To understand this evil twin pretender to the CMO, one must start by understanding its companion, the planned amortization class (PAC) CMO.

The reduced loan repayment uncertainty, or negative convexity, that makes stand-alone CMOs so attractive to investors led very large and influential bond investors to demand that underwriters create securities with ever-greater certainty as to the timing of cash flows. Achieving that desired payment preference, however, meant someone else would have to accept a CMO class with even higher than normal prepayment/deferral risk. Investment bankers therefore invented a PAC/companion as a pairing structure where the preferred PAC investors got a greater share of payments when mortgage prepayments slowed and a smaller share when loan repayments accelerated.

This created a need for investors willing to buy the toxic waste companion class so favored investors could get the more predictable cash flows with PAC bonds. Companion class bondholders would receive much faster prepayment when interest rates fell and much slower prepayment when rates rose, meaning that the effective maturity, or duration, of the security—and therefore its market value—could change greatly.

These companion securities were called sucker bonds for good reason. Holders of the evil twin bonds, which were generated to give preference to buyers of PAC bonds, got stuck with acceleratable negative convexity, a concept many investors and sponsors never understood.

With stable rates, companion class investors would be paid in one to three years, so special funds were created to buy short-term agency securities, financed by selling commercial paper to money market funds and other unsuspecting groups. If rates rose, of course, those short-term funds might see duration explode and only be paid in 20–25 years. Nobody can safely hedge that investment risk.

One rating agency, Standard & Poor's, tried to warn investors by forcing issuers of companion class CMOs to label them with an *r*. That was soon referred to as the scarlet letter of risk in mortgage finance.

Unfortunately, by the time the PAC/companion structure became common, federal income tax law had changed to confer a near-monopoly on CMO issuance that favored the federal housing agencies (GSEs). The real estate mortgage investment conduit (REMIC) tax structure became the exclusive legal format available for multiple class CMO securities. By the time S&P insisted on its *r* designation for companion class CMOs, roughly 95 percent of the sucker bonds were issued in CMOs created by the GSEs.

Being GSEs, they did not need or obtain ratings for the securities—but this did not change the riskiness of the securities they issued.

S&P's effort to warn investors, therefore, was futile. A security suitable for perhaps 0.5 percent of all mortgage market investors comprised as much as 30 percent of all CMO issuance as 1993 was coming to an end. Until then, Fed chairman Alan Greenspan suppressed the Fed funds rate after the recession of 1990/1991 emerged, but eventually rates had to rise.

At the end of 1993, the Fed began considering a preemptive increase in interest rates to discipline what it perceived as excessive speculation. The Fed's belated move to impose interest rate discipline would nearly destroy several money market funds because of the embedded timing risk of sucker bonds.

As short-term interest rates rose, several funds managed by Askin Capital Management that were created to hold companion class CMOs became unable to repay repo loans that Kidder, Peabody had made to the funds so that they could buy portfolios of companion class bonds. These loans were made because Kidder needed to sell the sucker bonds in order to dominate PAC issuance and corner a large part of the GSE CMO market.

The resulting bankruptcies ended Kidder, Peabody's role as an underwriter. Reverberations of the turmoil caused several money market funds to break the buck, an event that triggered a series of blunders that are key to dissection of the crises that followed in 1998, 2000, 2001, 2003, 2005, and 2007–9.

Banc One of Ohio was also caught in the duration explosion caused by the Fed's interest rate increase. In that era, Banc One had piled into interest rate swaps with Wall Street, basically betting that interest rates would stay low and stable. Before merging with First Chicago in 1998 (to become Bank One), Banc One reportedly had a negative carrying value of its derivatives portfolio that was roughly equal to the entire capital of the holding company.

Almost nobody inside or outside the regulatory community understood the term, much less the substance, of acceleratable negative convexity during this period in 1992–1994. As a result, the SEC thrashed around in a fog seeking ways to protect money market fund investors from a problem that the SEC had not defined. The agency enacted new money market fund rules in 1998 that, along with the absurd exclusivity of REMICs, were key contributors to every financial crisis since 1994.

Understood and offered properly, the acceleratable negative convexity of companion class CMOs is not inherently bad. It's complex. In the hands of investors or bank managers that do not understand the securities or abuse them to secretly speculate with other peoples' money, however, the securities are destructive toxic waste that allow investors to be duped by false promises of higher returns.

The beneficial economic attributes of stand-alone CMOs and the financing capacity that they represented generated history's first self-correcting virtuous economy in 1997. While many observers credit the policies of the Clinton administration for the relative prosperity experienced in the mid-1990s, the fact that nonbank financial companies could use vehicles such as stand-alone CMOs (and variations of this model) to raise capital played a big part in the 1990s' expansion of jobs and economic activity related to the residential housing and real estate sectors, and also a strong manufacturing recovery.

Starting in 1998, mistakes made by policy makers in response to the Kidder, Peabody collapse, which was caused by the 1994 companion class crisis, resulted in market changes that altered the use of these instruments. CMOs and their more exotic variants and derivatives became weapons of mass destruction in the hands of some of Wall Street's largest financial institutions. The basic model of the CMO was used by the large government-backed banks and GSEs (government-sponsored enterprises) to create off-balance sheet financial monopolies. The banks first gained control of the conforming residential mortgage market by capturing the inflow of mortgages to GSEs (Fannie Mae and Freddie Mac), then underwrote and delivered CMOs that the GSEs created as off-balance sheet debt (despite fully guaranteeing payment-a ridiculous result).

This unreported monopoly ballooned to enormity as international trade imbalances flooded the market and made it impossible to contain the growth of too-big-to-fail large U.S. banking firms and GSEs. They issued and hid mountains of off-balance sheet debt via CMOs and derivative permutations like collateralized loan obligations (CLOs) and collateralized debt obligations (CDOs). All of it was hidden from investors, rating agencies, and the capital standards of regulators. All told, the GSEs and largest U.S. banks created $30 trillion of hidden leverage (shadow banking) to seize control of the rest of the financial market and manipulate prices for all types of securities.

A decade of continuous blunders (from 1998 through 2008) inflated the bubble before the inevitable collapse that arises with every financial market monopoly. That bubble caused the financial Armageddon of 2007–2009.

When the two mortgage GSEs were forced into conservatorship early in September 2008, it opened a capital sinkhole that swallowed $1.6 trillion of U.S. loans, leading to the failure of Lehman Brothers a week later, American International Group (AIG) failed three days after that, and a near total failure of the entire system occurred by late October of 2008, as credit spreads widened to twice the level observed after the 1929 Crash.

This cascade of failures expanded a U.S. financial sinkhole to consume all $30 trillion of the secret excess U.S. leverage that had been created by the large bank monopoly. It exposed an even greater hole ($37 trillion) of even more obvious off-balance sheet manipulation and fraud elsewhere around the world. That's when the reins of economic power shifted away from large banks to a new generation of public political and monetary leaders. They built a bridge of government liquidity and, we hope, the cooperation needed to sustain that bridge until the United States and its allies can once more create a private financial system that will sustain stable growth. This is what is meant by the phrase *nationalization cum monetization.*

The stand-alone CMO is *the* essential instrument for sustained financial stability, but as the subprime debacle illustrates, abuse of the structure via deliberate acts of securities fraud must be contained. The CMO was invented to access a unique financial market opportunity that emerged in 1983, just as Fed Chairman Paul Volcker's cure for the Great Inflation of the 1970s was succeeding. The Fed's success allowed it to reduce short-term rates at a time when long-term rates remained unusually high. That created a huge profit opportunity for entrepreneurs that understood how to generate riskless arbitrages that spanned the difference between long- and short-term interest rates—what we call generically the *rate spread.*

What is unique about the stand-alone CMO is that it's the first (and only) financial instrument that actually adds value merely by changing the form of the underlying financial assets. The capacity for that transformational increase in value exists when credit spreads widen (the symptom of a financial crisis) and disappears when spreads narrow (consistent with a return to equilibrium).

That counter-cyclicality, in turn, gives stand-alone CMOs the capacity to prevent financial crises by drawing credit spreads toward equilibrium. As spreads widen, stand-alone CMOs generate risk-free profits that attract more and more transactions—a direct parallel to Bagehot's dictum about using high interest rates to attract capital back into markets in the 1800s. The transactions, in turn, generate countercyclical demand for assets—mainly mortgage loans—which reduces credit spreads just as widening tendencies (created by the procyclical demand associated with a panic) threaten to generate a crisis.

As more of the transactions are done, spreads narrow and profits from originating stand-alone CMOs shrink and eventually disappear. As equilibrium is regained, the transactions no longer generate risk-free profit. Therefore, their use automatically shrinks because profits are restricted to circumstances that are risk free. That makes stand-alone CMO transactions financial shock absorbers that, properly used, help to assure sustained financial stability. They solve the last major problem in macroeconomics.

On a level playing field of finance free of monopoly behavior by large banks and government-sponsored entities, this process can be monitored by a combination of:

- Total transparency (exemplified by the Fed's recent policy to telegraph and report everything it does and intends to do),
- Full reporting of daily bond market trades,

- Rules mandating that all financial transactions that generate *any* form of risk be required to provide full disclosure of *all* involved assets and liabilities.

That's the promise of the future, however. First, let's review how the United States has progressed with each of these requirements, beginning with circumstances that led to the 1969 appointment of the level playing field commission. All history of mankind's folly is a sad dialog. We will seek to add humor when possible. It is the ability of humans to laugh at the irony of their mistakes that makes any recital of our history palatable.

ECONOMIC EXPERIMENTS: FROM VIETNAM TO THE S&L CRISIS

In late 1967, President Johnson was contemplating a huge military build-up, hoping that an increased effort would end the war in Vietnam before the 1968 election. He asked Congress to approve a tax surcharge but did not reveal how much would be spent on the build-up. According to econometric models used at that time, a surcharge was necessary only if the administration was lying (and not just a little bit) about what it intended to spend.

Several runs of one model were offered to the U.S. Treasury Department, using reported budget data and assumptions about undisclosed expenditures. It soon became clear that the administration's intent was to hide an enormous level of spending for a war that was already tearing apart the fabric of American politics. The Johnson administration was lying about a huge expansion of the war. They were repeating an economic mistake dating to at least 1694, when the English parliament formed the Bank of England to hide funding of their king's desire for war with France.

The effort led to protests and backfired. President Johnson announced his retirement in 1968, after his defense secretary, Robert McNamara, left office because he opposed Johnson's build-up. McNamara went on to be president of the World Bank. The loss of life in Vietnam doubled before the war finally ended, and the impact of our many errors continues to affect that region even today. The 1967–1968 budget deceptions also continued and helped generate the Great Inflation of the 1970s.

After he took office, President Nixon appointed the level playing field commission to consider how the United States could reduce constraints on growth created by the silo-monopolies of finance that resulted from Depression-era controls on banking and financial markets known. Under the commission's December 1971 report, the first obvious candidate for reform was the government's financial hammer—the Fed's Regulation Q, which placed ceilings on deposit interest rates.

Because of Regulation Q, it was irrational for any bank to expand lending, which the nation needed for growth of capital. Regulation Q let the government cut off market access to liquidity by the simple expedient of reducing deposit rates below the level a bank needed to attract and retain necessary funding. The very notion of Regulation Q was inconsistent with a free market, but as we have discussed, there was nothing free market about the post-World War II regulatory environment. Banks were heavily regulated appendages of the federal government. Regulation Q was the essential string that tied the Depression-era package of financial reform together. Just as the prohibition on the ability of the Fed to pay interest on reserves stymied its lender role from 1913 to 2008, retaining Regulation Q made no sense if faster growth in the U.S. economy was desired.

Unfortunately, the Depression-era financial model revolved around the concept of prohibiting interest rate competition. The ability to control competition when raising deposits allowed regulators to prohibit credit expansion and block moral hazard speculation at will, but it also relegated the United States to substandard economic growth. Financial deregulation forced the United States to relearn a lesson in finance that seems impossible for many to understand. It's a lesson that FDR learned between the presidential campaign of 1932 and the harsh reality of March 1933, when most of the banks in the United States were closed. The nature of finance ensures that there is no space, no compromise, between total control and a free financial market. A free society accepts the existence of fraud, but seeks to lessen its impact by encouraging disclosure and remediation.

Unless there is total control, money is entirely fungible. Like water, money slips through any crack in any rule that is inconsistent with a free market. Absent total control, therefore, there must be a free and level playing field where only fraud is regulated to preserve a peaceful society. To ensure fairness, the process of market participation can be regulated, but a participant's access cannot. In the absence of a level playing field, there is no free market—only the sort of monopoly behavior that characterized the Gilded Age up to the Great Crash of 1929 and also the housing boom of the 2000s that led to the subprime crisis.

Using controls such as Regulation Q to prevent a total collapse, Depression-era laws created separate banking silos in which each type of financial institution had some form of monopoly control that allowed it to profit, but only if it did what government wanted. That concept of government monopoly cannot support any market society's capital needs and, in the 1960s, a lack of economic growth eventually drove the changes in policy that followed.

Thrift institutions that restricted themselves to making residential home loans were given a Regulation Q and tax advantage over commercial banks so that they could pay more interest on the savings accounts that supported their investments in 30-year mortgages. Since savings could be withdrawn with 30 days' notice or less, the thrift silo relied on the government to keep a positive spread between short- and long-term interest rates. When that positive yield spread disappeared with the great inflation of the late 1970s, the 1930s thrift model died.

Until the 1970s banks had the exclusive power to provide checking accounts. By law, thrifts and other financial firms could only pay depositors directly, thereby precluding third-party payment accounts. In addition, only banks were effectively allowed to make commercial loans, a business many banks had to relearn under rules of the Uniform Commercial Code put in place after 1951. Regulation Q let the federal government stamp out any hint of loan speculation. It could stop speculation in mortgages, for example, by lowering the Regulation Q margin between banks and thrifts, thereby forcing thrifts to stop lending. As a consequence, homebuilding rose and fell like a yo-yo under Regulation Q (see Figure 9.1 in Chapter 9) based on the whims of the federal government rather than market demand.

As fear generated by the Depression began to fade, lawyers and judges began to forget the reasons for all the anticompetitive rules dividing finance among separately regulated groups. In the mid-1970s, for example, a thrift firm in the Midwest decided to cross the line and compete with banks by offering customers accounts from which funds could be withdrawn by drafts payable to third parties.

The thrift consulted a lawyer who found no prohibition on offering the accounts. The UCC defines a check as a draft drawn on a bank and the lawyer's client wasn't a bank. How, therefore, could the thrift be offering a checking account?

The thrift jumped out of its silo and invaded bank turf. Courts eventually agreed that the offer was illegal because withdrawals at thrifts could not be paid to the third parties, only to the depositor. By then, however, federal law had changed to specifically allow the same thing for thrifts all around the country.

In the first stab at deregulation, banks were allowed an exemption from Regulation Q for short-term deposits of more than $100,000. The change was designed to permit large commercial banks a level playing field with issuers of commercial paper, thereby allowing them to gain access to more stable funding sources. Some bank clients were selling commercial paper to the public at rates higher than that allowed by Regulation Q, thus avoiding the bank monopoly on commercial loans to businesses.

As soon as deposits of more than $100,000 were freed from rate restraints, the free market began to operate. Families and brokers began aggregating deposits to get to the $100,000 level, creating the precursors of money market funds to take advantage of the higher rates offered on deregulated deposits. By 1980, Regulation Q had been abolished entirely.

The desire for greater economic growth began in the 1960s as Americans started to borrow from banks in order to invest greater and greater sums in the stock market. Regulation Q precluded banks from attracting consumer deposits, so depositors turned to purchasing stocks. The average daily trading volume on the New York Stock Exchange rose by more than 300 percent during the 1960s, while other markets likewise saw large increases in trading volume. Hurd Baruch, special counsel to the SEC during this period, described the market growth of the 1960s as a frenzied speculative bubble.

A combination of mounting technical problems and enormous growth in trading volume resulted in a near collapse of U.S. equity markets. Stocks lost a third of their value between May 1969 and May 1970. Operational and financial constraints caused the largest number of failures of securities firms since the 1930s. Over 160 members of the New York Stock Exchange failed during this period, and an even larger number of regional brokerages failed. So serious was the damage to public confidence in the markets during that period that Congress eventually passed the Securities Industry Protection Act, modeled after the Federal Deposit Insurance Act.

By the mid-1970s new forms of financial market speculation had been unleashed and were generating mini-panics. One of the most notable was the crisis involving real estate investment trusts, or REITs. In December 1973 a developer in Palm Beach, Florida, named Walter Kassuba, filed for bankruptcy and defaulted on numerous loans that had been made by REITs. The failure started a cascade of defaults that eventually caused many REITs to fail.

These failures, in turn, caused significant losses to commercial banks that had (1) made loans to REITs to fund the sponsoring banks' expanding commercial lending operations, (2) sold excess commercial real estate loans to REITs they sponsored, and (3) advised the same REITs on how to manage their portfolios. Almost nobody stopped to question whether this multifaceted involvement of the banks might create conflicts of interest that would allow rescission of any transaction that ended badly for REIT investors.

The assets held by REITs fell from almost $500 billion in 1974 to less than $25 billion by 1978. Large New York banks, such as Chase Manhattan and Bankers Trust, suffered serious losses because of defaults on commercial loans made by and to REITs. Throughout the nation, banks that had sponsored REITs found it necessary to repurchase many loans that they thought they had sold. Their sales came home as banks' conflicts of interest were exposed in court.

Two OPEC oil crunches, an expansion of banking and investment activity, and the accommodative monetary policies supporting the guns-and-butter policies of the Johnson and Nixon administrations all contributed to the

Great Inflation of the 1970s. The sharp increase in wage and price inflation caused the Fed to lose credibility until 1979, when Paul Volcker stepped in and took the painful steps needed to control inflation—and, most importantly, inflation expectations.

Without the protection of Regulation Q to control their cost of money, and as a necessary consequence of the Fed's actions to stem inflation, most traditional U.S. thrift institutions were rendered hopelessly insolvent by 1982.

If U.S. homebuilders that relied on mortgages originated by thrifts wished to survive, they had to figure out how to sell homes as mortgage interest rates ran as high as 17 percent per annum. Even with the steep inflation during and after the American Civil War, rates did not get that high.

For traditional thrifts, the problem extended far beyond the destruction of new lending business. By virtue of the incentives provided under federal law, almost all of the assets of thrift institutions were long-term fixed-rate home mortgages. That business model survived the Great Depression by letting thrifts work with customers to prevent foreclosures while banks (that only made short-term mortgages) were forced to foreclose rather than negotiate. When a borrower defaulted, the thrifts simply added small, deferred sums to the mortgage until the borrower got a job.

As a result of the thrifts' asset concentration in long-term mortgages, however, when interest rates on short-term deposits zoomed to 12 percent or more, the thrifts were stuck with long-term assets paying perhaps half the cost of deposits that were funding their mortgage loans. Readers who have seen the 1946 Frank Capra movie *It's a Wonderful Life* will recall James Stewart explaining to terrified customers that their savings financed the home mortgage loans of their neighbors.

The inflation of the late 1970s destroyed the 1930s thrift model. It left the firms without a survival plan. Reports of the time divided the U.S. thrift industry into 6-, 12-, 18-, and 24-month firms—with the designation signifying the amount of time that the thrift would survive. That number was calculated by dividing the firms' net worth by the monthly loss on their negative margin between asset earnings (low fixed-rate mortgage interest) and liability costs (rising deposit rates).

By 1982 there were *no* traditional thrifts with expected lifespans of more than 24 months: within that time, they would all become insolvent and be thrown into receivership. In 1982, Congress and the Reagan administration decided the next step in deregulation should be to let these zombie thrifts invest their way out of trouble by allowing them to make new commercial loans (thereby competing with the former commercial bank monopoly) at the prevailing high rates.

Mr. Reagan's conservative and very intelligent FDIC chair, Bill Seidman, was asked by reporters to comment after President Reagan signed the bill in the White House rose garden and proclaimed, "We have finally freed the free enterprise system." Mr. Seidman quietly said, "I don't see any of those guys asking for freedom from the government's guarantee of their liabilities."

After the dust cleared and his service to the nation as head of the RTC (the agency that cleared up the rubble of that 1982 error) was ending, the last question someone asked Seidman after a retirement speech at the Economic Club of Detroit was, "How much is this mess going to cost?"

Obviously irritated at having answered that question about 5,000 times, he told the audience, "I have no idea how much this will cost. Remember, this was the worst mistake in the history of government. The mistake occurred when we let those guys make loans that will never be collected. The government promised to pay their deposits, so whatever it costs we will have to pay it." Seidman understood the rule of financial stability, but the lesson did not stick. The projected cost of the 2007–2009 crisis peaked at roughly 100 times the initially-estimated cost of the S&L Crisis. By prompt action, moreover, the entire cost of the 2007–2009 crisis has now been recovered.

The cause of each crisis was identical. The government promised to pay investors in the banks that originated bad loans and purchased millions of mortgages and thousands of mortgage-backed securities. These securities were flawed when written and funded during the decade of market neglect and flawed policy that led to each financial collapse. The legacy of such transactions remains a barrier to economic recovery even today. We must end all forms of off-balance sheet speculation. Whatever the cost may be to fix those transactions, it must be paid.

So it is with all systemic financial crises—a nation's financial survival is at stake. Whatever it takes to fix the mess must be done. Blame can be sorted later, but the established process of resolution to end a crisis must be undertaken.

Before Mr. Seidman left office Congress passed a 1991 law that included a process empowering U.S. bank regulators to keep financial crises from destroying the economy. In a systemic meltdown, regulators could undertake whatever response was required to save the system. The law provided for reports to Congress when the authority was exercised. Whatever cost was involved, it would be funded, automatically, through increased premiums on insured bank deposits. For a variety of reasons, however, that law proved ineffective in the 2007–2009 crisis.

PENN SQUARE BANK AND THE PARTICIPATION PROBLEM

In the commercial banking world of the early 1980s, another problem arose that is likely to have far greater ramifications in the future than the better known aftermath of the 1980s thrift crisis. That problem is the loan participation debate generated by the failure of Penn Square Bank, a small Oklahoma shopping center bank in the midst of U.S. oil fields. That bank's failure destroyed two of America's leading banks and nearly toppled several more.

Global trade patterns funded this particular bubble, as was the case in 2008. To understand how it happened, consider the problem of the OPEC nations that sought to enforce their oil monopoly on the United States, a nation as rich in that resource as almost any on earth. The United States lets the price of its dollar float. When we export dollars to buy oil, if OPEC exporters converted those dollars into other currencies, the excess dollars would drive up the price of other currencies and drive the dollar down. That in turn would reduce the OPEC monopolists' profits on subsequent sales unless they charge ever-higher prices for oil.

To avoid a drag on profits without having to buy U.S. goods, OPEC monopolists invested in U.S. capital markets—which kept the dollar strong and generated greater liquidity for banks that make loans. This mercantilist process is as old as trade itself, and will become increasingly important to our narrative as we proceed from the worldwide blunders of the 1970s to far greater blunders of the decade from 1998 to 2008.

To expand oil production the United States of course pushed policies favoring loans to domestic oil producers. That greatly expanded Penn Square's business, to the point where it sought to gain access to other banks' deposits to make ever more oil patch loans. It is at that point where some unique ramifications arose by virtue of the terms banks use for loan participation agreements.

Loan participations are subordinate loans made to a lead bank—Penn Square, in this case—from other banks (the participants). They are documented using a false form (the sale of a partial asset) because at the time these interbank funding mechanisms were invented banks were prohibited from borrowing on a secured basis for fear of harming the rights of unsecured depositors. Because participation agreements are subordinate to the rights of all of the lead bank's depositors, the FDIC (as the deposit insurer and statutory receiver of a lead bank) finds participations a convenient way to protect its interests. This preference by the FDIC, of course, ignores the fact that the FDIC insures deposits at all U.S. banks. As such, the FDIC is merely trading its advantage at lead banks for the disadvantage of the participating banks that the FDIC also insures.

Penn Square found many banks willing to provide it with money for oil patch loans because the drag OPEC's monopoly caused for oil-consuming regions of the country left them with relatively few opportunities to create new loans. Penn Square had plenty of loans to sell and its borrowers found Penn Square able to assure them lots of standby liquidity by creating loans that funded new deposits that the borrowers made at Penn Square.

The participants could have been protected if they insisted on receiving a distinct loan to the ultimate borrower by the creation of a loan syndicate. That, however, was complicated and would have required Penn Square to grant participants direct access to arrangements with Penn Square's customers— reducing Penn Square's ability to generate more deposits.

As opposed to a syndicate of lenders, under which each bank makes loans to the customers, in a participation a lead bank merely declares that it has sold a pro rata share of the lead bank's loan to the participating bank and agrees to share repayments from the customer, pro rata, based on the amount each bank invests. The participations are documented as the sale of part of a loan, but there is no delivery of the note evidencing the loan to the participant, nor is there an agent that holds the loan in trust for each lending bank.

Absent a syndication or actual delivery of the note, sale of part of the loan is a legal impossibility under the U.S. Supreme Court's 1925 decision discussed earlier. Loan participations are, therefore, incomplete sales. The purported sale "imputes fraud conclusively" under the Supreme Court's 1925 ruling. Under the Uniform Fraudulent Transfer Act, the buyer can only acquire collateral rights, and then only if it takes proper steps to gain a security interest.

Thus, by nonbanking law, the participant bank made nothing more than an unsecured loan to the lead bank, Penn Square. Under U.S. law adopted after Penn Square went broke, moreover, unsecured loans to an FDIC in-sured bank are now subordinate to rights of depositors and to the FDIC as successor to depositors' rights in receivership. Participations were invented in this form long before enactment of state and federal laws that allow banks to achieve the same result as a participation using a secured borrowing, a model that would now meet the standards of the Supreme Court's 1925 ruling.

Part of the problem in policing the terms of loan participations is that the transactions, which are arguably a fraud, have been blessed and even encouraged by the FDIC and other regulators. Even if it was a fraud, regu-lators knew they could prevent receivers from asserting fraud claims and could cut off speculative abuses by lead banks that go broke.

All banks accounted for participation activities under regulatory ac-counting principles, or RAP, until 1989. Structures for participations could be written for most banks, therefore, without fear that the deceptions im-plicit in the transactions could spread to other institutions. In these lim-ited circumstances, allowing banks to exchange assets and diversify risk by borrowings written as participations, even if they were poorly documented subordinate borrowings by the lead bank, posed no risk to the government (assuming participants remained solvent).

If a participant in the lending relationship went broke, the lead bank still owned the loan and the cash flows from the loan payments. The regulators could sort out the arrangement as the need arose. If the lead bank went bust, the FDIC knew that the participant bank only had an unsecured (and by later law, subordinate) claim against the estate of the lead bank. In Penn Square's receivership, the FDIC could and did use the deceptions built into the participation documents to the advantage of the insolvent lead bank's estate and depositors.

Penn Square operated after Regulation Q and other relics of Depression-era controls were largely removed. As lead bank on many oil and gas loans in Oklahoma and Texas during the OPEC oil crises of the 1970s, Penn Square found it could double up on the normal rights of a lead bank by holding large (and therefore largely uninsured) deposits of borrowers.

These deposits were funded, in many cases, by loans that Penn Square participated (sometimes 90 percent or more) to other banks around the nation. Penn Square had all the deposits while participants had funded 90 percent or more of the loans, creating a massive mismatch of actual credit exposure. It was, in a very real sense, nothing but a Ponzi scheme funded with the deposits of other banks.

When Penn Square went into receivership, its loan participation practice allowed a depositor that borrowed from Penn Square to collect the uninsured part of its deposit merely by offsetting against borrowings. That meant borrowers from Penn Square were protected on their deposits in amounts that greatly exceeded the FDIC's normal insurance limit—even though in economic terms that money belonged to other banks.

When borrowers offset loans to collect the uninsured portions of their Penn Square deposits, participants of course claimed that the FDIC, as Penn Square's receiver, had to share the deposit offsets, pro rata, as loan proceeds. If the FDIC had agreed, it would have suffered much higher losses than those generated by the borrowers' recovery of uninsured deposits. It would have also had to turn over the participants' share (sometimes 90 percent or more) of the offsets, increasing the FDIC's exposure by a like amount.

So the FDIC told participants that the law gave them no ownership rights or security interest in Penn Square's loans or the associated deposits. Therefore, participating banks had no right to proceeds of the deposit offsets. Worse yet for participants, since the offsets had paid the loans, the FDIC noted that there was no further participation obligation of Penn Square. This meant that the participant banks would see no further share of the loan payments.

The failure of Penn Square Bank was a horrific event for those in the banking industry that had not abandoned informal participations in favor of the more complicated and legally correct syndication format. This systemic aspect of the Penn Square collapse also explains why then-Fed chairman Paul Volcker tried, unsuccessfully, to convince FDIC Chairman William

Isaac to provide open bank assistance that would bail out Penn Square rather than put it in receivership.

The FDIC's handling of the failure of Penn Square Bank in receivership was a brutal result for participating banks, and each court that considered the case ruled that the FDIC's position was correct. Participants that had paid for 90 percent of the balance of Penn Square's loans, thinking they bought 90 percent of the loan rights and cash flows, were left with 90 percent of nothing.

Participant banks were deceived by false forms that regulators approved as convenient for the banks they regulated, then shattered by the powers of those same regulators acting as bank receivers. As we discussed earlier with respect to state receivers for failed banks prior to the 1930s, the FDIC can enforce the true nature of transactions despite fraud committed by a regulated bank (and encouraged by regulators) before receivership.

Receivers "stand in the shoes of" innocent depositors of an insolvent bank who are likewise defrauded. As against other defrauded bank customers, receivers prevail on behalf of depositors because banks are government-sponsored entities for which, as a matter of public policy, the protection of depositors comes first. This is the fundamental legal principle that allows the FDIC to minimize losses when a bank fails, but also creates enormous risks for customers and counterparties of that bank that do not understand the law.

The FDIC's actions in the Penn Square receivership case pushed several participating banks into receivership —including some large national banks, such as Seafirst in Seattle in 1983 and Continental Illinois National Bank & Trust in Chicago in 1984. "Continental Illinois held a shocking $1 billion in participations from the Oklahoma bank Penn Square, which had 'grown pathologically,'" Robert Hetzel notes (Hetzel 2009). Another large participating bank, Chase Manhattan, struggled for many years thereafter and finally was merged into another bank.

U.S. banks are now permitted to borrow on a secured basis. So there is no harm at all in changing the forms for these transactions today. Yet in the early 2000s when accounting standard-setters were asked to consider accounting for participations as the subordinate borrowings they are, the FDIC supported maintenance of the deceptions created by deeming participation agreements to be partial sales. Although the FDIC also warned that it would do what it did to participants in the Penn Square loans if those circumstances arose again, the accounting deception was allowed to continue and to be expanded so that any bond owner can today create an off-balance sheet borrowing scam merely by declaring that it made a partial sale of its bonds.

Penn Square Bank's failure, combined with the thrift crisis of the 1980s, resulted in the revision of banking laws, elimination of a separate insurer of thrift deposits, and tighter regulatory control through the passage of the Financial Institutions Reform, Recovery, and Enforcement Act of 1989 and the Federal Deposit Insurance Corporation Improvement Act of 1991. But little or no change was made in the practice of selling participations in assets that are not true sales, either by regulators or the accounting profession.

Accounting standard-setters decided to go along and took no steps to minimize the deceptions inherent in these participations. These rules, moreover, now apply to *all* bond owners. They allow banks and others to magically generate off-balance sheet liabilities merely by declaring that some entity that pays them cash owns a partial asset despite having nothing more than the lead entity's unsecured promise of repayment.

Even today, accounting methods for participations allow the same type of frauds that led to the Penn Square disaster. Nobody can say when that dog will once more bite the U.S. economy, but it will surely bite again and cause far more harm than resulted from the Penn Square situation.

The FDIC does not seem to worry that others will abuse this scam to create systemic risk for the United States and the world. The fact that fraud helps the government generate nominal economic growth and avoid losses when banks fail cannot possibly justify this policy position by the FDIC, but that's a discussion for the next crisis. What started as a closely regulated scam has become an unlimited opportunity for investor deception.

We suggest laughter at this point—the alternative is to become quite sick.

THE REPURCHASE GAME

Another scam was uncovered at an early stage of deregulation when a Kansas City firm, Financial Corp, worked its way into the secondary group of repurchase agreement traders through which the Fed regulates the nation's money supply. At a time when banks were legally precluded from issuing secured borrowings, regulators created repo agreements in the form of a sale for use only with a specific class of securities—those issued by the federal government and its agencies. They did so wisely, because borrowing against U.S. bonds precludes the damaging effect of forced bond liquidation that could harm the entire Treasury market and disrupt monetary policy.

When applied to other assets and circumstances, however, repos quickly became another form for generating abusive off-balance sheet liability frauds.

The form of agreement in a repo says the asset is sold but the buyer and seller agree to specific repurchase terms using the sale price plus a rate of interest determined by the time period between sale and repurchase, ranging from overnight to the maturity date of the sold asset. In other words, the agreements are sales in name only. The seller retains all risk of the underlying asset by its agreement to repurchase the asset without regard to market value at time of repurchase or if the obligor (e.g., Greece) defaults. [1] Each and every term is identical to obligations of secured creditors and borrowers —except that many repos are still done without delivery of the underlying assets—making them unsecured loans rather than even superficial sales.

In a case concerning taxation of interest earned on the underlying assets, the U.S. Supreme Court ruled that the obligation of repurchase makes the ostensive seller of assets subject to repurchase in fact retain ownership, as everyone who understands the instruments expected. Except for a loophole by which Lehman Brothers generated a scam known as the Repo 105 (that it reflected as an asset sale for accounting), GAAP (generally accepted accounting principles) accounts for these transactions as borrowings—which they are.

Now, let's go back to the Kansas City firm. Financial Corp discovered that if it took possession of the securities it was obligated to resell, it could get still more leverage by selling the pledged collateral outright and pocketing the accrued interest portion of the underlying asset. That is to say, it stole the collateral.

When the firm went broke, after trying (unsuccessfully) to claim a privilege against self-incrimination, the head of the firm was forced to tell creditors what happened under limited use immunity. Without the need to use that testimony, authorities soon placed him in jail. Banks were able to recover their money under theft loss insurance, though many insurers amended their policies to eliminate that coverage after those claims were paid. But manipulations, made possible because the form and substance of these transactions are duplicitous, continue to interfere with efforts to stabilize financial markets. Jerry Markham notes that between 1977 and 1985, failures of government bond dealers dealing in repurchase transactions totaled about $1 billion (Markham 2002).

The Repo 105 used by Lehman exemplifies the trouble with any loophole in accounting for finance: money is entirely fungible. Therefore, any loophole eventually attracts enough bad transactions to generate a crisis, even if normal use of the technique is beneficial to the economy.

---

[1] A recent lawsuit on behalf of MF Global Securities against its auditor exposes the abuse of a repo to maturity exception to the reporting of repos as secured borrowings. MF reported repos to maturity as sales despite the effect of the transaction in creating a full-recourse borrowing identical to sales of acceptances that are reported as secured borrowings. By a recent ruling, repos to maturity are no longer accounted for as sales.

The loophole used in Repo 105 by Lehman Brothers was exposed and closed, but has now been reshaped as a derivative that preserves the deception. As with loan participation scams, poor accounting for repurchase transactions will eventually come back to bite the United States as more and more trades are written to take advantage of the loophole. Again, one of the aspects of a free society is that people will always try to bend or break the rules created to ensure financial stability. Damage is limited by laws that encourage and enforce remediation on behalf of those harmed.

By law, auditors are required to ensure that financial statements fairly state a firm's financial condition without regard to GAAP. The only solution that prevents deception is to insist that *all* transfers that are not complete (or true) sales under the Supreme Court's 1925 standard must be reported as debt under accounting rules. The appendix provides a worksheet and opinion terms to assist the reader in understanding how to meet the test for a true sale.

UNCONSOLIDATED FINANCE AFFILIATES OF MANUFACTURERS AND HOMEBUILDERS

Under Depression-era rules, the ability of financial firms to hide transactions using subsidiaries led to requirements after 1934 that those subsidiaries be included in consolidated reporting. Since productive sector entities used finance to support manufacturing, however, accounting continued to separate their manufacturing and financial affiliates to avoid confusion.

That was significant to the 1983 development of stand-alone CMOs by homebuilders. It gave innovators a measure of secrecy and market control that, like the temporary monopoly offered to inventors by patents, helped assure their ability to recover development costs. As financial market deregulation progressed, industrial firms were forced to bring their unconsolidated financial subsidiaries onto their balance sheet in the early 1990s, ending the separation of commercial and financial activities.

A few homebuilders, moreover, had created affiliated originators that were licensed to offer government-backed mortgages in the late 1970s. Originating conforming mortgages and selling GSE-guaranteed mortgage-backed securities gave the builders some relief from problems that deregulation and inflation-fighting caused to those builders' earlier and more traditional associations with local thrifts. Like all thrifts, they suffered as federally mandated changes in deposit rates (to effectuate monetary policy) created housing booms and busts that reinforced the nation's need to end Regulation Q.

After learning the process of creating and servicing mortgage-backed securities, a few builders found they could defer U.S. taxes by issuing builder bonds that were backed by home mortgages and issued by nonconsolidated finance subsidiaries of the builders. Under then-applicable tax law, if the builder or its subsidiary owned the mortgage, profits on the sale of that home were recognized only as the mortgage principal was paid. Borrowing against the value of the mortgage gave the builder cash to fund new developments while still deferring the profits on earlier home sales.

The builder bond structure was not new. It mimicked formats that predate the Depression. By creating bond liabilities to support the rentention of mortgages that the builders originated for customers, they could defer taxation for, quite literally, decades. That deferral offset some of the adverse impact on home sales caused by the very high mortgage interest rates that resulted when, under Chairman Volcker, the Fed took steps to end the Great Inflation of the 1970s.

The strategy was hidden from some competitors by the fact that builders were not required to consolidate debt of finance subsidiaries. Investment bankers eventually figured out the structures, however, and offered to help other builders join the party. When too many builders took advantage of the tax benefits, Congress eliminated the tax deferral under tax reforms enacted in the late 1980s.

During the regional recession that followed the 1980s thrift bubble/crisis, the builders' use of special-purpose bond issuing corporations proved beneficial to mortgagors and bond investors. Unlike the stalemate created by inability to reconcile unpaid mortgages with unsustainable mortgage securities after the 2007–2009 crisis, corporate mortgage bond issuers of the 1980s could file for reorganization in bankruptcy. That allowed modification of their mortgage assets and bond liabilities to match underlying borrowers' ability to pay and maximize the cash available to pay the issuers' bonds.

Many bondholders, of course, considered this use of the Bankruptcy Code an invasion on their rights. They were wrong, of course, but it would take twenty years to generate a new crisis during which the lack of adequate remediation would prove the point.

THE RISE OF CMO BONDS ISSUED BY HOMEBUILDERS

Tax benefits that later supported research to create stand-alone CMOs were first used to save the builders' business model from total elimination as mortgage rates hit 17 percent or more in 1981–1982. As the Fed's policies to end the great inflation of the 1970s succeeded, long-term rates fell rapidly. By the builders' experience gained issuing builder bonds, training and market opportunity combined in 1983 to open a profit opportunity unlike any other that the builders had seen.

They found an ability to buy government-backed mortgage securities to serve as 100 percent of the collateral needed to sell stand-alone CMOs.

Until others caught on, the builders could pay 97 percent of the bond proceeds for collateral, spend 2 percent on structuring costs and walk away from the closing with 1 percent of bond proceeds as pure profits, with no future obligations. The collateral, moreover, if issued a few months before the bond closing, might pay 2 to 3 percent higher interest rates than those paid on the CMO bonds.

It was an opportunity worthy of the label–an Alchemist's Dream. While the tax benefits originally allowed are no longer available, an opportunity for riskless arbitrage profit arises when normal financial markets are disrupted. A stand-alone CMO can be created without the participation of a monopoly bank or GSE, so it has enormous positive potential for the global economy. It allows nations to end the threat that supports too big to fail bailouts.

Regulators and economists frequently (and properly) refer to shadow banks as somehow evil, but in fact nonbank finance is a very important part of the private economy. Because anyone can create a stand-alone CMO when banks fail to do their job, these private sector innovations are the very structures needed to overcome crises and assure financial stability–provided they are not abused.

Understanding why this innovation only arose when it did (and not earlier) necessitates reflection on the times from many perspectives. Anyone wanting to better understand the structuring details on which we will now focus will find them in *The Law and Economics of Financial Markets* (Feldkamp, Lane, and Jung 2005). The process is hard to simplify, but here we go:

1. Start with mortgages originated on one new home at a time—they require individual management. Even if well underwritten, it is hard to tell when a particular homeowner will lose his or her job and need to default.
2. Accumulate a pool of loans and a professional manager to cost-average collection and spread the risk of individual default.
3. Build a nationally diversified pool of mortgages with good underwriting, professional loan collection, and insurance to cover normal default risk relating to individual, local, and regional economic slowdowns. The only remaining default risk is a macroeconomic national concern.
4. Add government mortgage payment guarantees that cover catastrophic national economic emergencies, and the remaining risk will relate only to the timing of loan repayment, not to default.

Let's now pause to restate the timing risk of these bonds—also known as negative convexity. It is very common for home mortgages to require payment in level installments for 30 years, whereby most principal is paid in the later years. Since most homes last far longer than 30 years, these terms are important stabilizers supporting homeownership. Investors in mortgages know that prepayment penalties don't work well to preclude early payment because millions of consumers are potential victims. Try as one may, it's impossible to control the risk that locally elected judges will side with voters over distant bankers and ignore prepayment penalties. Indeed, the 2010 Dodd-Frank law has largely prohibited prepayment penalties on first lien mortgages.

Most home mortgages can be prepaid without penalties and borrowers do so *very* quickly when interest rates fall. Conversely, when interest rates rise, low-rate mortgages almost *never* prepay. Both alternatives are disliked by investors, who naturally prefer to have a relatively stable maturity for their investments and certainly do not want early payment when rates fall or deferred payment when rates rise.

Think of the homeowner having the right to pay back the loan to the end investor at any time and without penalty. This is negative convexity, discussed in the earlier analysis of companion class scams. It means that even fully guaranteed mortgage securities trade at a rate spread over similar maturity U.S. Treasury obligations that cannot be prepaid, much like a corporate bond that has a call feature will also trade at a higher yield than a piece of straight corporate debt with no call option for the issuer.

Mortgage experts use the spread of newly issued market rate government-guaranteed mortgage-backed securities over 10-year Treasury securities to measure what investors demand at a given time to accept negative convexity risk. Using statistics that date from 1963 (see Figure 9.1 in Chapter 9), that spread has ranged from a tight spread of less than 50 basis points (suggesting a state of housing euphoria) to a wide spread of more than 250 basis points (a housing industry crisis).

More than almost any other factor, it is this spread that establishes demand for housing and mortgages. The math behind this is complex, but any major builder who looks at the chart of this spread points to times of tight spreads as a high point for builders, and vice versa when spreads are wide.

The point of equilibrium in that market seems to be about 150 basis points. When interest rates are expected to rise (or fall), that equilibrium point changes a bit to reflect changing demand, because prepayment and new origination expectations change (mortgages refinance more slowly when rates rise and faster when rates fall). The effect of spreads on housing activity will vary, moreover, depending on the variance in rate paid on a particular security compared to current market rates for new mortgage loans.

For simplicity, a perceived 150 basis point spread for mortgage securities means that an otherwise risk-free new mortgage will bear a yield 1.5 percent per annum higher than a 10-year U.S. Treasury security when the housing side of Adam Smith's great wheel of circulation is circulating smoothly at its lowest sustainable level of cost.

Now, let's go back and describe the last two steps for issuing stand-alone CMOs:

5. A simple mortgage security that is bought at a discount rate 2.5 percent per annum above a 10-year Treasury costs far less cash for an investor to buy than the same security would cost at a discount rate representing a 0.5 percent per annum spread.
6. If one can purchase mortgage securities at a 3 percent spread in a crisis, and finance the purchase 100 percent by selling bonds backed only by the mortgage securities, but with different maturities, at an average spread of 1 percent per annum over 10-year Treasuries, either the seller can keep 2 percent per annum or sell more bonds than it costs to purchase the mortgage securities.

That 2 percent difference in the spread between the simple mortgage security and the CMO with multiple bonds of differing maturities is the source of profit that became available to builders that figured out how to create a stand-alone CMO in 1983. They formed bond issuing subsidiaries (with no need for equity, because the bond structure was free of all default risk) that would (1) buy higher rate mortgage securities at 100 percent of the principal of the issued bonds and pocket the annual spread, (2) buy mortgage securities at a discount from principal and sell bonds up to 100 percent of the principal and keep the front end difference, or (3) in some cases, a little of both.

The profit from doing these deals for new mortgage originations rises as the spread between mortgages and Treasury bonds rises. Therefore, more transactions are done as spread rises, creating demand for more mortgages and increasing the amount of money available to build homes. That heightened demand, in turn, causes the spread to fall, until the reduction of profit for doing the transactions sufficiently reduces the number of transactions done to cause spreads to stabilize.

Over time, therefore, a housing market equilibrium is assured by stand-alone CMOs as the volume of transactions is allowed to ebb and flow freely.

The transactions are safe for anyone to create when the *only* risk is prepayment. They fit the definition of a riskless arbitrage that opens markets to greater competition and efficiency.

In 1983, the processes of U.S. financial regulation and deregulation had reached a point where each of the many market structures necessary for stand-alone CMOs to work existed. Their creation, moreover, was necessary because the U.S. thrift system (on which the Depression-era mortgage system relied) was rapidly disappearing. By luck and hard work, need and opportunity merged.

Where default is not a risk, generating different classes of bonds with different maturities lets investors that want early payment buy the first bonds to be paid and those that want progressively later payments to buy later maturities.

The overall average maturity of all CMOs issued using a pool of mortgages is necessarily the same as the mortgages backing the CMOs. Each class in a CMO, however, demands a smaller premium for negative convexity risk than the underlying mortgage pool. This is because a risk-free stand-alone CMO provides greater repayment certainty to each class by partnering each investor with the holders of the other classes. It is a partnering process that reduces the aggregate negative convexity premium of the aggregate mortgage investment.

Today, any first-year investment banker that sells CMOs has a computer program that will do all calculations for these transactions in less than a minute. When builders invented CMOs in 1983, however, the algorithms needed to translate standard mortgage prepayment experience into cash flows, aggregate the cash flows and allocate them to pay each class of bonds at different payment speeds (so each bond purchaser could be shown how their bond would pay in different circumstances), required several hours of time on the mainframe computers of major Wall Street investment banks.

The formulas that generate CMOs required months of work by PhD mathematicians. Explaining the models in terms the SEC and investors understood required bevies of lawyers and auditors. After the first deals were done, of course, all front-end costs were covered, making sustained equilibrium of the U.S. mortgage market a reasonable and attainable goal.

Because financial firms were required to consolidate debt issued by financial subsidiaries and homebuilders were not, the creative homebuilders that invented the stand-alone CMO were given the advantage of secrecy. That advantage ended, however, after 1986 when the real estate mortgage investment conduits, or REMICs, opened the housing finance market to financial firms and were then deemed exclusive for income tax purposes.

Wall Street firms successfully lobbied Congress to create REMICs as an exception to IRS regulations that sought to restrain issuance of a trust form of CMO invented by New York lawyers for an affiliate of Sears Roebuck & Co. Under the so-called Sears Regs, the IRS imposed double taxation on multiclass mortgage securities issued by passive trusts. This meant that the CMO trust as well as the investor paid taxes on the interest received from the underlying loans. Since stand-alone CMOs issued by affiliates of builders managed taxes by balancing interest income and expenses using consolidated taxation, the Sears Regs did not affect builder issuance of bonds.

Banks and others pushed for a REMIC exception to give them a way to compete for CMO issuance. After an introductory period, however, REMICs were deemed to be the only form for multiple maturity mortgage securities that could avoid the Sears Regs. Exclusivity had the effect of giving the large banks and mortgage GSEs a monopoly.

It is no coincidence, therefore, that REMICs displaced other types of mortgage-backed securities. They became the only viable choice and led to domination of CMO transactions by banks and federal housing finance agencies, the GSEs.

By the exclusivity REMICs required, tax law closed out competition from nonfinancial firms issuing bond forms of CMOs. Even after the IRS recognized that taxpayers should be able to choose structures that passed tax responsibility to participating owners (the check-the-box rules) as long as they maintain consistency, REMICs continue to sustain a monopoly position that favors GSEs a few large U.S. banks. That problem was a major underlying cause of the significant mortgage market disruptions that have occurred since the 1980s.

The too-big-to-fail (TBTF) banks used their cheap funding and other origination advantages gained under 1998 SEC rules to monopolize the loan issuance market, while the housing GSEs dominated the long end of the mortgage bond market with the aid of phony off balance sheet accounting and REMIC exclusivity. As the subprime market expanded, originating TBTF banks with a short-term funding advantage over nonbanks handed off the junk mortgages to the GSEs for the long bond market monopoly.

No private company or issuer of ABS (asset-backed securities) can compete with a GSE, especially when the GSE is allowed to use its government support to speculate, off-balance sheet, on securities where it remains as the ultimate obligor. The GSEs are fully liable, so it is outrageous to suggest that its obligations can be unreported. Yet that is exactly what both major housing finance GSEs (Fannie Mae and Freddie Mac) were allowed to do. It is equivalent to a manufacturer that buys its own debt, repackages it and resells it, then says it's not liable for its own debt. The only value to such thinking is that it proves, beyond all doubt, that the very concept of an off-balance sheet liability is duplicitous—a fraud.

The TBTF banks gained an advantage in markets for mortgage originations by funding transactions using commercial paper sold to money market funds (by the off-balance sheet abuse of short-term structured investment vehicles, or SIVs). The practice expanded rapidly after the adoption of the SEC's Rule 2a-7 amendments in 1998. This was a terrible blunder by Washington that guaranteed bank SIVs unlimited access to money market funds as warehouse lenders. That made the TBTF banks monopoly originators that, in turn, sold these mortgages to monopoly GSEs.

Between 1992 and the SEC's 1998 rule change, there continued to be enough independent competitors in the origination process to assure that there was at least some origination discipline. That ended in 1998.

The next development accelerating a decline in mortgage quality arose after 2001. Using credit default swaps, the giant insurer AIG became guarantor of almost any transaction, with ever-declining quality. That set off a race to the bottom of the quality chain, funded on the long side by the insatiable appetite of international trading partners seeking to export goods to the United States and rebalance their current account surpluses with capital account investments in GSE and TBTF bank mortgage securities that had direct or implicit U.S. government support.

Bradley Borden and David Reiss note that during the first decade of the twenty-first century, Wall Street firms abused the Internal Revenue Service rules regarding the tax exemption of REITS, bringing into question whether the vehicles used were ever properly constructed (Borden and Reiss 2013). Allegations in a 2012 suit filed by the New York attorney general details how loan originators and REMIC sponsors on Wall Street colluded to populate REMICs with mortgages that did not comply with the REMIC rules.

By the early 1990s, builders had largely stepped back from the CMO instruments they had invented. They saw that financial firms were using REMIC CMOs to bid down spreads between newly originated mortgage securities and 10-year Treasury bonds to levels that made the deals less profitable than other opportunities. So the business became monopolized by loopholes and gimmicks that gave large banks and GSEs unlimited leverage opportunities, off-balance sheet, thereby avoiding all regulatory capital rules.

The SEC's 1998 Rule 2a-7 changes further compounded the problem by granting banks monopsony power over money market funds. Diversified nonbank asset-backed securitizations that had neutralized the pricing power of bank-sponsored conduits between 1992 and 1998 were cut off. The rules subverted asset concentration limits that are supposed to force money market funds to buy no more than 5 percent of assets from a single entity. The SEC's changes permitted a single bank to be the sole source of credit deficiency support behind 20 or more SIVs and thereby to become the backer of 100 percent of all assets in a money market fund.

It is, therefore, understandable that bank-controlled conduits came to dominate short-term commercial paper (CP) issuance in U.S. financial markets. They recycled a major part of the $67 trillion international and domestic funding behind the series of market bubbles and crashes that occurred in the decade following 1998. It was a situation that not even the inherent stability of CMOs could rectify.[2]

Bank regulators, accountants, and the SEC essentially let a few large banks and the GSEs take near-total control of mortgage markets just as the mercantilist instincts of major exporting nations such as China began to flood the United States with unprecedented (and arguably, unneeded) liquidity. America's massive trade deficits resulted in an equally massive flow of dollars back into the U.S. financial markets, creating a ready supply of liquidity to fuel the boom in mortgage securities. Rate spreads fell as foreign

---

[2] For an in-depth discussion of the impact of the SEC's 1998 amendments to rule 2a-7, see Feldkamp (2005), pp. 223–232.

investors flooded U.S. markets to support their own age-old policies of mercantilism. The too-big-to-fail entities began to reduce the quality of underlying loans so they could buy them more cheaply and make front-ended profits. Builders dared not do that, because they were not too-big-to-fail banks and would have gone broke buying back the loans during a slump. So builders elected to profit by creating McMansions that few customers could afford in a mortgage origination process that had gone berserk.

By slipping risk in at the front end and using off-balance sheet liabilities to pretend risk did not exist when selling CMOs, financial firms succeeded in driving a magical product into the ground, along with the world's economy. As speculators learned how to short low-quality deals using derivatives, the race to the bottom accelerated. By 2008, modern history's greatest financial invention ended up nearly destroying the global economy.

Good stand-alone CMOs remain beneficial for the issuance of newly originated mortgages under stable market conditions, but only when the transactions are true riskless arbitrages and their use expands (and contracts) as market spreads for sound products dictate—otherwise they become instruments that support deliberate acts of securities fraud. When risky assets infect these transactions, unwinding the structures without the means to forgive or refund fraudulently contracted obligations is well-nigh impossible.

As a consequence, whenever an opportunity for abuse existed, CMOs issued between 1998 and 2008 generally increased market volatility. In their original form CMOs are instruments designed to be held to maturity. That intention cannot be fulfilled when a crisis necessitates the sale of CMOs by the initial holders of the instruments. We now know that when markets are destabilized by abuse, CMOs convert from countercyclical assets to procyclical instruments that intensify market instability. In short, they become weapons of mass destruction.

There is little doubt that Congress and regulators understand what is required. For the past 12 years (at least) proposals to permit restructuring of underwater mortgage loans have been presented to Congress. When a law similar to the one creating REMICs was enacted for the taxation of securities structures backed by nonmortgage financial assets (FASIT), there was no exclusivity provision. As noted above, the rationale of IRS check-the-box rules made REMICs' exclusivity a vestige of past illogic. Meanwhile, the SEC needs to address the real problem behind the break the buck crisis of 1994, namely the issue of negative convexity, and end the monopoly/monopsony it granted to the largest banks and GSEs with its 1998 Rule 2a-7 amendments.

These are steps in the best interest of creditors, debtors, the United States, and the world, yet Congress and the SEC have refused to do what must be done for at least a decade.

CHAPTER 9

Paradise Gained, Lost, Regained, and Destroyed (1992 to 2008)

In *The Law and Economics of Financial Markets*, the authors detail not only the construction and terms of stand-alone CMOs and other instruments, but also follow the money and track the trails of schemes generated during the period up to the date of that book's publication (Feldkamp, Lane, and Jung 2005). Covering all aspects of this time period is beyond the scope of any writing worth reading at this point. Much still remains to be done before we will know if the good created can be preserved despite all the bad that resulted from manipulation of the structures that create financial stability. Only then can a truly balanced history be compiled.

In the next section we provide an overview of empirical data compiled in five graphs, as well as a summarizing table. Much of this analysis is based on Fred's daily market observations (made in real time and transmitted regularly to global financial leaders), despite knowing the perils of that enterprise. Some readers will surely say the commentary misses important details. Others will find the summary overbearingly complex. To both groups, we apologize. This discussion is based upon a library of transaction documents that structured perhaps $3 trillion worth of funds flows during this period. That collection, however, is miniscule compared to all the contractual rights accumulated for investment participants.

EQUILIBRIUM ACHIEVED—JUST IN TIME

Figure 9.1 tracks the spread between (1) the rate charged on newly originated 30-year fixed-rate Fannie Mae/Freddie Mac-conforming U.S. residential mortgages, and (2) 10-year U.S. Treasury securities. It tracks the stability of U.S. mortgage markets for 50 years (from January 1, 1963 to October 17, 2013). This is the market on which the business of America's homebuilders, and the U.S. dream of homeownership, was built.

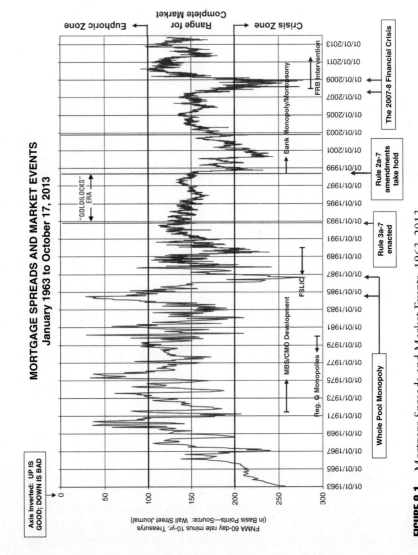

FIGURE 9.1 Mortgage Spreads and Market Events, 1963–2013

Source: Data for FNMA 60-day rate minus 10-year Treasuries from the *Wall Street Journal*, January 1, 1963–October 17, 2013.

The graph shows the market volatility before and during the phaseout of Regulation Q deposit controls (1960s and 1970s) and during the period after the first GNMA mortgage-backed security was issued (1971) until 2013. It also tracks the progress of mortgage markets: (1) as participants developed the stand-alone CMO, (2) when SEC rules enacted during Richard Breeden's term as chairman generated the Goldilocks era of 1993–1998, and (3) after the market was permanently disrupted by the foolish Rule 2a-7 amendments adopted in 1998 under Arthur Levitt, then chairman of the SEC. Only when the Fed determined that it had to intervene to stabilize this market at the end of 2007 did some semblance of the stability enjoyed by investors from 1993 to 1998 return.

Viewed overall, the Goldilocks era in the middle of the graph represents a brief period of stability in a long continuum of disruption. That six-year period represents what is best in U.S. market policy. To understand what fostered that equilibrium (and disrupted it in 1998) is to understand how the theory of market stability applies to market practice.

The market for mortgage-backed securities was severely disrupted by events in 1987, as explained in greater detail below. It recovered near-equilibrium by 1990 and generally flatlined for almost six years after the enactment of Rule 3a-7 under the Investment Company Act of 1940 and its companion shelf registration rules (1992).

When the SEC adopted Rule 3a-7 in 1992, it specifically excluded certain asset-backed issuers in its definition of an investment company. That created parity between issuers of securities backed by mortgages and those backed by other debt obligations. Markets responded favorably to this change—at least until the forces of market monopolization started to bubble up following amendments to the SEC's Rule 2a-7 (the 1940 rule governing money market funds) in 1998. As we've noted, that change led the United States into several financial crises, including (eventually) the crisis of 2007–2009.

It is important to understand the context behind these two key rule changes by the SEC. Financial markets had struggled for balance, from the 1987 stock market crash through George H. W. Bush's presidency, despite resolving many issues. A group of lawyers (including Fred) was asked to assess reasons for the market dysfunction. Each member of the group responded that mortgage finance markets were in equilibrium because of CMOs, but that an equivalent stabilizing instrument was not available for nonmortgage assets. Therefore, as investors' preferences changed from mortgages to shorter term securities, there was nothing comparable to the CMO in nonmortgage finance. Shorter maturity tranches of nonmortgage securitizations needed access to money market funds through introduction of the same legal exemptions that made mortgage deals work. The several years of SEC experience allowing an exemption to mortgage securities issuers made it clear that it was the structure of CMOs, not the backing of mortgages, that justified the broader exemption from limits normally applied to investment companies.

The SEC adopted Rule 3a-7 and new shelf-registration rules in December 1992, before Chairman Breeden left the SEC and after President Bill Clinton was elected. Many years later, one of Fred's clients who had relied on the rule gave Chairman Breeden a plaque measuring 36 by 48 inches for this achievement in front of several hundred executives. Since he left the SEC shortly after the rule was adopted, it was apparent that Chairman Breeden had little experience with just how important that move was for markets and the U.S. economy. In fact, the adoption of Rule 3a-7 in 1992 broke a logjam in the markets for nonmortgage securitizations and, in the process, helped make the Clinton presidency one of the most successful in the past half century in terms of economic growth.

Within months, people were able to bring CMO technology to non-mortgage assets and short-term mortgage tranches to money market funds. Implementation of Rule 3a-7 by the SEC was important for encouraging nonbank financial transactions. After General Motors lost $23 billion in 1992 and was within weeks of bankruptcy, a series of nonbank financings rescued GM and its GMAC financing unit with no public assistance. Market professionals created commercial paper backed by asset-backed securities (ABS) and mortgage-backed securities (MBS) using their creativity, Rule 3a-7, and lots of bells and whistles. The change enabled nonbank firms to safely compete with banks in selling this paper to money market funds.

Soon, however, scammers began to exploit the rule changes. As with any prohibition, every rule change carries both benefits and dangers for the market and society. Less than candid market participants soon created companion class CMOs that supported financial instruments that behaved like the ultrasafe current assets that were required for backing commercial paper sold to money market funds—but *only* when interest rates were low. By creating financial instruments whose negative convexity dramatically accelerates as market interest rates rise, the commercial paper backed by these instruments blew up as soon as the Fed caused a jump in mortgage rates early in 1994.

As previously noted, one casualty of that rate jump was Kidder, Peabody. The firm was owned by General Electric when the Askin funds went broke and could not repay Kidder on repo transactions. These short-term loans were backed by the companion class CMOs that suddenly went from a 2-year estimated maturity to 20 or more years, with a commensurate decline in price. Kidder was owned by GE's gilt-edged finance firm, General Electric Capital Corporation, and ended up in such bad shape that GE sold the shell of Kidder to PaineWebber and absorbed Kidder's assets in GE's long-term investment portfolio, where they languished until markets eventually recovered.

The SEC and other regulators certainly did not understand what had happened. The SEC later tried to convict one of the fund managers who had speculated on companion class CMOs as if they were short-term GSE securities. The fund's portfolio of short-term agency debt dropped 25 percent in value over one calendar quarter. That seems possible only in a case of fraud, but the SEC could not get a conviction. By 1998 it was clear that the SEC had never understood the acceleration of negative convexity that achieved this astonishing result. Obviously, they did not sufficiently explain the concept of option-adjusted duration to the jury in that case.[1]

Rather than fixing what really went wrong early in 1994, under Chairman Arthur Levitt the SEC enacted amendments to Rule 2a-7 in 1998. Those changes cut off access for good nonbank commercial paper (CP) issuers, handing the largest banks a monopoly over issuing asset-backed CP. Worse yet, the rules were written so that each bank-sponsored SIV could issue commercial paper for up to 5 percent of each money market fund's assets. This allowed a large bank (e.g., Citibank) to create 20 SIVs that the bank guaranteed and supply 100 percent of the commercial paper for every money market fund. Additionally, all of the assets were exempt from bank capital requirements because conduit SIVs were deemed off-balance sheet if just a miniscule amount of risk was owned by another investor. History would show that these arrangements were deliberate acts of fraud. To cite another example, Lehman Brothers, seems to have created its infamous Repo-105 transaction in part as a simple way to comply with the SEC's 1998 amendments to Rule 2a-7.

Simply stated, SEC Rule 3a-7 created the Goldilocks era in 1992 and the 1998 Rule 2a-7 amendments destroyed this equilibrium, creating a monopoly for the large banks and housing GSEs in the world of asset securitization. Fred Feldkamp's 2005 book provides details that bring the real-world financial consequences of the SEC's blunder into sharp focus, starting with the hedge fund crisis of 1998 (Feldkamp 2005).

How could a seemingly innocuous change to Investment Company Act Rule 2a-7, which nobody but a few short-term debt traders even noticed, cause the largest corporate debt crisis in eight years and destroy the virtuous cycle of liquidity that supported the first equilibrium in financial market

---

[1] Option-adjusted duration, or OAD, measures the convexity of a mortgage security. If you think of OAD as the time it takes for investors to recover their investment in an MBS, a change in duration for a so-called sucker bond (companion class CMO) from 2 years to 20 years because of a decline in loan repayments means that the return of capital will be significantly delayed. This results in a sharp drop in the value of the bond.

history? Consider the aggregate consequences that arose over the next four years. By the end of the third quarter of 2002, spreads had widened so far that unrated growth companies needed to pay about $170 billion per year more in interest costs (relative to AA-rated competitors). At a price-earnings ratio of 20 to 1, that implies a reduction in the value of corporate equities totaling $3.4 trillion. Not surprisingly, the Wall Street economist Larry Kudlow reported that stock markets fell by exactly the same amount ($3.4 trillion) during that period.

In 2009, we began to see that mortgage markets had recovered sufficiently to undertake new lending as a result of the Fed's market rebuilding programs. Through the Fed's intervention mortgage markets have been remarkably stable since 2009, despite enormous pressures. This has allowed some Americans to refinance their mortgages at historically low rates, although a number of structural impediments remain. The mortgage monopoly composed of the large banks and GSEs, for example, continues to use a variety of means to prevent homeowners from exercising their legal right to refinance. In order to restore the market to private-sector control, the United States will need to recreate the components that generated the 1993–1998 Goldilocks era. We urge three changes:

1. Fix the SEC's amendments to Rule 2a-7.
2. End the exclusivity of REMIC's for tax purposes so nonbanks can re-build private, stand-alone CMOs.
3. Create means for restructuring first mortgages on primary residences to establish sustainable repayment terms (the method most likely to succeed is to amend the U.S. Bankruptcy Code).

Figure 9.2 builds on the mortgage spread graph (Figure 9.1) to extend our market analysis to corporate bonds and stocks. It covers 25 years, from 1987 to 2012. The mortgage spread data in Figure 9.1 is represented by the dotted line in Figure 9.2 A dashed line represents the spread between high grade and high yield bonds in corporate bond markets during that period. That line uses two private-sector indices for corporate bonds calculated by different investment banks. The indices were published daily in the *Wall Street Journal* from 1987 onward.

As the 2007–2009 crisis began to affect the firms providing the corporate bond market data used for the dashed line in Figure 9.2, publication of the data became sporadic and, at least in our view, less trustworthy. These indices, however, were the best such data available until the SEC insisted on instantaneous reporting of corporate bond trades in 2005.

Figure 9.2 then correlates trends in mortgage and corporate bond markets with the daily closing price for the S&P 500 stock index (the solid line).

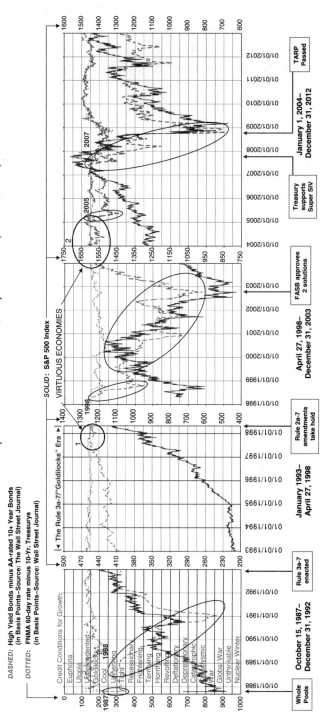

FIGURE 9.2 Crises and Recoveries, 1987–2012

Source: Data for high-yield bonds minus AA-rated 10+-year bonds and FNMA 60-day rate minus 10-year Treasuries (in basis points) from the *Wall Street Journal*, October 15, 1987–December 31, 2012.

The graph confirms the conclusion of Fed Chairman Bernanke and Kenneth Kuttner (see page 7) that changes in bond market spreads (risk) are a primary force in generating trends in equity markets.

Table 9.1 stands as strong evidence that the spreads shown in Figure 9.2 may, in fact, be the primary determinants of such trends. For any given time frame and level of cash flow available to support capital investment, Table 9.1 uses the sum of base rate and credit spread as the i in $FV = PV(1+i)^x$, the formula for compound interest. Bonds and stocks only have value by the application of that formula to an expected stream of future cash flows, and debt is prior to equity. It follows, therefore, that for any given term of repayment and level of cash flow it is only i that matters to investors. The table shows the value, today, of an assumed future cash flow for various base rate and spread assumptions. Table 9.1 shows how equity values change for each stated rate and spread assumption when debt is a fixed amount.

That is why rising credit spreads in Figure 9.2 (the dotted and dashed lines) depress equities (the solid line) and *vice versa*. The spread lines in this graph are, therefore, inverted to illustrate that inverse relationship. Both lines fall when spreads rise and *vice versa*. Thus, they show how changes in credit markets move equity markets.

In Fred Feldkamp's 2005 book, an earlier version of Figure 9.2 was used to track market solutions that created the first two virtuous (or Goldilocks) economies and to explain other matters shown on that graph (Feldkamp 2005).

TABLE 9.1   Up Is Bad; Down Is Good

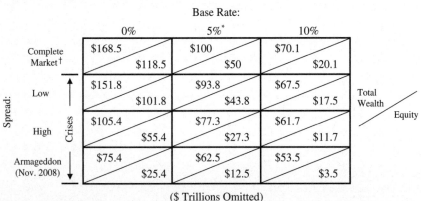

(\$ Trillions Omitted)

*The 2005 base rate of 5 percent generated a total capital market of roughly \$100 trillion, divided roughly 50-50 between debt and equity (Feldkamp 2005).

†A complete market (by definition of Adam Smith and the 1969 Level Playing Field Commission) produces a 150 basis point spread for long-term debt and a 250 basis point spread for equity cash flows.

The dotted line (mortgage spreads) trended toward equilibrium in 1990 because of orders issued by the SEC, affording exemptions to issuers of mortgage securities under the Investment Company Act of 1940 that allowed mortgage-backed securities markets to operate freely. As soon as risk-free arbitrages could be combined with stand-alone CMOs to moderate boom-bust cycles in mortgage markets, this graph shows that the U.S. mortgage market experienced (1) a few final growing pains after 1986, and (2) an enduring period of equilibrium from 1990 until the market disruption of 1998. Corporate bond markets were only freed of the restraints of that same 1940 act by Rule 3a-7, at the end of 1992. Those markets required several more years to stabilize and generate the virtuous economy of 1997–1998.

From 1998 through 2009, instability that arose in either or both of the mortgage or corporate debt markets triggered a series of financial crises. Starting in 2006, the losses embedded in off-balance sheet speculation by banks and the GSEs using low-grade mortgages (created to generate short-term profit supporting the compensation of bank managers) began to proliferate in the markets. When the piles of toxic waste mortgages that supported toxic CMOs and derivatives ceased to perform, losses were pushed on balance sheet. The fraud of off-balance sheet liability became obvious. As 2008 progressed, the likelihood of a $67 trillion write-down to equity loomed. Market confidence imploded. Prices fell and credit spreads exploded in both debt markets in Figure 9.2 (residential mortgages and bonds of growth firms). Due to a series of policy blunders, the resulting crisis was not contained until 2009, when losses in most financial institutions peaked.

In 2006, some of the most notorious issuers of toxic waste mortgages, such as Countrywide Financial and Washington Mutual, were showing severe signs of operation stress and were already shrinking in terms of assets and loan sales. Yet, investors and federal regulators ignored the warning signs.

With the benefit of hindsight, Figure 9.2 suggests that the responses of banks and GSEs to the early success of stand-alone CMOs was probably a major force behind the U.S. stock market crash of 1987. Looking at that period in Figures 9.1 and 9.2, one sees large spikes in spreads (declines in the graph line in Figure 9.1 and in the dotted and dashed lines in Figure 9.2) just before October 1987. That's the period when homebuilders, the entities with greatest need for stable funding for home mortgage origination, were being pushed out of the CMO market by the exclusivity of REMIC. Large banks, GSEs, and financial firms took over as just as Drexel Burnham's junk bond practice was starting to implode.

Investors who saw the negative implications of REMIC (through the monopoly it implied for financial institutions and GSEs) naturally sold CMOs. When they did, they discovered that there was no similar product available in the corporate bond market. That meant the United States was stuck with a return to the government-bank monopoly model for credit creation that had disrupted prosperity for both the United Kingdom and the United States since the Bank of England was created in 1694. The effect was amplified because the U.S. equity market used program trading in 1987 that relied on the mistaken sense that a credit market equilibrium had (at long last) been achieved. In such a situation, program trading becomes procyclical and exaggerates market reactions.

The belief that the market was balanced seemed logical. Relative stability had existed in corporate bonds for several years before 1987. Even the looming S&L crisis seemed to be an event U.S. corporate bond markets could handle. The variances in credit spreads during that period that these graphs show were observed only by a few people in the financial markets, since the data was neither readily available nor as reliable as it became after 2005.

In a credit market at equilibrium, each widening of the spread relationship is expected to generate counterdemands that will eventually reduce spread. By the fall of 1987, however, market imperfections caused U.S. investors' dreams of equilibrium to dissolve. Mortgage and corporate spreads spiked concurrently and generated no offsetting increase in investor demand. Investors, therefore, dumped stocks and program trading kicked in to generate a record-setting crash.

The October 1987 crisis generated the first exercise of the Greenspan put, a policy whereby the central bank used massive liquidity to prevent a sharp market correction. The Fed flooded markets with bank liquidity, as well as collateral, opening the doors to Treasury traders who could not cover short positions. Chris Whalen was working on the fixed-income desk at Bear, Stearns & Co. on the first day of the Fed's intervention, when every Treasury bond trader in London was short collateral as the New York equity market opened limit down. Enough banks bought enough bonds to reverse the spread spikes, however, and equity markets gradually rebounded. Without finishing the market reform process, however, the United States could not achieve sustained financial stability using private-sector demand to counterbalance procyclical, bank-dominated market panics. As evidenced by events of 2007–2009, markets will remain reliant on the Greenspan put until new policies create the necessary mechanics for a sustained period of private-sector equilibrium outside of the present bankcentric monopoly.

As discussed above, experts told the SEC that the fundamental problem behind the 1987 crash was failure to open markets for structures allowing nonmortgage financial assets (corporate bonds and other loans) equal access to markets that were opened for mortgages in 1986. That relief only came in 1992, however, after George H. W. Bush lost the 1992 election to Bill Clinton. In 1992, markets were recovering from three shocks that the first Bush Administration addressed but had not resolved quickly enough to win reelection:

- The S&L crisis
- The continuing effect of the failure to resolve corporate bond market issues
- A credit spread spike (and drop in demand for homes, cars, etc.) associated with Iraq's invasion of Kuwait at the end of 1990

Several very large U.S. firms (including IBM, Sears, and GM) that had the resources to survive crises for quite a while began to shake at their foundations by 1992. Then, at the end of 1992, the SEC implemented Rule 3a-7 and other reforms. This gave equal treatment to sound structures for private intermediation of nonmortgage financial assets. Congress had not yet eliminated the Glass-Steagall Act prohibitions on banks engaging in investment banking activities, so the 1992 reform generated a new market that nonbank brokerage firms could exploit, allowing interested entrepreneurs to fund nonmortgage loans outside the banking system and thereby support economic growth. From the 1988 S&L crisis until then, the United States suffered the usual shortage of business lending that lingers after any financial crisis when banks exercise monopoly lending power.

The initial impact of the SEC's 1992 reform was even more salutary than the 1983 success of stand-alone CMOs. Within a few years, Rule 3a-7 fostered the first virtuous economy. Much of that virtue arose as a result of one specific firm's financial needs—General Motors.

Operating and financial crises in the late 1980s and early 1990s led GM to deploy the countercyclical funding resources of its nonconsolidated GMAC financial arm. Before, during, and after the Great Depression, GM had successfully used GMAC's access to credit markets to ensure continuous funding for automobile dealers and consumers.

The economic impact of the 1987 crash, the 1989–1992 slump reflecting the cost of fixing the 1980s S&L mess, and the crisis of confidence caused by the oil and defense shocks associated with Iraq's invasion of Kuwait all contributed to reduce U.S. demand for automobiles. Without GMAC's access to commercial paper markets, GM's dealers and consumers had to compete for bank funding at a time when many bankers saw a need to retrench, further depleting sources to finance auto sales at exactly the time when liquidity support was badly needed.

The auto recession of the late 1980s and early 1990s, moreover, was compounded by the good news that the quick success of Desert Storm had reduced the demand pull of defense spending. The United States raised taxes under President Bush to fund Desert Storm and stabilize markets. When the war ended in about a week, increased taxes unmatched by expenditures created a drag on the economy as credit spreads failed to fall to levels allowing sufficient private-sector growth.

In addition, long-needed accounting reforms impacted GM and GMAC. GM did not consolidate GMAC before the 1990s, but was now required to do so. GMAC was structured with legal protections for unsecured creditors that addressed creditors' needs during the 1920s and the Great Depression. Those protections included a prohibition on secured borrowings without a general pledge to protect all creditors. While not framed as such, that no-pledge clause supported unsecured creditors against the fraud found in the famous 1925 U.S. Supreme Court opinion of Justice Brandeis.

Accounting consolidation had reinforced rating agency considerations that generated identical ratings for GM and GMAC, though GMAC's business model was demonstrably less cyclical than GM's. In addition, at the end of 1992, new accounting rules required GM to recognize previously unreported future health care commitments made to retired employees. All told, GM reported a massive loss of some $23 billion that year.

Well before the end of 1992, GM understood the implications of these market issues and accounting changes. GMAC diversified and lengthened its funding sources to reduce reliance on short-term commercial paper liabilities, even though short-term debt was less expensive than longer term debt. Its program was as successful as anyone could imagine, reducing dependence on commercial paper by about 40 percent.

Near the end of 1992, however, it was anticipated that GMAC would be downgraded by some major rating agencies. The record for commercial paper issuance at the next lower rating level, even with standby bank support and collateral, had recently been set by the troubled retailer Sears. Sears raised only one-sixth the amount of commercial paper GMAC expected to have outstanding at year end 1992. By its no-pledge commitment, moreover, GMAC could not secure its commercial paper as Sears had done. The vast bulk of GMAC's commercial paper would come due in less than 90 days.

For decades GM and GMAC had paid banks to stand by with funding commitments if a crisis arose. The crisis for which bank support was needed was happening. Even though much of GM's loss in 1992 was due to accounting changes that finally required recognition of retiree health costs, banks became reluctant to lend GM and GMAC what they needed. At the time, the JPMorgan crew that now leads major commercial lending was still at Chemical Bank (which later merged into JPMorgan Chase Bank). Chemical was selected to lead the world's banks (which had collectively taken at least $500 million in fees over the years to stand by) in a consortium to get GM over the funding hump.

After long and careful study, banks concluded that they could do it, but that it would mean GM-GMAC would need to pay about 400 basis points more than Ford for at least five years, and therefore GM would be broke. Some wondered if GM should just turn the shop over to the big banks, a situation nearly identical to what Mr. Morgan did for the owner of Tennessee Coal, Iron & Railroad in 1907. In that situation Morgan used cash from the U.S. Treasury to fund loans secured by the bonds of U.S. Steel and caused a transfer of TC&I to U.S. Steel for almost nothing.

In a sense, in the 1990s the bankers were replaying events that GM had experienced before the Great Depression. In 1910, a syndicate of bankers led by J.W. Seligman and Kuhn and Loeb took control over the General Motors Company from founder William C. Durant, the acclaimed master of the market. As we noted earlier, Durant was a Wall Street speculator who created what is today's GM through a series of audacious acquisitions of small auto manufacturers in the first two decades of the twentieth century.

Durant was a maker and loser of fabulous fortunes, but this meant that GM was entirely self-financed and was thus vulnerable to changes in markets and the broader economy. In 1915, however, Durant acquired Chevrolet and formed an alliance with the DuPont family to reclaim control. But this reprise was short-lived, and in 1920 Durant was forced out for the last time. In 1923, Alfred Sloan became GM's president.

The great management genius of Alfred Sloan made GM the most profitable company in the industry through the astute use of leverage and decentralized management. But the process of turning GM into the greatest industrial company the world had ever seen took years. GM survived the Great Depression and then grew enormously during WWII and afterward, using the model of leverage put in place by Sloan.

Seven decades later, banks extended a helping hand to GM in a new crisis, but with a 400-basis point upraised middle finger of interest cost. Moreover, the banks said they would likely continue to stick GM with that fee for perhaps five years, a cost that would force the company into bankruptcy. Barbara Tuchman and John Merriman note that governments, and merchants dealing with governments, have faced the same issue of punitive interest rates throughout the world and throughout the ages (Tuchman 1984; Merriman 2010).

Before the 1992 adoption of Rule 3a-7 by the SEC, the only way GM could fight the banks was to file for bankruptcy. Every merchant (and government) knows you don't piss off a banker. As 1993 began, Rule 3a-7 and the advent of CMO technology allowed GM and GMAC to create entirely new ABS markets for all of GMAC's assets. It was done with the help of banks, but outside the control of a bank monopoly on liquidity from deposits. The structures denied bankers the premiums they sought by going directly to the markets.

The process allowed GM to fund GMAC at rates below Ford and just above the U.S. Treasury by mid-February of 1993. Because GM showed a capacity to raise unlimited funds in the open market, when it came to pricing new bank funding that GM and GMAC sought in March of 1993, the upraised middle finger of bank credit spread was wiped out.

Bankruptcy filings rarely occur because liabilities exceed assets (called legal insolvency). They occur because an essential creditor demands payment and cannot be paid (equitable insolvency). If only a small amount of the more than $20 billion of commercial paper that GMAC had sold could not be paid as it matured in the first months of 1993 there would be no choice but to put GMAC (and probably GM as well) into bankruptcy reorganization.

Before the 2008 TARP legislation gave the government the ability to persuade banks to permit GM's reorganization on reasonable terms, nobody who understood the firm believed any reorganization plan would succeed.

Without a solution (no GM or GMAC treasury office financial planner could find one before the adoption of Rule 3a-7), it seemed inevitable that GM and GMAC would be forced to liquidate during the first three months of 1993. That would have left perhaps 2 million people instantly unemployed and the government's Pension Benefit Guaranty Corporation with a huge and nearly incalculable liability. In short, as Bill Clinton took office it appeared that the nation was staring into a chasm that might repeat the terrible events of 1933, when Michigan's banks went broke as FDR took office.

Applying the technology of stand-alone CMOs to generate new market structures under the SEC's 1992 Rule 3a-7, one writer who covered GM's crisis later noted that by the end of February 1993, the worst of GM's crisis was over.

The description of precisely how that happened was an empty space at the top of the page on which that writer declared the worst was over. GM's bleeding had stopped, but nobody knew why. Those involved in the salvation of GM have decorative plaques that describe the structures used to fund, over time, some $200 billion of GMAC's assets, representing a debt turnover of several trillion dollars.

After 127 years, the premium embedded in Bagehot's May 1866 dictum was overcome. No penalty rate was needed to attract necessary capital. GM's experience put the price of allowing a bank monopoly at 400 basis points (4 percent per annum) for five years. That necessary penalty from the banks was so high that it would have caused GM's bankruptcy even if *all* GMAC's commercial paper had been paid.

With the market freedom allowed by the SEC's adoption of Rule 3a-7 in 1992 there was no penalty. GMAC was funding at rates approaching those offered to the U.S. Treasury. Such is the power of free markets operating outside the control of a government-bank monopoly.

The structures GMAC created to fund short-term investors using Rule 3a-7 proved so protective of each and every investor (for each and every borrowing) that even the most conservative analysts deemed them risk free. The premium of Bagehot's dictum was overcome by creating the means for avoiding a funding monopoly. The world's leading central banks followed the same plan (and saved the entire financial world) after the crisis of 2007–2008.

The GM-GMAC resolution used stand-alone CMO technology to change everything in corporate debt markets. On both of the first two graphs in this book (Figures 9.1 and 9.2), the period from the end of 1992 to the second calendar quarter of 1998 is labeled the Goldilocks era. Led by manufacturers seeking only to use finance to maintain a stable great wheel of circulation (rather than to create profits by short-term speculation), for six years U.S. financial markets generated new demand for loans whenever spreads rose (preventing spikes in spread) and slowed the offering of new securities when spreads fell to levels consistent with credit market equilibrium (restraining euphoria). That's when U.S. markets proved the efficacy of the theory of financial stability presented herein and Adam Smith's reserve banking model.

The 400 basis point credit spread over Ford that GM was quoted by the banks (before Rule 3a-7 was adopted by the SEC) compares, quite frighteningly, with similar spikes of rising spreads charged after 1998. It was in the spring of 1998 that the very structures GMAC successfully used were cut off for broader application by amendments the SEC adopted to Rule 2a-7. The rule was supposed to save money market funds from problems (discussed above) that arose early in 1994. Not only did the Rule 2a-7 amendments fail to address the cause of the 1994 market disruption, they were designed, with the aid of bank representatives, so off-balance sheet bank SIVs gained a monopoly/monopsony over money market funds. It compelled markets to rely on too-big-to-fail banks by excluding nonbank issuers while favoring those banks.

Combined with the monopoly on long-term mortgage funding that the REMIC structure gave U.S. housing finance GSEs, the 1998 Rule 2a-7 amendments led to the near destruction of *all* money market funds (along with every other investment in the world) by 2008. Just a moment's glance at Charts 9.1, 9.2, and 9.3 reveals what is by far the worst example of a monopoly-driven financial disaster in modern time. The peak on those charts is twice as high as spike in spreads that followed the Crash of 1929 and precipitated the Great Depression.

We will use these three charts later to describe the events of 2007–2014. The discussion of how a new monopoly produced that spike begins now.

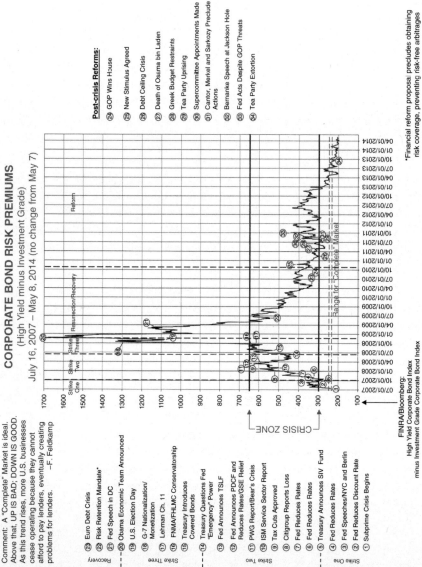

CORPORATE BOND RISK PREMIUMS

(High Yield minus Investment Grade)

July 16, 2007 – May 8, 2014 (no change from May 7)

Comment: A "Complete" Market is ideal. Above that, UP IS BAD; DOWN IS GOOD. As this trend rises, more U.S. businesses cease operating because they cannot afford to pay lenders, eventually creating problems for lenders.   —F. Feldkamp

FINRA/Bloomberg:
High Yield Corporate Bond Index
minus Investment Grade Corporate Bond Index

Post-crisis Reforms:

㉔ GOP Wins House
㉕ New Stimulus Agreed
㉖ Debt Ceiling Crisis
㉗ Death of Osama bin Laden
㉘ Greek Budget Restraints
㉙ Tea Party Uprising
㉚ Supercommittee Appointments Made
㉛ Cantor, Merkel and Sarkozy Preclude Actions
㉜ Bernanke Speech at Jackson Hole
㉝ Fed Acts Despite GOP Threats
㉞ Tea Party Extortion

Recovery
㉓ Euro Debt Crisis
㉒ Risk Retention Mandate*
㉑ Fed Speech in DC

Strike Three
⑳ Obama Economic Team Announced
⑲ U.S. Election Day
⑱ G-7 Nationalization/ Monetization
⑰ Lehman Ch. 11
⑯ FNMA/FHLMC Conservatorship
⑮ Treasury Introduces Covered Bonds
⑭ Treasury Questions Fed "Emergency" Power
⑬ Fed Announces TSLF

Strike Two
⑫ Fed Announces PDCF and Reduces Rates/GSE Relief
⑪ PWG Report/Bear's Crisis
⑩ ISM Service Sector Report
⑨ Tax Cuts Approved
⑧ Citigroup Reports Loss
⑦ Fed Reduces Rates
⑥ Fed Reduces Rates
⑤ Treasury Announces SIV Fund

Strike One
④ Fed Reduces Rates
③ Fed Speeches/NYC and Berlin
② Fed Reduces Discount Rate
① Subprime Crisis Begins

*Financial reform proposal precludes obtaining risk coverage, preventing risk-free arbitrages

CHART 9.1   Corporate Bond Risk Premiums, 2007–2014

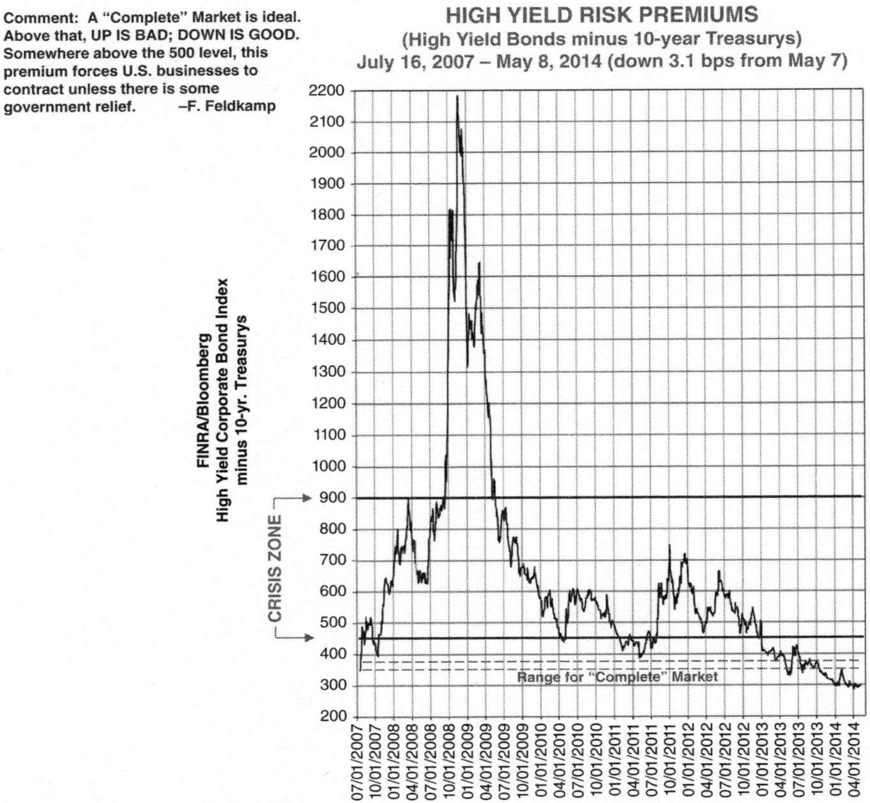
Comment: A "Complete" Market is ideal. Above that, UP IS BAD; DOWN IS GOOD. Somewhere above the 500 level, this premium forces U.S. businesses to contract unless there is some government relief. –F. Feldkamp
HIGH YIELD RISK PREMIUMS
(High Yield Bonds minus 10-year Treasurys)
July 16, 2007 – May 8, 2014 (down 3.1 bps from May 7)
FINRA/Bloomberg
High Yield Corporate Bond Index
minus 10-yr. Treasurys
CRISIS ZONE
Range for "Complete" Market
2200
2100
2000
1900
1800
1700
1600
1500
1400
1300
1200
1100
1000
900
800
700
600
500
400
300
200
07/01/2007
10/01/2007
01/01/2008
04/01/2008
07/01/2008
10/01/2008
01/01/2009
04/01/2009
07/01/2009
10/01/2009
01/01/2010
04/01/2010
07/01/2010
10/01/2010
01/01/2011
04/01/2011
07/01/2011
10/01/2011
01/01/2012
04/01/2012
07/01/2012
10/01/2012
01/01/2013
04/01/2013
07/01/2013
10/01/2013
01/01/2014
04/01/2014

CHART 9.2 High Yield Risk Premiums, 2007–2014

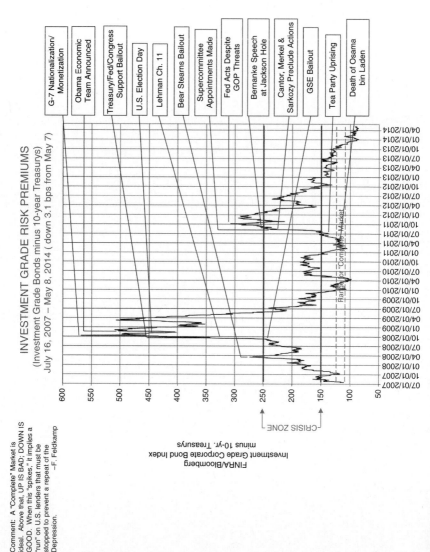

Comment: A "Complete" Market is ideal. Above that, UP IS BAD; DOWN IS GOOD. When this "spikes," it implies a "run" on U.S. lenders that must be stopped to prevent a repeat of the Depression.
–F. Feldkamp

INVESTMENT GRADE RISK PREMIUMS

(Investment Grade Bonds minus 10-year Treasurys)

July 16, 2007 – May 8, 2014 (down 3.1 bps from May 7)

G-7 Nationalization/ Monetization

Obama Economic Team Announced

Treasury/Fed/Congress Support Bailout

U.S. Election Day

Lehman Ch. 11

Bear Stearns Bailout

Supercommittee Appointments Made

Fed Acts Despite GOP Threats

Bernanke Speech at Jackson Hole

Cantor, Merkel & Sarkozy Preclude Actions

GSE Bailout

Tea Party Uprising

Death of Osama bin Laden

Range of "Complete" Market

CRISIS ZONE

FINRA/Bloomberg Investment Grade Corporate Bond Index minus 10-yr. Treasury

CHART 9.3 Investment Grade Risk Premiums, 2007–2014

1998: WHEN THE SEC DESTROYED A WONDROUS MACHINE

In 1994, equity markets began a four-year rise (before the post-1998 build-up to the tech bubble). Bill Clinton easily won reelection in 1996, in part because the financial markets were operating so well. The payroll contributions of baby boomers were at their peak, deficits were vanishing and economists were fretting about the disappearance of public Treasury debt. The markets were awash in cash and the nonbank private sector was raising capital in ways not seen since the 1920s.

Then came the hedge fund crisis of 1998 and the failure and rescue of Long Term Capital Management. Bond markets began falling out of sync as soon as the SEC adopted and implemented the 1998 amendments to Rule 2a-7 and destroyed the equilibrium generated by its 1992 reforms. When the 1998 amendments were announced and before they became effective, Fred attended a conference at which the SEC group that wrote the 1998 amendments bragged that they had solved the 1994 problem that caused some money market funds to break the buck. It was clear, however, that the staff did not understand the problem, much less the cure.

As discussed earlier, the 1994 problem arose from GSE sales in prior years of an enormous number of companion class CMOs. The securities are 100 percent free of default risk, but include terms that could extend repayment maturities (and the duration of the security) from less than a year to, in some cases, more than 25 years, if long-term interest rates rise by just a few percentage points.

The GSEs created and sold some 95 percent of these time-bomb securities. Many were used to back commercial paper that money market funds bought. The numbers sold were unimaginable to the creators of the structure. Drafters of the first such bonds believed no more than .05 percent of investors in mortgage-backed securities would find these risky securities suitable for purchase. It was impossible to contain the duration explosions embedded in them. Those explosions caused the bonds to abruptly stop paying and fall very rapidly in price (market value) whenever market interest rates rose.

In low-rate environments companion class bonds can support commercial paper, but they cannot support the issuance of any short-term debt when rates rise. As noted earlier, knowledgeable market participants openly refer to them as sucker bonds.

Because GSEs did not need to rate their bonds, a mandatory *r* rating disclosure of the volatility embedded in the securities was not included when GSE companion class CMOs were sold to short-term government bond funds. Those funds, in turn, sold commercial paper to money market funds, declaring the bonds' current assets suitable to support commercial paper issuance. The bond funds bought them because the securities paid a slightly higher interest rate than other short-term securities at a time that market rates were very low (a sign that some risk exists).

As soon as the Fed raised rates at the end of 1993 and early in 1994, buyers of these sucker bonds saw the value of their short-term bond portfolios drop by more than 25 percent in less than three months. For investors in traditional short-term government/agency debt, that impact was impossible to manage or understand. The hit to value made no mathematical sense except to those few people who understood the implications of a change in interest rates to the effective duration of companion class securities.

For those who got it, the effect was entirely logical, but the SEC commissioners and staff missed it. If one faces a rise in discount rates of 2 percent, and the maturity of affected assets increases by 25 years as a result of a rise in long-term rates, the affected debt securities *must* lose 25 percent in value. The moment rates rose, companion class CMOs could not be considered current assets. Since they could not then back the sale of new commercial paper, and stopped producing cash flows in amounts necessary to repay maturing commercial paper, money market funds that owned affected commercial paper couldn't be paid at maturity. It was a colossal blunder but one that was obvious to observers that understood these securities.

As previously noted, that is how the 1994 crisis was caused: by an acceleration of the negative convexity embedded in toxic waste securities, a hidden risk in creating a security that was so risky as to make it unsuitable for all but a very few investors. All the SEC had to do in 1998 was ban that feature from securities supporting commercial paper and other assets bought by money market funds. Instead, the SEC enacted rules that entirely missed the issue and handed a monopoly/monopsony over the market for asset-backed securities to the largest commercial banks and bank-supported SIVs that invested in companion class CMOs issued by the housing GSEs.

The SEC staff listened to bankers, wrote a rule that gave them a monopoly, and ruined the mechanisms that generated the first-ever debt market equilibrium. The staff then arrogantly announced that their new rules made it mathematically certain that money market funds would never again suffer a crisis. The general counsel of a major investment company who spoke at the 1998 conference Fred attended looked at drafters of the rule and declared that if they thought any rule could improve the judgment of a good investment manager or eliminate the errors of bad ones, the SEC was "even dumber than I thought."

The Rule 2a-7 amendments of 1998 created a monopoly for banks that reinforced, and was far worse than, the monopoly generated by the ill-conceived exclusivity of the REMIC tax structure. Not only did the SEC's 1998 rule miss the cause of the 1994 crisis and generate a monopoly that favored such absurdities as Lehman's Repo 105 deception, it created a bank monopsony. One bank, simply by generating 20 alter egos in the form of

SIVs, could now be the sole source backing 100 percent of all assets of money market funds. And the big banks, led by Citigroup and Lehman Brothers, more than vigorously availed themselves of that gift in the years leading up to the 2007 market meltdown.

The 1998 SEC amendments to Rule 2a-7 allowed money market funds to flood liquidity into ill-fated SIV funds (conduits used to hide off-balance sheet speculations by Citibank and other large banks) using whatever leverage the bank desired—with no capital support. While a few nonbank entities successfully passed through the minefield of the SEC's 1998 amendments, those amendments laid the foundation for each crisis thereafter.

Using a credit spread chart like the graphs in this book, Fred helped a client show the SEC staff precisely when and how the Rule 2a-7 amendments created the hedge fund crisis of the summer of 1998. The client showed that the usual suspect for the hedge fund crisis of 1998, Russia's default on a small bond issue, was simply irrelevant. The SEC responded by granting grandfather rights to certain structures created before the rule became effective.

That allowed the September 1998 resolution of Long Term Capital Management, but the staff said it would be embarrassing to change the rule itself so soon after adoption by the SEC's commissioners. The SEC staff knew the Commission had made a mistake, but was either too arrogant (or ashamed) to admit it erred.

Every subsequent effort to resolve the problem has likewise been too early. The defects have not been corrected. The unwise SEC rule remains in place today.

The SEC staff was also told by Fred's client that as grandfather rights wore off (as those securities repaid), another crisis would follow. As predicted, a liquidity crisis in 2000 led to the bursting of the tech bubble. George W. Bush won election during that crisis. Reviewing a spread chart Fred prepared in the fall of 2000, a senior Bush economic advisor called it "the scariest thing I've ever seen."

The crises associated with the 2001–2002 tech bubble and the events of September 11, 2001, and the crisis that ended the 2004 virtuous economy, can also be traced to the same 1998 warp in market function that the SEC created with the 1998 amendments to Rule 2a-7. In 2008, the entire money market fund industry had to be guaranteed by the US Treasury in order to cleanse it of bank-originated toxic waste that predictably found its way into the funds through Rule 2a-7. That problem included the Repo 105 abuse Lehman used for short-term funding of toxic mortgages that the firm traded.

Being cut off from access to money market funds, structures by which creative entrepreneurs intermediated loans to stabilize markets in 1992–1998 were abandoned. Over time, it became clear that stable funding through money market funds was available only to banks. So many nonbank firms became (or acquired) banks to compete with the advantages given to banks by the SEC with the 1998 amendment to Rule 2a-7.

By the end of 2008, the surviving broker dealers (such as Goldman Sachs and Morgan Stanley) were all forced to become bank holding companies, at least in name. None of these ersatz banks, however, could compete with the funding monopoly of a money center bank.

THE BUILD-UP TO DISASTER (2001 TO 2007)

As we've noted, the SEC's 1998 rule change created a financial monopoly for banks. Throughout history, every financial monopoly has spawned a disaster— call it a suicide monopoly, the title of an article Fred wrote years ago.

Once the SEC gave them a monopoly, the banks compounded risk by overfunding markets to gain still greater control, a standard practice of monopolists. It is important to mention that the self-destructive behavior of the big banks in the 1998–2008 period almost precisely mirrors the anticompetitive behavior of JPMorgan and the money trusts of a century before discussed earlier in this narrative.

Low spreads led to reduced margins that fostered excessive leverage to generate the same profit level using off-balance sheet liabilities. Secret leverage increased the number and amount of transactions while hiding the need for additional capital from regulators. The process raised fees for management compensation and left losses for creditors, owners, and ultimately the taxpayer, both in terms of cash and lost economic value, growth, and opportunities. It was fraud, committed by the bankers of Wall Street and London and their monopoly partners in Washington and elsewhere.

The sources of liquidity to fund bank speculations also grew. In addition to oil exporting nations, expansion of worldwide trade created a surge in export-driven trade surpluses in Germany, Japan, and less developed nations (led by China, India, and Brazil).

As capital needs shrank at U.S. productive-sector firms that were losing jobs, mercantilist exporting nations were in an ever-increasing search for U.S.-backed investments to avoid currency changes that might dampen their export-fed growth. They turned to U.S. mortgage securities issued by the U.S. GSEs. Underwriting standards of the GSEs dropped and that allowed bankers to seek lesser and lesser quality credits and higher fees, while hiding their new leverage for loan origination off-balance sheet.

In that way, managers of the monopoly avoided the need for new capital and continued to receive big compensation packages even as investors' risks ballooned.

As non-U.S. investors needed still more investments in the United States to address the export desires of their nations' leaders, foreign banks recycled some $30 trillion into the United States. Creative investors found new ways to generate mortgage-backed securities in which the credit quality of the underlying assets became irrelevant. Indeed, with the creation of new credit default swaps (CDSs) after 2001, sound underwriting actually became a detriment to the sale of new GSE securities and other securities backed by subprime mortgages.

The CDS debacle emerged when some investors began to note the trend downward in terms of the quality of mortgage underwriting that began in the late 1990s and decided to pursue a strategy that would reward them as mortgage defaults inevitably rose. Following the 2001 change in management at AIG, one of the largest U.S. issuers of CDSs, investors were able to short specific mortgage-backed securities without actually owning the shorted securities—naked shorting.

Gilded Age robber barons like Daniel Drew well understood the process, but they were discouraged from pursuing such naked short trades because it was considered conversion (theft) to sell assets that one did not own. By SEC rules, shorting of normal investment assets is allowed only when one finds an owner willing to lend securities that the short trader can deliver if the short is called. The beauty of a CDS is that regulators of that market allowed anyone to buy a short position, without having to own or borrow the underlying asset.

It was a short-seller's dream come true. Whether they understood the implications of what they were saying may be debated forever, but it is well documented that Robert Rubin, Alan Greenspan, and Lawrence Summers openly advocated deregulation of the markets where these CDSs were written and sold. Indeed, Mr. Greenspan is famously quoted as saying fraud is self-regulating (a quote he must now surely regret).

As a result, when the modern-day mortgage shorts could persuade originators to create mortgages that had little or no chance of paying, their potential for profit was only limited by the risk of insolvency at the CDS issuer. Due to its size and acquired too-big-to-fail status, that is what, in September 2008, made the name AIG a household word everywhere.

In this tragic comedy of blunder, a bubble funded by international trade was allowed to expand to $67 trillion, off-balance sheet, by managers seeking ever-greater compensation and investors who discovered that they could profit on others' stupidity as credit quality dropped. It is for this reason that U.S. leaders who in the late 1990s and early 2000s advocated deregulation of the CDS market are now deemed pariahs by those that understand this defect in their leadership. Greenspan, Rubin and Summers are very smart people, but they blundered on this issue in a way that does not foster trust.

Naked shorting cannot be justified. It is fraud because it allows an investor to feign a desire to sell assets and profit when that false pretense drives the assets' value down.[2] Unless a short investor has the ability to sell the assets in question, the pretense of a sale is duplicity, per se. To allow markets to be driven by false pretense is to deny investors a right of honesty.

Naked shorting is a deliberately incomplete sale. It is fraud by the law of Moses and by the test set forth by Justice Louis Brandeis 90 years ago in the *Benedict* decision. As soon as resourceful traders found that this fraud was actually deemed lawful in the United States in 2000, it took little time before mortgage shorts drew out the issuance of innumerable mortgage securities backed by increasingly dumb and dumber loans. The lower the quality of loans in a pool, the more the CDS short traders loved the deals.

Soon after the PhD mathematician CEO of AIG Financial Products (AIGFP) retired in 2001, his firm became the largest collector of the other side of the shorts' CDS trades. Its 2008 demise was made certain by that blunder.

With this ridiculous dynamic in place, short traders hunted for ever-worse securities to enhance their prospects for profit. Foreign mercantilists (the long side of the mortgage trades) still needed to buy ever-more U.S. mortgage securities to give them U.S. capital market investments that absorbed the current account surpluses and thereby supported their nations' export and investment goals.

It was folly. As with any investment mania, none of the participants stopped to consider the illogic of their actions.

ENLIGHTENMENT IGNORED—RESULT: ARMAGEDDON (2007 TO 2009)

Given what we discussed in the previous two sections, it should be clear that the 2007–2009 financial crisis was accelerated by worldwide forces much larger than the deceptions of U.S. banks and other financial asset traders. The crisis began with subprime mortgage debt and derivatives, but the causes of the crisis were far larger and more profound. It was caused by, and part of, a buildup of $67 trillion of worldwide imbalances that arose from mercantilist patterns of international trade (and the related financial flows) and hidden from scrutiny as off-balance sheet liabilities. Those patterns are as old as trade itself.

Economists from Adam Smith forward have criticized mercantilist trade patterns from all perspectives. As usual, the mercantilists will be financial

---

[2] A similar pretense is reportedly used in certain high-frequency trading schemes. A false sell signal is used to attract buyers, who are then outrun to exchanges and fronted to lock in higher sale prices.

losers as the crisis resolves. Having ignored centuries of warnings, however, the mercantilists have little basis to cry foul when their losses mount. The world's major exporting nations understood they were importing excessive amounts of foreign currency from trading partners—their accumulated current account surpluses. As a result, their currency would rise in value (reducing exports) if they did not reinvest imported cash in the capital markets of the importing nations that exported their currency to buy the mercantilists' exports. This dynamic is exemplified by what we now see between the United States and China (where restructuring is progressing) and between Germany and Greece (where inevitable restructuring was stalled by politics—trapping Greece in a depression from which it now, finally, appears to be emerging).

A mercantilist exporter's strategy is to import jobs and build factories. To achieve that, it must prevent currency readjustments that naturally occur when a net-exporter's positive current account balances are either converted to local currency or exchanged for other currency. For example, the currency of a major exporter (e.g., China and Japan) would certainly rise relative to dollars if it dumped the extra dollars paid by the United States for net imports bought from China or Japan, respectively. Alternatively, of course, the exporters could buy goods for import, but that obviously contradicts their mercantilist strategy.

One way or another, a high level of exports necessarily translates into the need for a net exporter to (1) import, (2) sell imported currency, or (3) invest money into the capital market of the importer of the exporter's goods. Setting up sovereign investment funds is just one way of achieving (3).

For decades, net-exporter nations with trade surpluses with the United States chose (3). The United States was importing so many goods that U.S. producers had no need to build factories or other value-added capital goods. That bid down the cost of U.S. capital to record lows. At that point, what's left? The largest non-plant/equipment capital asset most easily expanded by excessive investment and leverage is land and housing. Whether done by the exporting nation or by others supporting housing in importing nations, the standard result of mercantilism is a real estate bubble.

Direct ownership of U.S. land and homes subjects an exporter to U.S. real estate taxes. Therefore, the capital investment of choice for U.S. -related trade imbalance dollars (roughly $30 trillion in aggregate as of 2006) became U.S. mortgages, especially mortgages in a REMIC-type vehicle, which qualify for tax-free treatment. That means U.S. citizens bear the real estate tax burden while the exporting nations get interest (often exempt from U.S. taxation by treaty). Through GSEs, moreover, the U.S. helped exporters hide their strategy by failing to report the GSEs' obligations on balance sheet. In the end, however, mercantilists eventually make up in capital losses whatever they gain by exporting goods.

So, to absorb trade imbalances, exporting nations bought whatever mortgage securities U.S. financial gurus invented. In the past, that's how Japan became the victim of capital market speculations in the United States (e.g., Rockefeller Center and all the schemes related in *F.I.A.S.C.O.*, a mid-1990s book by Frank Portnoy, professor of law and finance at the University of San Diego, that led to some reform of U.S. derivative markets).

Over time, a $30 trillion current account imbalance created an insatiable demand for U.S. mortgages. Investing that much money requires many financial machines. One must also force-feed a lot of mortgages to a *lot* of borrowers to satisfy that level of foreign demand for investible assets. Achim Deubel makes this very point: "If you import capital on this scale for such a long time, misallocation is preordained" (Deubel 2012). It is not at all difficult, therefore, to understand the size of the forces that brought the world to the point of Armageddon in late 2008 via the devices of poorly underwritten subprime mortgages and fraudulent documentation of prime mortgages, all hidden as off-balance sheet debt of GSEs, major banks and AIG.

As we have said before, everyone is to blame yet it is hard to blame anyone. International folly was the overriding player in all this. Indeed, the role of international capital flows in fueling the mortgage boom of the 2000s recalls the warning of John Maynard Keynes about the dangers of free trade. He wrote

> *I sympathize, therefore, with those who would minimize, rather than with those who would maximize, economic entanglement among nations. Ideas, knowledge, science, hospitality, travel—these are the things which should of their nature be international. But let goods be homespun whenever it is reasonably and conveniently possible, and, above all, let finance be primarily national. Yet, at the same time, those who seek to disembarrass a country of its entanglements should be very slow and wary. It should not be a matter of tearing up roots but of slowly training a plant to grow in a different direction. (Keynes 1933)*

With that introduction to what created the subprime crisis, let's look at the day-by-day agony of steps leading to that financial disaster. Fred compiled his list of these steps from comments he circulated to correspondents, in real time, between July 2007 and November 20, 2008. Charts 9.1, 9.2, and 9.3 and Table 9.1 compile the daily data and translate the patterns shown into their economic impact, respectively. Each chart tracks a particular credit market spread. The numbered events marked on Chart 9.1 correlate with the descriptions—offered by Fred as the events occurred—that follow in the "Twenty Events That Led to Bankruptcy" section. Each was significant when it occurred, based on bond investors' concurrent market reaction. We will review the numbered events on Chart 9.1 and sometimes reference events noted on Chart 9.3

Chart 9.1 tracks the difference between daily indices for U.S. high grade (investment grade) and high yield corporate bonds from FINRA (Financial Industry Regulatory Authority). It uses the bond trade data the SEC began to mandate in 2005. This is the spread that most closely correlates to the daily cost of Adam Smith's great wheel of circulation, as measured by the U.S. bond market. Chart 9.2 shows high yield bonds minus 10-year Treasuries, the daily sum of the spreads from Charts 9.1 and 9.3. It represents a high-level look at the 2007–2009 crisis and its aftermath from the perspective of the U.S. government; events are not marked on it.

Chart 9.3 tracks the daily spread between high-grade corporate bonds and the market rate for 10-year Treasury notes. It measures banks' ability to meet the needs of borrowers and shows when they cannot do so because they are having a difficult time funding themselves.

All three charts cover the period from July 16, 2007 to May 8, 2014. July 2007 marks when a refusal by Bear, Stearns to support investors in a couple of their mortgage funds triggered widespread concern that AIG might actually default. That caused what was then the biggest one-month spread spike seen in these relationships since 2005 (when the SEC mandated publication of the bond trading data on which the charts are based). That July spike was soon to be dwarfed by events that occurred between September 6 and November 20, 2008.

The peak of the lines on all of these charts represents a point at which just about every major private-sector enterprise in the United States and every nation in the world was in a state of equitable insolvency (unable to pay debts as they became due). As the principal of one of the largest hedge funds in the world remarked to Chris in 2010, "for a few months we were all broke." After describing events leading to the subprime crisis, we'll use Charts 9.1, 9.2, and 9.3 to trace the world's recovery after November 20, 2008.

Table 9.1 shows the impact of changing credit spreads. It uses the formula for compound interest to show that each basis point of change in spreads above the complete market level of Charts 9.1, 9.2, and 9.3 represents a $10 billion (per annum) impact on the wealth production of the US. Thus, each 100 basis point rise (1 percent per annum increase in spread) reduces annual wealth generation of the U.S. economy by $1 trillion (and *vice versa* when spreads fall).

With that, it's pretty easy to understand why we refer to the 2008 spike of spreads as Armageddon.[3]

---

[3] In comparison, it has been estimated that recently criticized high frequency trading (HFT) practices transfer about $8 billion per annum from investors to traders, a less than one basis point rise on Charts 9.1, 9.2, and 9.3 At its peak, the 2008 crisis was 2,000 times as great. The far greater danger of HFT issues is a possibility that investors will lose confidence in the U.S. rule of law and flee U.S. markets.

TWENTY EVENTS THAT LED TO BANKRUPTCY

These are the events Fred found most notable for their instant impact on markets. In each case, the market impact became apparent each day, at 5:30 P.M. Eastern time in the United States, when FINRA published that day's bond trading data.

Investors' reactions to events are almost always assured to be correct because, as a group, their judgment is, *per force*, final. They are, after all, the market. For example, when the U.S. space shuttle Challenger exploded, the stock of the firm that manufactured the boosters which released burning gasses that caused the explosion dropped almost immediately. It would take years for experts to pinpoint a precise cause, but every television screen showed hot gasses leaking from the side of a booster.

Investors in free markets do not wait for absolute proof, they react to the sensible logic of the moment. If gasses are leaking from the side rather than boosting the rockets from their bases it was time to sell first and seek answers later. That same reaction has driven all free financial markets from inception. It is only during the past few decades, however, that disclosures were refined to allow full democratization of credit decisions.

Subprime Crisis Begins (Chart 9.1, Event 1)

Subprime mortgage specialists began to suffer losses in 2006. Their problems were widely discussed among financial experts, but major firms that bought mortgages and securities from them continued supporting their investments until July 2007. As we've already noted, some of the more aggressive loan originators, such as Countrywide and Washington Mutual, were then showing signs of operational stress. Yet most market participants were either unaware of these developments or unwilling to take notice of the obvious signs of danger. This lack of recognition of the obvious signs of market stress was significant because, as former Federal Reserve Bank of New York President E. Gerald Corrigan once wryly noted, the very definition of a systemic event is when markets are surprised.

That surprise came in July 2007 when Bear, Stearns revealed it would no longer support two mortgage investment funds it sponsored. People in Bear, Stearns' mortgage group had a long history in that market. Some were at Kidder, Peabody when the 1994 crisis, triggered by increases in the Fed funds rate, exploded the toxic waste securities of Fannie Mae and Freddie Mac that hid huge amounts of negative convexity, as discussed earlier.

If experts at Bear, Stearns & Co. and other firms lost enough faith in the market to back away from losses in funds they helped create, it was clear that a *lot* of trouble lay ahead. Chris participated in a meeting of some of the largest hedge funds in the world during this time period and none of these firms were facing Bear, Stearns in the markets. By June of 2007, Merrill Lynch was threatening to liquidate almost $1 billion worth of mortgage securities seized from the Bear, Stearns hedge funds sending "shudders across Wall Street," as Mark Pittman of Bloomberg News reported at the time.

To cover a default on mortgage paper sponsored by firms such as Bear, Stearns and others, many investors purchased insurance in the form of CDSs issued (or supported) by AIG Financial Products. As the magnitude of expected defaults increased, some very large-buy side entities began to question AIG's ability to survive. Credit spreads spiked 100 basis points in a week or so. That represented a $1 trillion hit to the annual wealth-generating capacity of the U.S. economy. For the first time in years a financial crisis loomed.

Fed Reduces Discount Rate (Chart 9.1, Event 2)

As Event 1 triggered the interest rate-spread spike shown on Chart 9.1, the spread for U.S. banks (see Chart 9.3) popped up into the crisis zone (marked on all three charts). Businesses and banks were experiencing the same funding concerns. The Fed reduced the discount rate. That meant the Fed was giving banks with good assets that needed funds a right to borrow more cheaply. That right is rarely used, however, because it means a bank would disclose it was not able to address funding needs anonymously in the Fed funds market.

Chairman Bernanke and Vice Chairman Kohn both knew—or should have known—the meaning of the rise in spreads that had just occurred. Was the Fed indicating that the situation was worse than expected, or was the Fed signaling that it was having trouble understanding what caused the rise in spread? Either way, this relief led to a further increase in credit spreads. The minutes of the Federal Open Market Committee (FOMC) meeting for this period suggest that most Fed officials still did not understand just how serious was the loss of investor confidence in mortgage markets.

Fed Speeches in NYC and Berlin (Chart 9.1, Event 3)

In mid-September of 2007, Mr. Kohn made a speech in New York City that demonstrated that the Fed understood exactly what was going on in the U.S. markets in macroeconomic terms. The next day, Mr. Bernanke gave the keynote address at a Berlin gathering to celebrate the fiftieth anniversary of the post-war Bundesbank. It was a discussion of international imbalances.

Shortly after he began, Bernanke stated an equation that proved the Fed understood all the worldwide issues that led to the crisis:

> *National income accounting identities imply that the current account deficit equals the excess of domestic investment in capital goods, including housing, over domestic savings . . .*
> Bernanke, *"Global Imbalances: Recent Developments and Prospects,"* Berlin, September 11, 2007.

The audience included representatives of central banks and finance ministries from around the globe. In terms that are inoffensive yet obvious to any economist with international trade experience, he told the world that the United States and all the exporting nations had created a huge mortgage bubble (and muddle). By those same words, he dismissed arguments that this was just a U.S. problem.

But neither Bernanke nor Kohn then had a full appreciation for just how the market reaction to fraud and malfeasance by leading Wall Street firms would soon destabilize the entire financial system.

The cause was an accumulated international trade imbalance that every major trading nation on earth had ignored for its own national purposes. For the most part, moreover, that imbalance ($30 trillion for the United States and $67 trillion worldwide) was hidden as off-balance sheet liabilities of GSEs and government guaranteed banks, using various accounting gimmicks. The logical (indeed, axiomatic) consequence of these accumulated imbalances was enormous, but Bernanke made clear that there was no reason why a world built from the ashes of the worst war in history by forgiveness of debt (and worse deeds) could not resolve these imbalances peacefully.

Fed Reduces Rates (Chart 9.1, Event 4)

After Messrs. Kohn and Bernanke returned to Washington, the FOMC met and announced it was cutting the Fed funds target rate. This time, there was no doubt about the Fed's actions. Investors responded by reducing credit spreads. By mid-October of 2007 it appeared the crisis was over. Investors were confident that leadership of the U.S. Fed would act, and do so properly, as the need arose.

Treasury Announces SIV Fund (Chart 9.1, Event 5)

In October 2007, Treasury Secretary Paulson made what could be the dumbest economic policy move since the Great Depression. Most errors leading to the Great Depression were, with hindsight, due to legal restraints, and not the Treasury's fault. His announcement that Treasury would support creation of a master liquidity enhancement conduit (or Super SIV fund) was a monumental blunder. It destroyed the positive impact of the Fed's decisive action in September of 2007 and focused investor attention on problems at the largest U.S. banks, especially Citigroup.

At the time, Citibank was literally choking on its own SIVs (off-balance sheet entities, fully guaranteed by Citibank, where it hid rampant speculation). Investors were redeeming obligations of the SIVs in droves. Paulson, being a relationship banker for Goldman Sachs and not a financial technician, probably did not think of the Super SIV idea himself. The reasons behind the Super SIV idea are consistent with the discussion in the book up to this point: namely, the SEC's adoption of amendments to Rule 2a-7 in 1998 and the monopoly that resulted in the market for asset-backed commercial paper.

In the fall of 2007, attention became focused on specific SIVs that were unable to find buyers for their commercial paper. As these SIVs were forced to redeem commercial paper for cash, sponsoring banks were being forced (by prior agreements) to take the vehicles onto their balance sheets and recognize previously hidden losses, effectively admitting that the transactions to create the SIVs had been a sham. A number of large banks met with officials at the U.S. Treasury to craft a solution for the problem that would not force the repatriation of these off-balance sheet vehicles back onto the books of the sponsoring institutions.

The Super SIV proposal was the result. Paulson met with members of the national media in an attempt to sell the idea, but was remarkably inarticulate in those meetings. New York Fed President Timothy Geithner, who was closely tied politically to former Treasury Secretary and Citigroup Chairman Robert Rubin, also supported the plan in meetings with investors and journalists in New York.

Fred Feldkamp was traveling in France with his wife at the time of the announcement. He had logged on to U.S. business websites to see the news from home and was flabbergasted by an announcement that the U.S. Treasury would support a special investment vehicle (SIV) that would take on the losses from off-balance sheet investment gambles by Citigroup. The plan had plenty of critics, including former Federal Reserve chief Alan Greenspan, who suggested that the Super SIV could do more harm than good. That was, perhaps, the understatement of the decade. Fred relayed grave concerns to clients and correspondents.

When Treasury announced its Super SIV plan in October of 2007, in a joint press release with JPMorgan Chase, Citigroup, and Bank of America, the Federal Reserve made no comment on the plan (then or later). The fact that Secretary Paulson had not sought the endorsement or involvement of the Fed, the FDIC, and other federal bank regulators speaks volumes for the hastiness and lack of thought behind the proposal. Again, Paulson was not a banking expert by training and it seems extremely unlikely that the idea was his own, but he is ultimately responsible for assuring that whatever he proposes is credible.

By embracing this proposal, Treasury Secretary Paulson unknowingly risked doom for the entire U.S. financial system. By saying that the U.S. Treasury needed to save Citibank he was undermining the system. But, as soon as he spoke, Paulson couldn't retract the announcement. The markets reacted badly to the concept, which could not possibly succeed. There was no legal foundation upon which the United States could absorb such losses without putting Citibank in receivership and, perhaps, invoking systemic failure provisions of a 1991 law that seemed entirely inapplicable at that point. The 2007 summer crisis was over but the crisis of that fall was, by that announcement, just starting.

In November 2008, strategist Ed Yardeni stated that "everything that [Hank] Paulson has done or endorsed has worsened the credit crisis and sent stocks reeling . . . Paulson's Super-SIV proposal was a distraction that went nowhere. It was the first clue that he likes half-baked schemes that are hard to implement." He then continued to list over a dozen of Paulson's most egregious errors, including, "Letting investment banks borrow from the Fed's discount window just after Bear, Stearns failed suggests that letting the firm go was done as a risky gesture to the principle of avoiding moral hazard, which has subsequently been thrown out the window (Pethokoukis 2008)."

The message Secretary Paulson conveyed with the Super SIV proposal was that a leading U.S. money-center bank was broke and that the top three banks in terms of assets in the United States required extraordinary assistance. Even if true, no responsible financial leader would say that without having the FDIC prepared to take over the banks that very day. Over its 75 years of receivership experience, the public procedure of the FDIC has been to never discuss a particular bank's problems unless it has been seized by that agency.

Worse yet, officials at Citigroup seemed to be behind the proposal, further undermining confidence in the bank. By mid-December 2007, Treasury and the banks were forced to abandon the Super SIV plan and Citigroup announced it would take the $49 billion in assets held by its seven SIVs back onto its balance sheet. Revelation of this heretofore hidden leverage only increased market uncertainty and nervousness regarding Citigroup's soundness. The use of SIVs to fund assets off-balance sheet was shown to be a sham and a pretense on the part of Citigroup, which had to accept the fact that these transactions were in fact secured borrowings and thus fraud on its face, to paraphrase Justice Brandeis.

Chairman Bernanke had settled the nervousness of the investment world by his Berlin speech in September. All of the major counterparties in the U.S. financial markets knew that Citibank had big troubles, but the bank was not having difficulty funding deposits as it relied on too-big-to-fail policies. Going forward with the Super SIV proposal would certainly trigger an electronic run by uninsured depositors at every major U.S. bank, but the damage was done.

The proposal about a year later to buy bad assets from the banks under the TARP law came from the same failed logic as the Super SIV proposal. With one brief respite in March of 2008, Secretary Paulson's announcement began the process leading to an Armageddon that all but bankrupted the world thirteen months later.

Fed Reduces Rates (Chart 9.1, Events 6 and 7)

Twice after the Treasury's October 2007 SIV blunder, the FOMC announced cuts in the Fed funds target rate. In each case, however, credit spreads widened, illustrating the loss of confidence and credibility that had been suffered by U.S. officials because of Hank Paulson's folly. It was unclear to the markets who was in charge of U.S. monetary policy. If it was Secretary Paulson, then the SIV announcement proved he was dangerous. If it was Fed Chairman Bernanke and Vice Chairman Kohn, then they needed to do things more assertively than the business as usual rate cuts. After Paulson's comments pushed U.S. credit spreads well into the crisis zones on Charts 9.1, 9.2, and 9.3, the need for even more decisive action grew with each passing day.

Citigroup Reports Loss (Chart 9.1, Event 8)

Most investors understand the accounting processes by which losses on bank loans lag their internal realization at banks. At year-end 2007, Citigroup's losses were not of a size that came close to justifying Paulson's SIV announcement. Investors therefore understood the Paulson proposal to mean that things were, in fact, far worse at Citibank than implied by the bank's public disclosure. The assumption behind the Super SIV proposal, at least as explained by Treasury officials, was that the prices for mortgage-backed securities inside the SIVs were below intrinsic value, but nobody in the market believed that fiction. To believe that meant the law of compound interest had ceased to function.

Soon after the bank's announcement, investors bid U.S. credit spreads to a level that was 400 basis points higher than when Treasury announced the Super SIV fund. Investors in U.S. markets were now seeing wealth depressed by $4 trillion per year compared to market conditions after the rally that followed the September 2007 speeches by Kohn and Bernanke.

This put the wealth effect in reverse, and in a very short period of time. More action was clearly required. In his 2014 book, *Stress Test*, Tim

Geithner notes that this is the time when Chairman Bernanke decided history would judge him based on what would occur in the economy, not what he would wish to occur. Therefore, rather than appease doubters among his colleagues at the Fed, he decided it was necessary for him to push what he understood to be correct.

With hindsight, Mr. Bernanke's advice, judgment, and actions proved remarkably accurate, saving the world from what might have become a worse calamity than the Great Depression and the war that followed it.

Tax Cuts Approved (Chart 9.1, Event 9)

Early 2008 was the beginning of an election year. Congress had no reason to support the lame duck Bush administration, but self-preservation prevailed and Congress cut taxes in an effort to stimulate a recovery. Economists were recognizing that the United States (and the world) faced a debt-contraction deflation scenario not unlike the Great Depression. The tax cuts helped, however, since the U.S. economy had officially been in recession since 2006. The Economic Stimulus Act of 2008 and the American Recovery and Reinvestment Act of 2009 took the federal budget deficit from low single-digits in 2007 to almost 10 percent of GDP. But even with the tax cuts, the financial crisis continued to grow, albeit at a slower pace.

After the tax cuts passed, spreads fell by more than 100 basis points, reducing the relative drag on wealth production by $1 trillion, to only $3 trillion per year. A $1 trillion per annum benefit was enough improvement in credit spreads to pay for the tax cuts, however, and then some.

ISM Service Sector Report (Chart 9.1, Event 10)

The next shoe to drop in the expansion of the financial crisis was the ISM (Institute of Supply Management) Service Sector Report of January 2008. It showed a sharper than expected contraction in the service sector of the economy. Contractions in this very large sector demonstrated what economists had feared, namely a deflationary contraction in demand. The economic problem was far larger than Congress or the Bush Administration seemed to understand. Spreads expanded after the report was released and pushed the rate of wealth contraction back up to $4 trillion per year.

Then came March 2008.

PWG Report and Bear's Crisis (Chart 9.1, Event 11)

The first of these combined events confirmed what many suspected after the SIV announcement—Treasury (which headed PWG, the President's Working

Group) did not have a clue about what to do. If you look at Chart 9.3, you will see that spreads for banks and other high-grade bond issuers immediately rose *above* that chart's crisis zone. That's one reason Bear, Stearns found it could not fund overnight needs. It was in a state of equitable (if not legal) insolvency and many other firms on Wall Street were heading in the same direction. Buy side firms (institutions that buy investment services) were turning away from the smaller dealers in droves.

The funding crisis affecting Bear, Stearns & Co. was the first such situation that appeared to justify exercising the 1991 systemic relief authority granted in reforms enacted in response to the 1980s S&L crisis. After months of conflict, the Bear, Stearns resolution and takeover, moreover, showed that someone in DC understood what was required when a systemic failure occurs.

Bear, Stearns faced equitable insolvency when spreads skyrocketed and it needed assistance to fund ongoing debt payment obligations. The acquisition of Bear, Stearns followed the basic playbook of larger firms buying smaller failed securities dealers that goes back a century, except that (1) a federal guaranty of the dealer's assets was needed (like those offered by FDIC in bank receiverships) and (2) Bear Stearns was not placed in receivership. That's how Bear, Stearns' sale revealed a fundamental flaw in the 1991 legal architecture—receivership proceedings were not available. The Bear, Stearns insolvency, moreover, was not the end of the crisis.

Helped greatly by aggressive moves by the Fed to provide liquidity to markets and specific institutions (discussed below), credit spreads fell more than 150 basis points after Bear was sold to JPMorgan Chase. Chairman Bernanke told a congressional hearing in April 2008 that the U.S. government had saved Bear, Stearns from bankruptcy because a collapse of the investment bank would have reverberated throughout the economy—increasing the risk of lower incomes, lower home values, and unemployment for ordinary Americans. Again, the worry was the very deflation that the ISM report had illustrated.

JPMorgan Chase initially agreed to purchase Bear, Stearns & Co. for $2 per share in March of 2008, but the employees and large shareholders of Bear resisted. Bear CEO Alan Schwartz had told employees that the firm's building on Madison Avenue was worth $8 per share, so the deal started to fall apart as Bear, Stearns threatened to undo its government-supported sale and bailout by filing for reorganization under Chapter 11 of the U.S. Bankruptcy Code.

As discussed earlier in regard to concerns over the ability of subsequently appointed state receivers to undermine Fed assistance to banks before the FDIC was created in 1933, without the appointment of a receiver, bankruptcy raised the possibility of a challenge to assistance the Fed provided to JPMorgan. The threat worked. Bear, Stearns' shareholders received $10 per share to go along with the JPMorgan purchase.

Former Treasury secretary, Goldman Sachs CEO, and Citigroup executive Robert Rubin incorrectly described the situation involving Bear, Stearns & Co as uncharted waters, in a March 2008 interview with the *Wall Street Journal*. The problem that arose in Bear's situation is *very* well-known and fully understood by the FDIC. It has decades of experience with assistance provided (1) in bank receiverships, and (2) by experimentation with open bank assistance programs.

Unless assistance is carefully planned and implemented to eliminate benefits for shareholders and managers who conducted operations in a manner that created the need for assistance in the first place, (1) assistance that is successful will have bailed out those that caused the problem, and (2) assistance that is not successful will be seen as a waste of taxpayer money. It is irresponsible for Congress to provide means for granting government support to any firm without taking the steps needed to assure that the investment is both wise and effective.

Equitable insolvency occurs, by definition, without notice. When a firm's equitable insolvency threatens the U.S. financial system, there is no time to analyze and assure the wisdom and effectiveness of supporting action. That could take months (e.g., the 2009 reorganizations of GM and Chrysler). Therefore, without the means for instantaneous elimination of managers and shareholders, it cannot be a long-term U.S. financial market policy to offer the Greenspan put without first placing firms that receive assistance into receivership. By U.S. law, instant elimination of managers and shareholders is only available in court-ordered receivership proceedings.

In 2010, the Dodd-Frank Orderly Liquidation Authority (OLA) resolved the problem that the Bear, Stearns situation had exposed by forcing each systemically significant entity that needs federal assistance into receivership under federal law. Payment of depositors and creditors is required before shareholders have any rights in receivership. If the federal government uses debt to bail out the entity, the FDIC serves as receiver under OLA. If it must inject capital, that investment is senior to rights of prereceivership shareholders, and managers can be replaced at will.

The OLA assures taxpayers that the government's assistance will be repaid before anything can be paid to former owners of the assisted entity. This has been the case for U.S. banks since 1933, but the shareholders of Bear, Stearns were spared that standard receivership consequence. It is obvious from the comments of Mr. Rubin, moreover, that Wall Street executives either do not understand or remain unwilling to accept this eminently logical policy requirement. Many still complain that OLA goes too far.

In view of what was revealed in the case of Bear, Stearns, it remains one of the more surprising aspects of the post-2008 period that many observers in the world of finance and economics have still not figured out why government assistance was not available to continue the operation of Lehman

Brothers. The Bush administration proved it would not repeat what happened in the Bear, Stearns resolution when it refused to compensate even the preferred shareholders of Fannie Mae and Freddie Mac when those GSEs were placed in conservatorship the week before Lehman failed.

Before the 2010 OLA, consent to total loss would have been required from thousands of Lehman shareholders to end their rights and still there would have been bankruptcy threats. Except as permitted by TARP, assistance to GM and Chrysler was only provided after the firms filed for Chapter 11. That is standard when providing major funding to troubled firms. It reduces the need to compensate shareholders exposed by Bear, Stearns (but only receivership eliminates that threat). But, then again, most people have never been involved in a bank receivership proceeding and so they do not know the difference between a receivership and a Chapter 11 bankruptcy.

Since the flaws in U.S. law that were exposed when Bear, Stearns became equitably insolvent were not yet resolved, bankruptcy was the only choice for Lehman Brothers in September of 2008. Without a statute prescribing receivership, proof of intentional fraud or outright theft would have been required to put Lehman in an equity receivership under supervision of a federal district judge. We will explain later that there was a second reason the 1991 FDICIA law allowing FDIC assistance could not be used for Lehman. Finally, since there was no collateral of assured value at the time, neither the Fed nor the Treasury would get involved when Lehman failed.

The FDIC did not have authority on its own to bail out the parent of a broker-dealer. Even though Lehman did own a small FDIC insured thrift that it used as a conduit for mortgage securitization activities, there was no means for its assistance that would have helped. In the previous two years, Lehman had tried unsuccessfully to sell itself but could not strike a deal, in part because nobody in the firm could attest to the firm's mortgage assets. Thus, unless someone would have bought Lehman without U.S. assistance (and Barclays Bank decided it would not do so until after Lehman was put in Chapter 11 bankruptcy proceedings), the only choice facing Lehman management (and the firms' creditors) was Chapter 11, with SIPC (Securities Investor Protection Corporation) as its designated trustee for customer accounts.

If a systemically important financial firm is assisted in the future, the FDIC will be named receiver for the firm. The government's priority status is then assured and shareholders will get nothing until all investments by government and other creditors are paid in full. Thus, to those who understand the difference between Chapter 11 and FDIC receivership and agree with the process, Dodd-Frank does not permit future bailouts. The financial system can be saved by preventing failure of one firm in triggering the loss of many other firms, as we do with insured banks Those who consider any intervention—even to save the system—a bailout, however, do not perceive Dodd-Frank as solving the problem.

Fed Announces the PDCF and Reduces Rates; GSE Relief (Chart 9.1, Event 12)

Just days after the acquisition of Bear, Stearns & Co., the Fed put in place the Primary Dealer Credit Facility (PDCF). This was an overnight loan facility that provided funding to primary dealers in exchange for a specified range of eligible collateral and was intended to foster the functioning of financial markets more generally. The PDCF began operations March 17, 2008, and was closed February 1, 2010. Had the facility been in place just a few weeks earlier, the sale of Bear, Stearns & Co. to JPMorgan Chase might not have been necessary.

The Fed also substantially lowered interest rates and put in place other credit facilities to address the wholesale collapse of the institutional credit markets. By this combined package, the Fed used emergency lending authority to extend relief beyond banks in the form of a credit facility to make loans against collateral pledged by any primary dealer. At the same time, the FOMC announced a further rate reduction and relief to assure the continuing function of the government's troubled mortgage GSEs, Fannie Mae and Freddie Mac.

By these actions, it was clear the Fed knew the crisis extended beyond the banking system. Finding some way to reduce spreads in mortgage markets was necessary.

Fed Announces the TSLF (Chart 9.1, Event 13)

Though not yet willing to reduce mortgage spreads by direct investments in mortgage securities, the Fed's Term Securities Lending Facility (TSLF) made clear that the Fed understood that without a vibrant mortgage market the nation faced a serious risk of long-term deflation. Under the TSLF, the Fed offered Treasury securities held by the System Open Market Account (SOMA) for loan over a one-month term against other program-eligible general collateral. The TSLF was announced on March 11, 2008, and the first auction was conducted on March 27, 2008. The TSLF was closed on February 1, 2010.

Via the TSLF, the Fed agreed to lend Treasury securities based on pledges of GSE mortgage-backed securities to dealers for terms during which the dealers could exchange Treasury securities to raise money to purchase more mortgage-backed securities. Spreads in mortgage markets responded favorably.

After the steps taken by the Fed described above, corporate bond credit spreads fell by a bit less than 200 basis points and stabilized until June of 2008.

Treasury Questions Fed Emergency Power (Chart 9.1, Event 14)

By June it seemed possible that the beneficial effects of the Fed's actions had begun to stabilize U.S. credit markets. Credit spreads were still well into the crisis zone on Charts 9.1, 9.2, and 9.3 but had come down significantly.

Yet due to the widespread panic in the markets and also among the public, spreads remained considerably higher than they were when Secretary Paulson announced Treasury support for the Super SIV fund, a move that could only be legitimized by an emergency.

One might have thought that in the wake of the Treasury's abortive attempt to float the idea of a Super SIV fund, the agency might have learned a lesson in humility. Nevertheless, Treasury publicly questioned whether the Fed could continue exercising its emergency powers. The short-term effect of this public statement by Treasury was a flight by investors that had bought securities of GSEs and primary dealers, in partial reliance on the Fed's March actions described above.

Corporate bond credit spreads quickly shot back up to where they were when Bear, Stearns failed. Investors, therefore, answered Treasury's question. They sold enough bonds to assure that an emergency still existed. This action of the Treasury, and the market reaction, opened the path to even more dreadful events in September 2008.

Treasury Introduces Covered Bonds (Chart 9.1, Event 15)

Not content with its failure with respect to the Super SIV fund and by questioning the Fed's emergency lending operations, the Treasury under Hank Paulson came up with yet another dumb idea: using covered bonds to finance home mortgages.

The proposal was not well considered, and further eroded confidence in U.S. Treasury officials. Former Treasury secretary Lawrence Summers noted in the *Financial Times* on November 2, 2011: "[D]ubious assertions by policymakers end up undermining confidence. Like the 13th chime of a clock, policymakers who deny the obvious or claim to know the unknowable call into question all that they say."

Paulson's covered bond proposal ultimately went nowhere on Capitol Hill. Not surprisingly, coincident with the appearance of the covered bond proposal, credit spreads soon rose (for the first time) *above* the crisis zone on Chart 9.1

Covered bonds are securities that are secured by a specific pool of mortgages, known as the cover pool, but remain on the books of the financial institution. In that sense, covered bonds are different from an MBS in that the collateral is not sold by the sponsor to another entity prior to the issuance of securities. Covered bonds have worked to finance mortgages in nations such as Germany and Denmark using a collective system of mortgage trusts that are still part of the issuing banks. By these arrangements, issuers guaranty repayment of bonds secured by mortgages when the bond terms to maturity do not match those of underlying mortgages. Providing this type of guaranty requires credit controls like those of the 1930s, controls that have historically proved unworkable in the United States (see our earlier discussion of what occurred during the 1960s). The U.S. economy and mortgage market is too large and diverse for such a vehicle to be successful.

Using covered bonds requires that banks guarantee reinvestment of early mortgage payments (so they will support later bond payments) and that bond payments that are not made from mortgage proceeds (due to unexpected delays) will be funded by the bank's payment of the bonds from other funds. We've seen that GSEs can do this in the United States, but private-sector entities that are not insured by the government cannot. Thus, covered bonds create a more entrenched government monopoly of mortgage credit.

The covered bond proposal was just another path to a government-bank financial monopoly, in this case proposed by Hank Paulson, the former CEO of Goldman Sachs. The large banks supported the proposal on Capitol Hill, where it was championed by Rep. Scott Garrett (D-NJ). But FDIC Chairman Sheila Bair made clear that the agency opposed the proposal, because in the event that the issuing bank failed, covered bonds might ultimately increase the cost of a collapse to the FDIC's insurance fund. In a conversation between Garret's staff and a member of the Bair kitchen cabinet, it was made clear that the FDIC would not tolerate legislation that allowed assets other than residential mortgages in any legislative proposal sponsored by Garrett and his supporters. The FDIC also stated unequivocally that a covered bond could only have a 2 percent overcollateralization rate, meaning that only prime mortgages would be allowed.

The United States has a much more active credit environment than Germany and other Northern European nations, where covered bonds are used. Some U.S. enterprises (largely in New York) issued bonds in this form before the Great Depression and just about all of the issuers went broke. That's why participants in private-sector U.S. mortgage markets (i.e., non-GSEs) promise only to pay bonds from proceeds of the mortgages as they are received. It is economically and financially impossible for a private issuer to guarantee the payment of principal and interest on the bonds if the underlying mortgages prepay less rapidly than planned because interest rates have risen. Indeed, the notion of converting GSEs into issuers of covered bonds had such an adverse effect on market confidence that the GSEs were pushed into conservatorship within a couple of months after Paulson's proposal.

GSE Conservatorship (Chart 9.1, Event 16)

On September 6, 2008, the director of the Federal Housing Finance Agency (FHFA), James B. Lockhart III, announced his decision to place two government-sponsored enterprises, Fannie Mae and Freddie Mac, into conservatorship.

The run on collateral and liquidity that had begun in 2007 with the closure or failure of nonbank mortgage issuers (such as New Century Financial, Freemont, and Ameriquest) and continued with Bear, Stearns had finally run up the credit ladder to the GSEs.

This event intensified and expanded the 2007–2009 financial crash. The significance of the conservatorship of the GSEs is clear from a puzzling difference in market reactions shown by Charts 9.1 and 9.3. The spread on Chart 9.1 actually fell (roughly 50 basis points) for a few days after this event.

Generally, that would be a $500 billion gain for the economy. That change in spreads made no sense, however, so Fred started asking questions of people in Washington, DC.

As part of the conservatorships, all GSE preferred stock would have to be written off. It seemed the Treasury wanted to show investors that the United States would not make another mistake like the one that gave Bear, Stearns' shareholders $10 per share before repayment of U.S. assistance. So, the Treasury decided to discipline investors that bought the GSEs' preferred securities.

While it can be argued that the private investors were really superfluous to the financial soundness of the GSEs, which ultimately required the backing of the U.S. government, the timing of the Treasury's actions was once again unfortunate and served to damage market confidence even more. Many of the holders of GSE preferred securities were other financial institutions, which now had to write down these investments to zero. The decision by Secretary Paulson was the equivalent of firing a gun before removing it from the holster and thereby shooting off your foot.

Holders of GSE preferred stock included U.S. commercial banks that had been allowed by regulators (that report to the Treasury, of course) to use the stock as primary capital. Treasury's attempt to restore market discipline caused loss of commercial banks' capital at precisely the wrong time. Those securities were capital backing for $1.6 trillion of loans by banks to U.S. consumers and businesses.

Chart 9.3 shows the consequence: spreads for high grade bonds of banks jumped by a record amount compared to 10-year Treasury bonds. The graph line on Chart 9.1 fell only because banks' funding costs zoomed up far faster than more risky high yield corporate bonds. The write-off of GSE preferred stock approved by the Paulson Treasury triggered a run on the bonds of high grade banks. Banks' bonds were soon trading at higher rates than when Bear, Stearns was forced out of business. Moreover, to make up for the lost capital, many banks began shrinking their assets by demanding repayment of otherwise well-performing commercial loans to U.S. businesses.

The GSE conservatorship, therefore, triggered a classic bank run.

Events of the following weeks, including the failure of Lehman Brothers and the government rescue of AIG, are the ones most people remember from that period and are the events that led to TARP. But it was the elimination of the GSE preferred stock, we believe, that caused the spike in credit spreads which ultimately destroyed Lehman and nearly wiped out every corporate debtor in the United States. Once again, Hank Paulson proved that during 2008 he was the chief source of instability in the U.S. financial markets. History may prove otherwise, but after the fall of the GSEs it seems that the Paulson Treasury decided it should get out of the way of the Federal Reserve Board and let Ben do it.

Better late than never.

Lehman Chapter 11 (Chart 9.1, Event 17)

On the next Sunday following conservatorship of the GSEs, Lehman Brothers filed for Chapter 11. Unlike the collapse of Bear, Stearns before Lehman, and the AIG situation after, there was no systemic failure relief for Lehman. The only reason given to distinguish the assistance given Bear, Stearns and AIG, but not Lehman, was that assisting Lehman was illegal. The reality, in terms of the market, is that the failure of Lehman was unexpected and thus accelerated what had started with the GSE conservatorships and eventually became the largest systemic event since the bank holiday of 1933.

In addition to the matters discussed above raised by the Bear, Stearns transactions, the 1991 FDICIA established a specific process to make any such assistance legal. No responsible entity starts an approval process for something like this if the process cannot be finished. Therefore, the Treasury, the Fed, and the FDIC (all of which must act to make the assistance legal) certainly conducted research to learn what would be required to obtain all requisite approvals before taking the first step in that direction.

The law says two-thirds of the Board of Governors of the Federal Reserve System and of the FDIC's board of directors must approve assistance. After that, authorization must be given by the Secretary of the Treasury of the United States upon consultation with the President of the United States. Nothing in the law authorizes delegation of that authority in the event of a conflict of interest.

Even if the FDIC and Fed had approved assistance for Lehman, Secretary Paulson and President Bush both had relatives who worked at Lehman. Short of resignations at the highest national level (which could have proven disastrous at that point), therefore, it would be hard to see how any authorization process to legally assist Lehman could proceed to conclusion. Two of the essential approvals required action by persons with a conflict of interest. If an action cannot be completed, the best legal advice is to take no action and declare illegality the reason. Between the lack of clear authority in the law for a government receivership of a nonbank firm and these personal conflicts, it seems that no action was the only course available.

In several respects, the failure to fund Lehman belongs in the same category with inability of the Fed to follow Bagehot's dictum between 1929 and 1933. The 1991 FDICIA law did not provide for the receivership process by which the 1933 FDIC law overcame risk that any assistance to Lehman could later be challenged. Moreover, Congress demanded presidential consultation and Treasury secretary authorization under the 1991 law before there could be assistance to Lehman. In each case, the hurdles could not, it appears, be overcome. So, assistance by Treasury or a takeover by the FDIC was illegal under the laws that existed at the time. And, interestingly enough, Lehman apparently could not borrow from the Fed based upon good collateral.

The arguments made by members of the economics profession that Lehman should not have been allowed to fail miss this key point. For reasons of the law and also personal conflict, the firm could not be saved. Only persons that do not deserve our trust act contrary to the rule of law. When a law bars action, leaders must suck it up and move on to find other means for attaining a goal.

The sad conclusion seems to be that the Treasury, through the missteps we have discussed above during 2008, accelerated the crisis and ultimately made the sale or salvation of Lehman Brothers impossible. Treasury Secretary Paulson should have cooperated with (and supported) Chairman Bernanke much more forcefully and much earlier in the crisis. Such cooperation might have prevented the collapse that followed Lehman's bankruptcy. But when looking at the narrow question of whether the U.S. government could save Lehman Brothers in September 2008, if the above analysis of actions in response to the Lehman situation is correct, Messrs. Paulson and Bernanke and the other regulators have our praise. They made the required decision, disastrous as it may have been.

Lehman's bankruptcy had a disastrous effect on the world. It triggered (1) the loss of AIG within three days, (2) the insolvency and rare emergency seizure of Washington Mutual (WaMu) by Thursday of that week, (3) forced sale of Wachovia Corp. a week later, and (4) the biggest financial crisis in world history within 60 days. The impact was so disastrous, however, that it forced the United States to take actions that saved the world from financial ruin within six months. More than five years later, the problems caused by the Lehman surprise persist. But that's because the problems, even in hindsight, were far worse than almost anyone believed at the time.

In the 60 days after Lehman fell, further adverse credit spread trends tore another $10.5 trillion from the annual growth capacity of the U.S. economy. The world faced a $67 trillion hole in the accumulated balance sheet of worldwide wealth caused by the creation of fraudulent securities. About half of that wealth was destroyed before the bleeding ended. But most important, by the cooperative efforts of two presidents and some truly remarkable leadership at the Fed, the worldwide bleeding of economic capital ended quickly. Investors have now enjoyed several years of recovery.

Unlike the mistakes that led to the Great Depression, world leaders have, for the most part, not fanned the flames of world war. While there are people and nations in very bad economic circumstances at the moment, there are signs of recovery (and new bubbles) sprouting in many places around the world. It is only by continued benevolence and empathy that the world will fully recover. Let's now finish the path to Armageddon so we can get on to some overall comments and discuss the resurrection and recovery phases of the crisis.

G-7 Nationalization cum Monetization (Chart 9.1, Event 18)

From Lehman's filing until the G-7 nations acted in concert to effectively guarantee the entire remaining financial market, spreads zoomed up in a manner that has never previously been observed in real time. Chart 9.3—bank spreads—displays a near vertical climb from the GSE takeover to this point. Between September 6 and the beginning of October, Treasury Secretary Paulson devised yet another ill-considered scheme, the Troubled Asset Relief Program, or TARP. Like the abortive Super SIV proposal authored by the Paulson Treasury, the idea behind TARP was to somehow purchase bad assets from banks—an idea that was yet another nonstarter. Neither Paulson nor the senior career officials at the Treasury apparently understood that having the U.S. government buy bad assets from the commercial banking industry was legally and financially impossible.

Not only was it functionally impossible for the Treasury to actually purchase these assets from private banks under current law—a reality that only became clear just before President Bush left office—but once again the Paulson Treasury was signaling to the markets that there was an immediate problem with the largest U.S. banks when in fact none existed. Ed Yardeni again comments on Paulson's missteps in 2008:

> *As a method for buying "troubled assets," TARP was a bad idea. By inciting a panic, and sending the global economy into a tailspin, however, the law passed because it became essential. Claiming that the Treasury could purchase one-of-a-kind troubled assets in reverse auctions made no sense. The RTC [Resolution Trust Corporation]*

solution to the S&L crisis of the early 1990s won't work to end this crisis.

Richard Kovacevich, chairman of Wells Fargo from 2001–2009, vociferously objected to the TARP proposal and confronted Paulson and Federal Reserve Bank of New York President Timothy Geithner after the legislation eventually was passed by Congress. Kovacevich castigated Secretary Paulson in a January 5, 2012 interview with the PBS program *Frontline* and illustrated why the approach by the Federal Reserve Board was far superior to the proposals by Treasury:

> *I have no issue if a financial institution needs money. It's not bankrupt, it's not failing, but it's got liquidity issues. It can be rescued; it can give back. If the government wants to give money to a financial institution to get them through a crisis, to make sure the crisis doesn't expand, they need the money, I have no issue with that. That's been done a lot over a long period of time. My objection was that if you give it to people who are perceived not to need it, it's going to destroy confidence in the industry; it's not going to restore confidence in the industry. And that's exactly what happened. They exacerbated the panic.*

Mr. Kovacevich is an outstanding banker who demonstrated extraordinary confidence in the U.S. power to recover from the crisis when he outbid an FDIC-backed package to acquire Wachovia Corp. His bank is primarily a West Coast firm, however, and his comments on the need for capital infusions were not shared by colleagues on the East Coast. In hindsight, the capital infusions had the effect of calming investors to such a degree that they were a key turning point in the crisis.

As the Fed and Treasury struggled to fashion a reasonable response to the crisis, events continued to unfold. It was early October when Wells Fargo announced the competing proposal to purchase Wachovia Corp. that did not require assistance from the FDIC. That same day, Congress passed the Emergency Economic Stabilization Act, which provided the legal authority for the Treasury to spend $700 billion under the TARP program. Three days later and perhaps more significantly, the Fed relied on the same law in announcing that it would pay interest on depository institutions' reserve balances. The Fed also put in place another emergency facility for commercial paper.

There was one sharp upward spike in credit spreads when Congress initially rejected TARP and one enormous recovery when Congress approved TARP. The TARP originally proposed by Secretary Paulson soon proved senseless. Just about everyone came to a conclusion that there was no possible way to extract enough of America's troubled assets from their deeply embedded positions for a troubled asset relief program to work. Weeks went by during which officials at the Treasury tried in vain to make the asset purchase model workable. Credit spreads immediately resumed an unprecedented upward path toward the destruction of everything in finance that we hold dear (and essential for a functioning economy).

While the Paulson Treasury was struggling to fashion a reasonable approach to the crisis, the Fed did the only reasonable thing it could and provided liquidity to the markets in vast and increasing amounts. On September 19, 2008, the U.S. Treasury announced the establishment of a temporary guarantee program to protect shareholders of money market mutual funds—and on September 29 officially opened the program to eligible money market funds. By no coincidence, the FDIC announced the emergency increase of federal deposit insurance to $250,000 from $100,000 and blanket coverage of all transaction accounts via the Transaction Account Guarantee Program. The Fed also was deeply involved in the rescue of AIG in the early days of October, adding still more liquidity to the system during those terrible days.

By the middle of October 2008, Paulson and Bernanke moved to the *only* economic solution that works: nationalization *cum* monetization. Since all money originates with the government, when the system falls apart government needs to step in and take over the means of monetary intermediation. Government must temporarily fill the hole generated by a crisis to prevent all of the private capital in the system from being consumed. Once confidence returns, it must then turn the intermediation process back over to the private sector. In specific terms, the Treasury changed plans and decided to make investments in banks to shore up their capital rather than attempt to purchase bad assets from these banks. That same day, the FDIC provided yet another significant liquidity facility for uninsured deposits that again helped to reassure businesses that their funds would be safe in America's banking institutions.

Nationalization cum monetization is the only known process that works in these situations, and it did in this one. Markets confirmed that it worked by another huge recovery in spread following the actions by the Fed and other G-7 central banks. The credit spreads shown on Chart 9.3 finally began to decline. One last issue, however, required resolution before the graph lines on Chart 9.1 would confirm those on Chart 9.3.

U.S. Election Day (Chart 9.1, Event 19)

Between the G-7 nationalization of major financial institutions and the U.S. election, it became clear that Mr. Obama would win. Investors in the

United States have (perhaps with good reason) grown insecure whenever one political party holds all the levers of power in Washington. That election gave the presidency and control of both houses of Congress to Democrats. Obviously, people didn't want the GOP to continue to have power, but did they really want a political monopoly for Democrats? Both parties are equally disparaged by a large portion of Americans.

Investors did not know what that election result might do to our financial system. For reasons discussed above, investors don't like the financial system that created the subprime crisis. But most Americans likewise understand that we cannot revert to the Depression-era model of government control that caused an 87 percent contraction in business and consumer lending between 1929 and 1955, and helped create the Great Inflation (and contraction) of the 1970s and 1980s. Therefore, because of this basic uncertainty over economic leadership, credit spreads were to skyrocket one more time.

Obama Economic Team Announced (Chart 9.1, Event 20)

On November 20, 2008, President-Elect Obama announced the proposed heads for several financial service areas of the new administration and his White House economic team. Sheila Bair would stay as FDIC Chair. Mr. Bernanke was praised at the Fed. Tim Geithner was selected as Secretary of Treasury and Larry Summers was to be an advisor to Mr. Obama. In effect, the status quo was confirmed both with respect to economic policy and also defense, where President Bush's Defense Secretary Robert Gates agreed to stay on and did not even require confirmation by the Senate.

Lots of people have said lots of things, good and bad, about each of these selections. It is only the reaction of investors, however, that really matters, and investors primarily means bond buyers. If bond investors like what the United States is doing, they vote by investing more money in the United States and spreads fall (and vice versa when they dislike something). Confirming more than twenty years of day-by-day observation by Fred, when bond spreads fall, equity markets and the economy rise (and vice versa when they rise). This follows because the law of compound interest works.

That investors approved was soon clear. From the date of Mr. Obama's announcement to his January 20, 2009, inauguration, the corporate bond spread on Chart 9.1 fell more than 750 basis points, a $7.5 trillion boost to the annual wealth-generation potential of the U.S. economy. A long road to recovery lay ahead, but the United States and worldwide financial system was resurrected in the 60 days after November 20, 2008.

AIG: One More Event from 2008 and a Math Footnote

Absent from the above list of events is the bailout of AIG that began a few days after Lehman's bankruptcy filing. AIG's failure did not change the course of credit markets—those markets were already plummeting at the fastest rate anyone had ever seen (for reasons explained above). AIG, however, represented the largest accumulation of toxic waste in the U.S. generated by all the bad policy judgments made since 1998 and so is worth discussing.

AIG Financial Products (AIGFP) was founded in 1987 by three Drexel Burnham Lambert traders and led by financial scholar Howard Sosin. They convinced AIG CEO Hank Greenberg to branch out from his core insurance business by creating a division focused on complex derivatives trades that took advantage of AIG's AAA credit rating. Significantly, Sosin brought two other DBL bankers, Thomas R. Savage and Joseph Cassano, along with him.[4]

Much of the activities of AIGFP were largely the creation of Tom Savage's math genius. He became CEO in 1988 after a career at First Boston and DBL. He wrote many of the algorithms that allowed the creation of stand-alone CMOs. He understood the complexities of insurance, securities, and derivatives in ways that few do. During much of the period that Savage ran AIGFP, it seemed clear to most observers who dealt with the firm that its aggregate liabilities (whether measured today, 40 years into the future, or at any point between) would always be far less than its aggregate assets and that its cash flows would always be favorable by every conceivable measure.

Savage decided to retire in 2001 at a young age to take up passions in life other than math. When he left, AIGFP had over $500 million in revenue and was a major profit center for AIG. A couple of years before he left, however, Savage gave the green light to Cassano to start writing insurance on the default of bonds issued by JPMorgan. Using the work of a Yale professor named Gary Gorton, AIGFP wrote default protection on these securities on the assumption that the likelihood of a payout was remote because the money center bank was too big to fail.

The involvement of AIGFP in credit default insurance accelerated and expanded significantly after the departure of Savage. Not content with the

---

[4] See Robert O'Harrow Jr. and Brady Dennis, "The Beautiful Machine" (first of three parts), *Washington Post*, December 29, 2008, www.washingtonpost.com/wp-dyn/content/article/2008/12/28/AR2008122801916_pf.html. See also "A Crack in the System," December 30, 2008, www.washingtonpost.com/wp-dyn/content/article/2008/12/29/AR2008122902670_pf.html, and "Downgrades and Downfall," December 31, 2008, www.washingtonpost.com/wp-dyn/content/article/2008/12/30/AR2008123003431_pf.html, (second and third of three parts, respectively).

pedestrian growth profiles of underwriting property and casualty insurance and investing the proceeds, AIG made a decision to chase revenue and earnings growth by moving up the risk curve in all types of CDSs after Cassano replaced Savage. For example, AIG wrote default insurance on collateralized debt obligations (CDOs), then purchased the senior and subordinated tranches of the same security. Specifically, AIG went from the low-beta, low-growth world of underwriting real-world risks (such as ships sinking and hurricanes) to the high-beta world of financial products.

According to a schedule prepared by Goldman Sachs for the Financial Crisis Inquiry Commission (detailing trades on its notorious Abacus synthetic CDOs), AIG bought subordinate tranches of Abacus 2005-3, Abacus 2005-CB1, and Abacus 2005-2. The other big investor in the subordinated tranches was Goldman's own CDO desk.

Writing insurance on the default of a corporate or mortgage bond or an executive facing a shareholder lawsuit are risks that are highly correlated to the financial markets, while writing risk on a ship sinking is uncorrelated to the markets. Going back to the founding of the Lloyds of London insurance market, writing insurance was seen as a natural hedge by farmers whose primary activity was agriculture. Hank Greenberg, the managers of AIGFP, and the board of AIG made the fundamental error of thinking that writing risk on loan or bond defaults, or other highly correlated risks, was nearly as profitable *in risk-adjusted terms* as simply writing insurance policies. In fact, even though AIGFP was reporting impressive revenue and earnings, it was actually losing money when measured against the risks taken.

In a September 2008 interview in the *Institutional Risk Analyst*, Robert Arvanitis of Risk Finance Advisors, who worked at AIG during its heyday and then at Merrill Lynch, described the monumental error in judgment committed by AIG as well as other insurers in chasing high-beta financial risk:

> *Low beta is uncorrelated, non-market risk. This is the type of risk that insurers used to price the sinking of ships, hurricanes. Nonmarket, uncorrelated risks. Now 300 years before Harry Markowitz, landed English gentry instinctively realized that their money came from land rents and crops, so they put some of their money to work by investing in Lloyds of London. If the crop was good this year, but a few ships sank, you made money on crops and lost on ships. The next year, the crops were lousy but no ships sank, so you made money on insurance. Lloyds was the insurance industry's first effort at diversification and they stuck to their knitting and underwrote real-world risk events like hurricanes and fires, which were uncorrelated to other markets. The insurance industry grew out of its crib and now does more and more underwriting in high-beta risks. They*

sell liability insurance, D&O coverage, surety, and, good lord, they even get into bond insurance. CDS is a bridge even further removed from the basic, low-beta model from which insurance comes. The risk taken by insurers is more and more high beta, and by doing so they spoiled a perfectly good racket.

By virtue of its perceived success in writing CDSs, AIGFP filled a void in terms of providing liquidity to the financial derivatives markets—it became the market maker for unregulated derivatives trading in contracts that nobody else wanted—and also took a lot of financial and liquidity risk that neither its traders nor its managers understood. In effect, AIG became a one-firm clearing house for a whole class of CDS contracts that were not well understood on Wall Street. Generally, a clearing house must be regulated because it is where all incomplete trades of any participant in a market will end up when the participant becomes insolvent. Without the power of a federal receiver to sort out the trades on behalf of innocent creditors, any clearing house can be driven broke if it makes even one small error (in finance, *any* error can morph into an overnight nightmare).

AIGFP's master craftsmen thought that they understood the problems and how to protect the firm. Almost nobody, however, could anticipate what would happen as CDS investors and the dealers who trade in these unregulated insurance contracts began to gang up on less sophisticated players. AIG thought it was a dealer in CDS, but in fact is was a retail customer at the mercy of derivatives dealer banks like JPMorgan and Goldman Sachs. It belonged in the same category as the mortgage issuers that originated and sold securities backed by dumb and dumber loans to mercantilist exporting nations and other sucker bond buyers. Those risks, moreover, related to long-term assets: meaning portfolio growth necessarily masks the extent of deferred risks. It took years for the risks of Drexel's 1980s junk bond monopoly to mature. When it did, the risk was more than 15 times as great as initially estimated.

If that wasn't bad enough, AIGFP's parent firm, AIG, was structured so that all its units had access to cheap money by a joint and several guaranty that allowed each unit to finance at AIG's valued AAA rating level. It was an idea that was "very good indeed" when times were good. In bad times, however, that idea proved "horrid."

In the rating game, an airplane example is used to differentiate good and bad corporate structures. Each unit within the enterprise is an engine. A plane with two is safer than a plane with one if either engine can lift the plane. If both engines are required, however, two engines are more risky than one (because there is twice the risk of failure). In fact, all of the insurance units of AIG had cross-guaranteed one another and were infected by the CDS default risk of AIGFP, meaning that the firms could not be broken without catastrophic results. When AIGFP flipped, from an engine that lifted everyone to one that could not do so, this cross-guarantee caused everything to collapse at once.

The day after Lehman failed, Fred was asked by someone from Washington, DC, who was participating in these market events why the government should save an insurance company that's not federally regulated. Knowing the likely CDS exposure of AIGFP at that point (every U.S. credit, all the way up the quality ladder to GE, was at risk of being unable to pay short-term debt, necessitating bankruptcy), if AIG was the entity at risk, the reason to fund it through the crisis was clear. Without saving the CDS clearing house on which everyone relied every participating member is likely to fail. Going back to Bagehot's dictum, AIG deserved punishment for being supremely stupid, but the cost of any punitive action to the rest of the market was prohibitive. Moreover, the AIG joint and several guaranty among entities drove the risk of AIGFP into each and every insurer AIG owned. Fred said federal assistance was probably the only option.

Due to AIG's enormous size, international spread, and intercompany guaranty agreement, failure to fund AIGFP would likely bankrupt all of AIG's many affiliates and force the insurance units into state receiverships, under which protecting policyholders was the first concern. That in turn would likely result in bankruptcy for just about every large bank, broker, and insurance firm in the world, without regard to whether they were active counterparties to AIG.

Unlike Lehman, AIG had plenty of good collateral to offer and presented no conflict of interest. Nothing could be done to prevent Lehman's failure. Bagehot's dictum, however, certainly justified becoming a lender of last resort to save AIG. Doing so prevented a spread of the run that Lehman's bankruptcy and the GSE conservatorships triggered to all the areas, worldwide, where AIG had relationships.

What would it have cost to let all those entities fail? Let's turn to Table 9.1.

Each of the 12 boxes within Table 9.1 reflects the total wealth (upper left) and equity (lower right) implications for different bond market scenarios. Across the top are three assumptions for the base rate (the rate for risk-free U.S. debt). Along the left side are four spread assumptions. The top-center box shows the approximate total wealth (stocks and bonds) of the United States in 2005 ($100 trillion) and the amount of that wealth represented by equity (about $50 trillion).

Markets in 2005 were as close as we've come to a complete market, in which 10-year Treasury bonds sold at about 5 percent rates and spreads were low (estimated in footnote 2 of the table).

Applying reverse math to total wealth and total debt in 2005, we can calculate the level of annual cash flow that supports that level of wealth. We can then use the same cash flow to calculate the eleven other boxes using different base rates and spread assumptions.

The results correlate with expectations reflected in markets and observed in day-by-day analyses since 1998 (and reverse analysis back to 1987). While equity markets did not hit bottom until March 2009, investors likely perceived that the Fed would push rates to 0 percent, if necessary, by late November 2008. Using that as the base rate and adding spreads observed in November 2008, total wealth was going down 25 percent (to $75.4 trillion).

Since $50 trillion of debt would have first dibs on that wealth, the equity component of total wealth would be seen by investors as declining about 50 percent, to $25.4 trillion.

Table 9.1 also shows what the impact would have been if the deflation scenario solution used early in the Great Depression had been chosen by the Fed in 2008. If rates had been pushed up to 10 percent to support the dollar (or whatever reason may have been argued to justify this step), the table shows that application of the formula for compound interest pushes 2005 total wealth down to $53.5 trillion and 2005 net equity down by 93 *percent*, from $50 trillion *to just $3.5 trillion*, a rate of decline consistent with the Depression-era experience.

In 1933, Irving Fisher, considered by many observers to be the greatest U.S. economist of all, analyzed what amounts to a deflation solution of liquidating bad debt. He compared it to a physician who recommends that a pneumonia patient do nothing and let the disease run its course. Sadly, some doctors elected to Congress seem to advise economic solutions of this type.

If AIG had been allowed to die and spreads rose by a few hundred more basis points as a result, Fisher's 1933 prediction of total worldwide bankruptcy could have come true. The equity of the global economy would have been consumed, leaving no foundation upon which to rebuild. Of course, like J. Pierpont Morgan and Henry Ford in their day, those who advocate the liquidation of bad debts (as occurred in the 1930s) would have sold every investment other than cash before implementing the advice. Henry Ford, when confronted by representatives of the Hoover Administration early in 1933, dismissed their warnings about the effect of looming bank failures and merely said that he would rebuild on his own. As a result, the likes of Morgan and Ford alone would have money and could buy up everything as everyone else went broke. But, then again, maybe that's the reason they urge an otherwise insane course of action.

CHAPTER 10

Resurrection, Recovery, and Reform (2008 to 2014)

Returning to Charts 9.1, 9.2, and 9.3, we'll now cover the recovery after 2008 and discuss what remains to be done. Again using references to the numbers on Chart 9.1, we now look at a few of the key events that occurred during the period of recovery and how those affected credit spreads.

BERNANKE SPEECH IN DC (CHART 9.1, EVENT 21)

The fact that the United States and the world somehow made it through 2008 intact is largely the result of the actions taken by the Federal Reserve. As we have discussed, the Treasury under Secretary Paulson was a source of instability and uncertainty during this period, although he now appears to take credit for saving the world. In fact the lion's share of the credit belongs to the members of the Federal Reserve Board and the thousands of regulators, lawyers, and financial professionals who labored long to save the global financial system. Mistakes were made. Some were unwound and others have been left unresolved for future crisis resolutions.

The following year was also difficult, for a variety of reasons. First and foremost, the peak losses for U.S. banks came during 2009 along with increasing revelations about the scope and magnitude of losses to be taken by investors in all types of securities. It would take several more years before a true picture of the damage done by the latest cycle of fraud on Wall Street was assembled.

Another source of instability came amidst continued questions about the direction to be taken by the Obama administration. Uncertainty arose early in 2009 as some issues with Mr. Geithner's tax returns and other distractions led people to question his choice as secretary of the Treasury. As president of the Federal Reserve Bank of New York, he had been one of the few people who had successfully challenged the thinking of Alan Greenspan. Rather than confront Greenspan's belief that "fraud is self-regulating" (a view that reveals an enormous gap in Mr. Greenspan's understanding of finance and its realities) and that derivatives need no regulation, Mr. Geithner and other regulators undertook a probe of New York banks and found a huge gap in the documentation of derivatives contracts.

Regardless of what one sees as the merits or risks of unregulated derivatives, without documentation of the parties' rights and obligations it is impossible for anyone to enforce those contracts. Off-balance sheet liabilities had to be discoverable at some point. Mr. Geithner convinced major banks that they needed to catch up on their documentation of trades, thereby beginning the process of creating a regulated central clearing house under the auspices of the Depository Trust and Clearing Corporation (DTCC). This documentation at least provides regulators with the ability to unwind the market when necessary.

What Geithner did proved invaluable as the subprime crisis unfolded, but it was long overdue. The New York derivatives dealers created a market that was deliberately opaque and dragged their feet on making basic changes and reforms to the OTC (over the counter) derivatives markets. Going back to the early 1990s, just when the big banks were preparing the ground work to install their monopoly over the market for mortgage finance, the former head of the New York Fed, E. Gerald Corrigan, joined Goldman Sachs and commenced a decade-long rear guard effort to slow the regulation of the OTC derivatives markets. Corrigan dismantled the dealer surveillance function at the Fed of New York in 1993 before leaving to join Goldman, and since then, has spent time obfuscating the need to bring the deliberately inefficient and murky ghetto called OTC derivatives (including credit default swaps) into the light.

Were Justice Brandeis alive today, he would no doubt condemn much of the OTC derivatives market as "a fraud on its face" because participants purport to sell assets they neither own nor can borrow and deliver.

During the debates over appointing Mr. Geithner, and for a period as he was getting his feet wet as head of the U.S. Treasury, spreads rose nearly 200 basis points, costing investors about $2 trillion of the $7.5 trillion regained between November 20, 2008, and Mr. Obama's inauguration. As things were beginning to look pretty awful, Chairman Bernanke gave a March 2009 speech that made it clear the Fed would do whatever it took to keep the nation's financial market operating.

Congress followed with a stimulus plan that Mr. Obama supported and signed. Markets rewarded everyone with a wonderful recovery. Stocks bottomed out in March 2009 and started what is now recognized as one of the most remarkable upswings in history. By June 2009, credit spreads fell another 600 basis points—enhancing the wealth generation capacity of the United States by another $6 trillion per year.

EURO DEBT CRISIS (CHART 9.1, EVENT 23)

Once it became clear that the United States would take the necessary steps to prevent naked short bond trades using CDSs from gaining too-big-to-fail status in American banks, investors specializing in that strategy found a back door to the same game. They began shorting bonds of weaker nations participating in the euro, using CDSs issued by the major U.S. banks.

If the shorts could create havoc in Europe and use the veiled threat of another European war by destroying the euro, they might force the United States to pay up on CDSs backing weak nations' bonds. Conservative leaders in France and Germany embraced punitive austerity positions that might have permitted the strategy to work.

Investors pushed U.S. corporate spreads up about 100 basis points (see Chart 9.1) before leaders in Europe began to figure out they were being played. The impact on bank spreads (see Chart 9.3) was even more noteworthy. Before these events in Europe became major news, trends had returned to the complete market band associated with credit markets at equilibrium (again, see Chart 9.3).

The rise of bank spreads observed on Chart 9.3 reversed when passage of the 2010 Dodd-Frank law made it clear that the U.S. depositor preference rule would limit unsecured CDS holder recoveries to the amount of a U.S. issuer's capital (whether it was a bank or not) after depositors were paid in full. When the size of the financial and economic problems in Europe became clear, however, the spread for banks rose again. This was primarily over concern that the United States would have to pay if Europe's financial infrastructure collapsed, despite the prohibition on bank rescues or bailouts of managers and owners of nonbanks by the Orderly Liquidation Authority provision of the Dodd-Frank law.

It looked like short sellers, including those engaging in naked shorts using CDSs, were in the process of creating a classic collision-course problem.

As rhetoric in Europe cooled and reheated in the months and years to follow, those ups and downs spilled back into U.S. credit markets.

GOP WINS HOUSE (CHART 9.1, EVENT 24)

Spreads in the United States fell (see Charts 9.1 and 9.3) during most of 2010 as U.S. markets recovered. Scholars of the U.S. Constitution understand that a majority of the House of Representatives shifting from one party to the other represents a change of government in Washington, DC. Senators have staggered six-year terms and are therefore a bit immune to party rhetoric, but public anger at the behavior of Wall Street and the government bailouts for large banks (e.g., Citibank and Bank of America) reached a high tide in 2010. The House is the people's chamber. It is where the strongest populist views get expressed. It is also the chamber where, for example, all tax legislation must originate.

The resurrection-recovery phase of the crisis, however, ended in the United States as the Dodd-Frank law passed. With the passage of the legislation, it was less likely that an event similar to the crisis that accompanied the House rejection of TARP would recur. Spreads rose a bit after the election results, but not by an alarming amount. But markets clearly anticipated a political fight now that the House was in Republican hands.

NEW STIMULUS AGREEMENT (CHART 9.1, EVENT 25)

It is not uncommon for politically sensitive matters to be resolved after an upcoming Congress is elected. Reelected members have the longest possible period of time to adjust their pitches for the next election at this point. Lame duck members and carryover senators have their maximum capacity for statesmanship in these postelection sessions. In any event, Congress enacted a stimulus bill. During the next three months corporate bond spreads fell to the bottom of the crisis zone for the first time since October 2007, shortly after Mr. Paulson announced the disastrous Super SIV fund (see Chart 9.1). Meanwhile, the bank spread fell back into the complete market zone (see Chart 9.3).

DEBT CEILING CRISIS (CHART 9.1, EVENT 26)

Just as it looked safe in U.S. financial markets, the relatively new politicians that took office in the new Congress began to make it clear that they did not care if the United States defaulted on its debt—they wanted budget austerity when it was clear that sound economics demanded a more benevolent approach.

The attitude of Republicans is understandable from a certain nineteenth-century perspective, but flies in the face of the needs of a modern society. The fact is that the red states where the GOP is strongest did not experience a housing boom and bust, nor do red states house the large financial institutions that received extraordinary government bailouts. Income levels, home prices, and other measures of economic affluence are lower in Republican red states than in the blue states where Democrats largely predominate. As a result, making arguments against bailouts for big banks and reigning in government have always played well in the red states as a group. Few people, moreover, can distinguish between the essential need to preserve systemic safety by preventing a temporary crisis from destroying debt generally and the bailout of management and shareholders that occurred when Bear Stearns, Citibank, and Bank of America were resolved without forcing the firms into receivership.

With the economy at least stabilized, Wall Street began to look for opportunities. Nonfinancial firms in the United States that produce and export goods were now in a very strong financial position, in part because low interest rates allowed corporations to re-fund liabilities and make investments at an extremely low funding cost. The weaknesses appeared to be lack of recovery in the financial sector and the mortgage hangover that continues even today.

The problems in banks were a logical result of balance sheets with too many bad assets and off-balance sheet liabilities that overhung reported assets and liabilities but were next to impossible to understand. Moreover, the flat labor market meant borrowers were reluctant to generate new loans that would lift the banks. Democrats argued a traditional Keynesian line that new demand for goods, funded with debt, was needed to generate new business loans. But consumers seemed oblivious to such arguments in 2010 and were instead focused on paying down debt and limiting consumption.

In many instances, corporate borrowers had so much cash that accessing new debt was not a priority. As a result, business lending languished, in sync with reduced consumer lending.

DEATH OF OSAMA BIN LADEN (CHART 9.1, EVENT 27)

Some events affect markets by generating a collective sigh of relief among investors. Successfully ending the threat this man posed to everyone's freedom caused a short-term recovery in U.S. credit markets, lowering credit spreads to a point below the crisis zone on Chart 9.1.

GREEK BUDGET RESTRAINTS (CHART 9.1, EVENT 28)

Bin Laden's death was soon trumped by new events in Europe. Pushing austerity on Greece generated disturbances and a Greek political crisis. That round of the euro crisis ended with the adoption of Greek budget restraints— but the resulting calm would not last.

In the summer of 2011, events combined to raise the corporate bond spread (see Chart 9.1) about 100 basis points. The same events pushed the spread for banks above the top of the crisis zone on Chart 9.3, highlighting the need for more action on both sides of the Atlantic Ocean.

TEA PARTY UPRISING (CHART 9.1, EVENT 29)

The Tea Party represents a political reaction against the perceived dominance of a center-left, corporate statism that they see as having controlled American politics since the Great Depression. The components of the Tea Party agenda includes devotion to small government and civil liberties, neither of which is bad in and of itself. But their thinking on fiscal matters is decidedly angry and self-destructive. It echoes the sort of selfishness and narrow-mindedness that we have discussed with respect to the likes of J. P. Morgan and Henry Ford. As with several proposals made by Treasury Secretary Paulson in 2008, the agenda of the Tea Party in the U.S. House of Representatives confirms a simple observation by German theologian Dietrich Bonhoeffer:

Folly is a greater enemy of the good than evil.

Why would a rising group in American politics think that it could succeed by defaulting on U.S. obligations, thereby destroying the fabric of America's rule of law? The United States makes humorous movies about blundering nations that think that they can succeed by doing demonstrably dumb things so others (generally the United States) will pay money to save them. In this case, however, a group convinced the Republican House majority that sabotage was the only way to prevent the continued and uncontrolled growth of government. Unable to succeed at the ballot box, they decided to embrace political terrorism by holding financial markets hostage.

For several decades, active lobbyists like Grover Norquist, founder of Americans for Tax Reform, have become personally successful advancing an idea that the government should be starved of revenue in order to limit its growth. The science of macroeconomics, however, shows that taxing, spending, borrowing, and repaying debt are of little concern to a reserve currency sovereign, as long as it demonstrates continuing respect for its obligations. That's because, absent a total waste of men and materials (as in a war), for each person harmed by changing a nation's fiscal patterns, someone else benefits.

Thus economists recognize the far greater economic significance of changes in credit spreads. High spreads unnecessarily weigh down the great wheel of circulation. The payment of spreads produces no offsetting macroeconomic benefit at any level that exceeds the cost of keeping the wheel turning.

Debate over taxation divides a nation and leads to less effective governance, but since one group will benefit by any change, all such groups lobby, and that benefits politicians and lobbyists. So we will never stop debating fiscal policy. All people naturally like to receive more government benefits or less of a tax burden.

By reaching the point at which their only argument was whether to pay government debt, however, the Tea Party strategy failed miserably. That point was reached in July and August of 2011. Credit spreads widened by roughly 100 basis points as the end result of GOP strategy, national default, became clear. Apparently nobody told the Tea Party that a 100 basis-point rise in spreads represents a near-certain loss of roughly $1 trillion per year in accumulated wealth in the United States. The nation's $15 trillion national debt looms *much* larger against $50 trillion of U.S. wealth than against $100 trillion.

For a while, the Tea Party, with support of the second-ranking Republican in the U.S. House of Representatives, stood firm. They threatened to force the United States to default on its debt rather than do what every sane investor in the world was begging the country to do—spend its way out of a recession. One of many reasons money was flowing into U.S. debt securities at the time, despite in some cases a negative effective yield, was because of the belief that the United States would follow past practice and spend until the financial crisis went away. After that, investors assumed, its ability to repay would be assured by economic growth.

When any nation's investors are begging it to borrow money and spend it (indeed, paying the nation to take the money) at zero cost, only fools ask questions. When rates begin to rise above 0 percent (after inflation is taken into account), there is plenty of time to return intermediation levers back to the private sector. When interest rates are below the rate of inflation (going back to the work of Irving Fisher) it is time to borrow and spend until that changes and the crisis that led to negative interest rates in the first place fades from memory.

There were certainly many worthwhile projects that the United States could have funded to improve infrastructure that would have added value at a rate above the cost of the funds investors offered to provide. But sadly, it appears that most members of Congress do not understand the previous several sentences (or, do not think their constituents would reelect them if they admitted such knowledge).

Part of the rise in U.S. spreads certainly related to the difficulty Europe seemed to be having with default by smaller nations in the eurozone. Why would leaders of France and Germany announce that the eurozone project, the best hope for long-term peace in history, should be weakened by demanding that people in some nations that overspent buying German goods should be starved into understanding the need to be more frugal? Did France forget the World War I lesson about demanding reparations? Did Germany forget what happened when the United States and its allies forgave Germany's prewar debts, squelched demands for reparations after World War II, and actually gave Germany enough in loans and trade benefits to fully recover?

In any event, the combined follies of Europe and Republican efforts to achieve austerity by a debt default pushed the bank spread above the crisis zone until calm returned to Europe in 2012 (see Chart 9.3). Probably by virtue of the extraordinary recovery in financial conditions within the productive sectors of the U.S. economy, the impact of events in Europe on U.S. business borrowers was not nearly as alarming as it was for banks (see Chart 9.1).

BERNANKE SPEECH AT JACKSON HOLE (CHART 9.1, EVENT 32)

Mr. Bernanke used the occasion of a speech at Jackson Hole, Wyoming, to make clear the Fed's intent to keep on buying securities until its dual mandate was achieved—price stability and full employment that is consistent with price stability. While nobody actually believes that the Fed can print jobs with the same ease and facility that it prints money, the statement was reassuring. By leaving that commitment open-ended, Mr. Bernanke told the shorts to buzz off. If the group in charge of a reserve currency that is perceived as infinitely elastic is willing to do whatever is needed to bring economic recovery, shorting that position is utter folly.

FED ACTS DESPITE GOP THREATS (CHART 9.1, EVENT 33)

Some GOP leaders tried to intimidate the Fed into a less active position, believing as they do that the Fed is facilitating the growth of government in Washington, DC. While the Fed has been concerned (and at times obsessed) with preserving the ability of the Treasury to borrow, the view of many Washington politicians about the role of the central bank sometimes hovers at about a second-grade level.

Failing to stand up to a bully is always a mistake. When that happens between Congress (or the president) and the Fed, we know from past experience that the Fed's credibility as an institution is undermined. The negative ramifications of such interference can last a long time.

When the Fed made clear its intention not to cower to GOP threats, short-sellers of debt realized they had almost no chance to succeed. From and after October 2012, several more skirmishes resulted from disagreements in Europe. Once the ECB (European Central Bank) took a firm position that it would similarly defend the euro from attacks, spreads all moved below the crisis zone shown on Charts 9.1, 9.2, and 9.3.

All three charts have shown a spread at (or even below) the complete market equilibrium level since the end of 2012. We will certainly see spreads rise as future events impact investors, but we now have all the precedents needed to instruct fiscal and monetary policy leaders on steps to reverse and prevent any recurrence of the horrific events of 2007–2008.

As is customary when credit spreads are low and stable, equity markets have risen strongly. Since low and stable credit spreads are the ideal conditions for productive sector growth, rising equity prices are both logical and beneficial. When the productive side of the economy's private sector expands, cash flow increases. When cash flow rises at a rate that exceeds the effect of increasing interest rates, total wealth (shown on Table 9.1) will expand, allowing debt and/or equity to rise even as interest rates must rise to preclude inflation. Rising values are what will permit policy makers to take additional steps to assure a balanced and brighter economic future. The only question is how long it will take for policy makers to actually turn these hopes into concrete reality.

While monetary policy has proven itself, U.S. market policy still has a long way to go. We need continuing reforms to be in a position where private-sector participants will be able to pick up the slack in terms of credit creation, much less to reabsorb the Fed's investments without generating a new crisis.

TEA PARTY EXTORTION (CHART 9.1, EVENT 34)

After the U.S. government's fiscal year came to a close in September 2013, Republicans in Congress again aligned themselves with the Tea Party and demanded that the U.S. government be shut down. Worse yet, at least for a while, it appeared the Tea Party might actually push the GOP into committing political suicide by forcing the United States to default on its financial obligations. The target of this extortion was at first the Affordable Health Care Act, which Mr. Obama and the Democrats passed in March 2010 over unanimous Republican opposition. Later targets arose, but the whole concept of using default as a political tool proved to be a farce.

Again, outmaneuvered at the ballot box and even on the floor of the House, the Republicans decided to try political terrorism. The results were appalling for the GOP and could have been even worse for the markets.

The United States pays some 80 million separate obligations each month. When Richard Nixon sought to unilaterally sequester some payments to whip inflation, Congress wrote a law making that illegal. As a result, the U.S.

Treasury created the equivalent of a massive automated teller machine. Anyone seeking payment must prove eligibility and, if proved, the machine automatically pays each and every bill that comes in. The only thing that stops the process is if the ATM runs out of money.

This process is appropriate because discretion is simply not feasible. It would take an army of people to decide which of 80 million monthly U.S. payment obligations to pay and which to ignore. If the ATM suddenly stopped, about 4 million bugs (obligations to pay) would slam (full speed) against the inside of the machine's windshield on that day and on each workday thereafter. One day's accumulation of bugs could gum up the process for months. Every bank and investor in the world that made commitments to buy or invest in reliance on payment by the United States would suddenly be without those funds.

How many members of Congress would be retired at the next election if social security payments froze for a few days? Just as Hank Paulson eventually learned to get out of the way and let the Federal Reserve do its job by acting positively to avoid a deflationary death spiral, Republicans in Congress need to recall the advice of New York Congressman Jack Kemp and tell voters how they propose to improve the economy rather than destroy it.

Never in modern financial history has any responsible person or group suggested such a disastrous course for this (or any other developed) nation. In 2011, the economies of Europe and other areas of the world were still teetering on edge after the subprime financial crisis when Congress threatened a debt ceiling crisis. That made the 2011 Tea Party uprising pretty scary for U.S. investors. The 2013 extortion was so absurd, however, that markets reacted by generating less than 8 percent of the credit spread spike that was observed in 2011. In simple terms, the market dismissed the 2013 Tea Party extortion for what it was, a ridiculous and petulant display.

The 2011 battle proved that the disruption of responsible governance can generate a large, negative, and instantly demonstrable impact on markets. The 2013 battle proved that investors and responsible leaders recognize political lunacy. They rose above the clamor of competing talking heads and ignored the ravings of the Tea Party. The crisis ended October 16, 2013, when GOP House leaders wisely agreed with a Senate proposal to end the shutdown and continue paying obligations that Congress had already approved. The final tally showed that 80 GOP representatives and more than 40 GOP senators joined with the Democrats to remove the threat of a new financial crisis.

That leaves less than 10 GOP senators and about 65 percent of House Republicans to be educated about the need for (and the process to achieve) financial stability by assured fiscal responsibility. That education is easy. Charts 9.1, 9.2, and 9.3 provide unmistakable and unimpeachable proof for what is, and is not, responsible fiscal policy. Table 9.1 puts the benefit/cost in dollar terms.

To show the calamity of causing a crisis, contemplate Chart 9.2. On that chart, up is bad and down is good. The gigantic mountain centered on November 20, 2008, is, in fact, the abyss into which the economy of the entire world fell, and would likely fall again if the United States actually defaulted on its obligations. That mountain is twice as high as the one that led to the Great Depression. To repeat that blunder would combine political suicide for the GOP with worldwide economic catastrophe.

On Table 9.2, each basis point by which credit spreads exceed those of a complete market equilibrium represents a $10 billion annual drain on the production of U.S. national wealth. Since most of the world's corporate bond intermediation is done in the United States, moreover, whatever harms U.S. bond markets similarly impacts the rest of the world, roughly doubling the total damage. At the depth of the recent abyss—November 20, 2008— that means U.S. wealth was shrinking at the rate of roughly $17 trillion per year ($34 trillion globally). No person with intelligence and/or compassion would knowingly use a threat of such decimation to support any political or personal agenda. The weapon of default must be banned.

If Republicans want to reduce the size of government or repeal the Affordable Health Care Act, then they need to make that case to the voters and win the mandate for change on election day. If they win, there is nothing wrong with adjusting the size of the federal government in line with voters' wishes. In that case, investors' daily responses to each new policy will also equally instruct the victors as to how to implement change constructively.

The only thing proven by these Tea Party struggles is that utter stupidity is not good policy. If that lesson sinks in, the skirmishes of 2011 and 2013 will not have been a total waste. Talk constructively about creating jobs, cutting taxes, and reducing the size of government, and Republicans will attract more voters and greater approval from the financial markets. The same simple test applies for Republicans as for Democrats: If your proposals make stock prices rise and keep bond spreads low and stable, then you know that you are on the right track.

CHAPTER 11

Different Circumstances Require Different Solutions

As Franklin Roosevelt was inaugurated, the banks that served Michigan had failed and the Great Depression had decimated Detroit. The entire country was on its knees. Six decades later, as Bill Clinton took office, the resources of GM's finance subsidiary, GMAC, needed to be tapped to their limit to fund GM through a crisis following a reported loss of more than $20 billion. As Barack Obama took office in 2009, GM reported a loss of more than $30 billion and the whole world was in a state of equitable insolvency.

Key GM leaders, however, had learned that for the first time in post–World War II history it was possible for GM to restructure under U.S. bankruptcy law. Implementation of TARP by Congress and the Bush Administration gave the U.S. government a stake in large U.S. banks and thus a significant voice in major decisions of the banking system that would be a major voting block for any successful Chapter 11 filing. That meant the government could prevent a calamitous loss to the Pension Benefit Guaranty Corporation by convincing bankers to allow GM and Chrysler a fresh start, making each sufficiently free of prior debts to succeed.

To accelerate the reorganization process, GM hired the legendary New York lawyer Harvey Miller, who succeeded in gaining court approval to sell the U.S. operating assets of Lehman Brothers to Barclays Bank within a week after Lehman filed for bankruptcy protection. A structure similar to the one GM would follow in 2009 had been used for Japan's largest bankruptcy, the 1998–2001 corporate reorganization of Japan Lease, sponsored by a GMAC subsidiary.

The sale process used in the Lehman, GM, and Chrysler bankruptcies is allowed under Section 363 of the U.S. Bankruptcy Code. Lehman used it to sell operating assets to Barclays and Nomura. GM's leaders were well aware of that sale process. By spring of 2009, the reorganizations of GM (considered impossible in 1993) and Chrysler (that had required a special act of Congress in the early 1980s) were both in place.

Ford was not reorganized via a legal bankruptcy, but was restructured in an economic sense. In 2006, Ford hired former Boeing CEO Alan Mulally and borrowed $23.6 billion secured by all of the assets of the company. Even Ford's blue oval was hocked to the bankers. That bold move gave Ford sufficient cash to survive the liquidity crisis of 2008–2009, the crisis that forced GM and Chrysler to seek $17 billion of bankruptcy court-approved financing from the federal government to reorganize in 2009. The astute 2006 move to raise cash allowed the Ford family to maintain control of Ford Motor Company while GM and Chrysler shareholders were effectively wiped out via massive dilution in Chapter 11(the government's loans to reorganize GM and Chrysler have been repaid in full).

"It was a defining moment for us," Mr. Mulally said in reference to the 2006 borrowings during an interview with the *New York Times* after just 90 days on the job. "But they never would have been willing to lend us the money if we weren't on a different path."

Although Ford took a different path to avoid the crisis of 2007–2008, many key Ford suppliers only survived because of the successful GM and Chrysler reorganizations. Mr. Mulally acknowledged the industry-wide benefits of the 2009 reorganizations. Had GM and Chrysler been allowed to fail, Ford's loss of shared critical suppliers might have precluded the success of its voluntary restructuring.

By 2013, however, Detroit itself needed restructuring.

The financial experiences of the United States during the 1930s and 1990s, and in 2008, are instructive for understanding what is required to regain and sustain worldwide financial stability. When events compel a contraction of debt, the faster and more decisively the world acts to counteract that contraction, the better for all concerned.

The first step, as we have described in this book, is for monetary authorities to lend aggressively to prevent contagion from wiping out the nation's wealth. Unreported debt must be absorbed, but without destroying confidence in the economy. Step two, however, is more difficult. It involves restructuring bad debts and companies so that the stabilized economy can grow and create opportunities. The restructurings of GM, Chrysler, and Ford are examples of success. The U.S. housing sector is an example of failure—at least so far.

Action is best accomplished by the private sector, applying the examples of Ford in 2006 and GM and GMAC in 1993 that we discussed earlier in this narrative. The only action required from Washington is enactment of rules opening markets and enough attention from officials to make sure the parties that need to act keep working in that direction. Sadly, while the

Fed did what was necessary to save the global financial system via massive liquidity, the second phase of restructuring has not occurred.

When private-sector remedies fail, government must act and when it does so properly, a crisis can be averted. The GM and Chrysler bankruptcies, and the ongoing restructuring of Detroit's debt, are examples of cases in which uniform bankruptcy laws compel adverse parties to reconcile. When necessary, government itself can be called on to participate.

If parties and the government cannot reconcile debt, then authority to do so must be placed with judges who will hear all sides and resolve debt sensibly, without resorting to the remedy of prison (except when theft occurs, as in the Bernard Madoff and Allen Stanford cases). Failure to follow that approach repeats past blunders. Such a failure is the primary factor now holding the housing sector and the U.S. economy back. In the 1930s, millions of Americans were caught in the deflationary downdraft after the real estate markets began to crack in the late 1920s. Those markets did not recover until the 1950s and, in some cases, the 1970s.

During the 2006–2009 subprime mortgage crisis, roughly 25 percent of all homes became worth less than the mortgage loans they secured. All steps short of court process have been tried without success. The pass-through structure used for REMIC-based securitizations precludes the entities that created the securities affected by these underwater mortgages from seeking relief in bankruptcy reorganization (as was done for bond structures affected by declining values in the U.S. regional crisis of the 1980s in the Southwest). Congress, moreover, has thus far refused to allow first mortgages on primary residences to be restructured by mortgagors in bankruptcy courts.

Without further action, nobody can say when matters will align to achieve the personal and household debt restructuring that must be done to fully revive the U.S. housing industry. It is absolutely certain, however, that the uncollected and uncollectable housing debt of millions of Americans must be forgiven, or restructured at levels that can be paid. Only then will the U.S. economy start to clear so a full housing and jobs recovery will become possible.

Eliminating the exclusivity of REMIC would allow new forms of debt-like CMOs where corporate issuers of bonds can, in cases of demonstrated need, restructure future-originated securities, and the mortgages that secure them, to maximize debt recoveries if a similar crisis occurs in the future. That process succeeded for issuers of builder bonds that failed in the regional S&L crisis of the 1980s.

Existing REMICs cannot use Chapter 11 to achieve that result because those entities are passive trusts that are not considered debtors. If Congress made it clear that REMICs qualified for bankruptcy, moreover, there might be constitutional conflicts relating to rights of existing guarantors and bondholders. Therefore, the only available process for restructuring today's underwater REMIC-entrapped mortgages would appear to be special bankruptcy proceedings where mortgagors apply for relief and judges are authorized to rewrite the obligations so they can be paid.

At the end of December 2013, data from RealtyTrac showed that 18 percent of homes (nationally) remain underwater, meaning the homeowner owes more than the property is believed to be worth. At the bottom end of the scale, there were still 9.3 million deeply underwater homes that were in that hole by 25 percent or more at the end of 2013. In fact, at the end of 2013, six states were at least 10 points above the national average of 18 percent: Nevada (38%), Florida (34%), Illinois (32%), Michigan (31%), Missouri (28%), and Ohio (28%).

The fact that many homes remain under water (and not foreclosed upon) probably helped push up home prices in 2013 by constraining the supply of homes for sale. But this is a short-term positive for home prices and a long-term negative for the U.S. economy. Each time prices rise appreciably, another part of the overhang comes to market, raising the supply of homes for sale and pushing prices lower in a repeating and very depressing cycle that will require many years to work through.

To clear standard mortgage underwriting guidelines (largely ignored in the subprime boom years), a home's value must generally exceed 125 percent of a new mortgage (an 80 percent loan-to-value ratio). On homes with higher loan to value mortgages (based on prerecession values) the seller must write a check at the closing unless the prior mortgagee accepts a debt write-off (a short sale). When a short sale occurs, moreover, the seller is often required to write a check to the government because forgiveness of debt creates taxable income. When mortgages are embedded in REMIC trusts, consent to a short sale is problematic, at best.

This has been a major obstacle to the Fed's efforts to boost consumption and job creation via low interest rates and quantitative easing. Indeed, if you think of the Fed's efforts to reflate the U.S. economy between 2008 and today as the first step in a national economic recovery, the second step must be to restructure the remaining underwater mortgages on residential homes. Unlike commercial mortgages, which can be restructured in Chapter 11, the practical and legal obstacles to fixing single family mortgages are a significant obstacle to economic growth—especially if home prices level off in 2014 after several years of improvement.

The last time we had a national calamity in housing like today's (overhang of underwater, and barely above-water, mortgages) was the Great Depression. It took from the late 1920s until the 1970s arrival of the REIT and a tax shelter craze to finally allow states like Florida to clear an overhang dating to the land bust of 1927. Everything and everyone in real estate finance simply froze in fear from 1929–1941. World War II disrupted normal economics for another decade. It took the growth of the 1950s and 1960s to get to a point where inflation pushed housing up enough to free Florida and other states from the deflationary vise that started to hit it in the late 1920s.

The Fed has done what it can to deal with the overhang of housing by stoking up leverage via mortgage purchases, but more must be done. By its mandate to maintain price stability, there is little more that the Fed should do. The appalling volume numbers for bank mortgage lending as 2014 began bear grim testament to the inability of the Fed to address all the underlying causes for slow housing and credit creation.

The clear alternative is restructuring, but Congress must allow that by using its exclusive authority to pass bankruptcy laws. Pushed by a banking sector that would be forced to accept what are now built-in (hidden) losses, Congress has stubbornly resisted the changes needed to make effective restructuring work. Pre-REMIC builder bonds (discussed earlier) could be restructured because corporate subsidiaries owned the mortgages and issued nonrecourse bonds secured by those mortgages. Those issuers were able to restructure their mortgage assets and align them with the rights of their bondholders. Through the exclusivity of REMIC, however, today's underwater mortgages are in trusts. REMIC trustees are not debtors that own mortgages as assets and can seek relief to restructure mortgage-backed debt. Undoing existing REMICs, moreover, raises issues regarding freedom of contract.

Nobody except Congress has the Constitutional power to do what's needed. We need to remove the prohibition on bankruptcy judges restructuring first mortgage loans on primary residences to give mortgagors judicially reviewed relief and extend a tax deferral for mortgage debt forgiveness. The chances of this happening are just about zero, however, in the near term. A logjam of interlocking rights among dispersed bondholders, trustees, servicers, and guarantors prevents creating another path to restructuring. In past crises, one or more of the nation's leading banks (often it was Citibank) indicated the time for resolving unpaid debts by announcing an enormous write-down of assets. Since the result is then a tangible valuation that the bank's assets can actually support, the bank becomes stronger, assuming it survives. In this crisis, it does not appear that any bank can yet take steps to restructure underwater mortgages and thereby help the economy to truly clear.

Keep in mind, moreover, that many millions of those underwater mortgages are owned by investors through securities guaranteed by Uncle Sam's GSEs. Any rewrite of the guaranteed senior mortgages in bankruptcy is likely to discharge subordinate mortgages that banks made as home equity loans.

In many cases, trustees and the banks that made the subordinate loans are one and the same. That conflict creates a big incentive to freeze the reconciliation process and defer losses on the subordinate loans (some banks think that will eventually force Uncle Sam to take the entire loss—nobody, of course, wants to say that to taxpayers, however).

In the 1930s, there were several government agencies that had the power to restructure loans—and it still took decades for the overhang to clear. In 2014, there does not yet seem to be a national will to address these issues. So, we continue to struggle with millions of unresolvable mortgages that preclude the prerequisite rise of value needed to stir faster growth.

Without the usual accelerator of economic recovery—rising housing starts—resolution of the financial crisis started with expansion of the next longest term assets that consumers buy—cars. Thus, it made sense to push through a restructuring of GM, Chrysler, and Ford. What the Fed achieved with low interest rates and QE was to preserve the productive capacity of the U.S. economy.

When businesses are building employment, restructuring personal finance can follow. We appear well on the way toward the first goal but the second remains blocked, largely by the housing debacle. Until either the passage of time or government action, or both, resolves the problem of underwater mortgages, therefore, the well-being of financial institutions, consumers, and the U.S. economy as a whole faces significant headwinds.

We will demonstrate a full recovery from the Armageddon of 2008 if and when the Fed is able to stop asset purchases and normalize interest rates without harming the recovery. The depth of the crisis and the magnitude of assistance needed to bridge a $67 trillion chasm give meaning to warnings of the Fed and other central bankers that low rates can be anticipated for an extended period of time.

Without a stronger recovery the Fed is not likely to sell any significant portion of its portfolio. In the event that the Fed does sell assets it will be due to a rise in real demand from investors. That will signal the healing process is advancing and that its policy has worked to preserve equity and generate a return of private demand for financial assets. Only then can we safely declare success.

The Theory of
Financial Stability

Statement: Rule of Law + Freedom + Transparency → Equilibrium

*I*n markets in which all participants' rights as issuers, obligors, creditors, and owners are justly supported and all are granted free and equal access to generate financial arbitrage transactions that are riskless, subject to:

- *Adequate constraints against fraud,*
- *Anonymous and timely reporting of trades, and*
- *Requirements to fairly state their financial condition,*

financial stability will be established by supply and demand at a price that represents the minimum sustainable cost of intermediation.

When market prices or spreads for credit establish that one or more of the conditions for sustained financial stability cannot be achieved effectively by private-sector participants, monetary authorities should undertake such transactions as are necessary and consistent with their mandates to minimize the cost of intermediation while encouraging steps to regain a level of private-sector participation that allows monetary authorities to suspend such transactions and unwind positions previously acquired. The actions by the Federal Reserve since 2008 that are illustrated in Part One of this book provide an excellent case in point. Likewise, when legal rights are not aligned correctly, political authorities should act as needed to correct defects in market regulation while avoiding the creation of market control.

CHAPTER 13

Saying versus Doing

Needless to say, doing what is required to maintain financial stability is much, much, much more difficult than saying it.

Fraud, defined in simple terms as the use of two measures, was banned by the Jews about 4,000 years ago. Two millennia later, high priests of the Temple in Jerusalem helped fund their work by the fraud of manipulating two currencies (Roman and Temple money) for gain, at the expense of religious pilgrims. A rabbi that founded a new religion sought to expose that fraud by forcing open competition that would relieve pilgrims from that burden of financial manipulation. The priests and Roman authorities, with consent of some of the very people Jesus sought to help (and silence from His closest friends), ordered His execution.

None of them understood how to change course. Few had any idea why Christ sought to push money changers into an open market. Most pilgrims did not see that fraudulent profits on lambs sold for their Passover sacrifices were hidden in the duplicity of controlled exchange rates.

The money changers could not do business in Temple currency on the streets of a Roman city. The Temple priests had families to raise and a Temple to run using their share of the money changers' profits. Moving the exchange process outside the Temple would have at least brought competition and, at worst, arrest for undermining Rome's taxation to support an occupying army.

Nobody understood how the transparency of an open market would have helped, and fear of change is an almost universal human reaction.

Forty years later Rome destroyed the Temple that protected the high priests' exchange fraud. A similar result occurred after Renaissance popes used duplicity to manipulate Christ's teachings for political and personal gain. Rome was sacked in 1527 by troops of Holy Roman Emperor Charles V, soon after the Protestant Reformation was born.

Kings abused financial systems and revolts followed, most notably in England, the United States, and France. Yet each nation's political leaders still abuse finance today. Nearly 500 years have passed since the sacking of Rome and we still fight the same battles over the ultimate questions of how to achieve open financial markets, financial fairness, and productive sector efficiency.

In Ukraine, for example, western banks helped to finance real estate development that enriched "self-made" billionaire kleptocrats and left thousands saddled with odious mortgage debt. Only when corruption reached extreme levels did the free markets respond and displace the wrongdoers.

We now have proof, by observing credit spreads, that the solution of free markets works, and the mathematics to precisely measure the impact of investors' responses to policy changes. Yet leaders of the world's most populous nation still circulate memoranda explicitly rejecting Western notions about the freedom, rule of law, individual rights, and transparency that prevent financial crises. Notwithstanding proof of error, nations still seek to rule by authoritarian direction and economic monopoly.

Ironically, rejection of the obvious truth of free markets is occurring even as a growing body of statistics and analysis proves that all crises are caused by the collapse of bubbles. The latest example is that of mercantilist nations such as China, which generated vast amounts of bad debt during several decades of excesses. China's leaders and bankers now seek to hide errors of financial judgment beneath authoritarian controls. The markets will ultimately win.

In the United States, despite lessons of the Great Depression, Congress continues to block the means for reconciliation of mortgage market errors that continue to block recovery from the 2007–2009 financial crisis. Congress alone has authority to enact uniform laws on bankruptcies throughout the United States. The United States needs a uniform process for reconciling unrecoverable mortgage balances and millions of lost and destroyed mortgage records.

In what may be the ultimate blunder, we now know that some of the largest banks in the United States cannot sell or resolve loans currently held on their books because they cannot locate the records needed to document claims. Many lenders voluntarily destroyed documents that recorded changes in title and replaced them with electronic files that proved entirely unreliable. Without proof, it is impossible for anyone to identify the actual rights and obligations of deceived borrowers and lenders.

In that morass, even a perfectly structured debt-trading market cannot function. Debtors have a right to insist on protection from double payment by insisting creditors prove that promissory notes debtors signed were not delivered to others who can later present those notes and collect again. Eight years after the start of the crisis, unresolved issues in the housing sector remain a dead weight around the neck of consumers, lenders, taxpayers, and markets. That is why at the end of 2013 nearly a quarter-trillion dollars' worth of distressed single-family mortgage loans remained on the books of U.S. banks. There are hundreds of billions more owned by REMIC trusts that cannot be restructured.

Human folly precludes most people from reconciling their own financial errors—that is why the U.S. Constitution explicitly directed Congress to create processes for bankruptcy to do that for them. The power to establish uniform laws for bankruptcies was given to elected officials so that past abuses by priests and kings (with similar human failings) would not be repeated to the benefit of a few and detriment of many. Article I of the U.S. Constitution gave Congress power to create bankruptcy courts because the Founders recognized that prompt resolution of insolvency was necessary for a healthy and prosperous society. So far in this crisis, however, their wisdom seems lost on a generation of officials worried alternatively about pleasing the largest financial institutions and political radicals that might cause them to lose elections.

There are followers of Christ who still don't understand the admonition against the duplicity of fraud. Financiers and the appraisers, auditors, and attorneys who serve them still seek to deploy different measures so as to benefit themselves over disadvantaged customers, shareholders, and fellow citizens. The use of different accounting regimes for investors, regulators, and tax authorities in the United States is an example of such muddled thinking.

Unlike the money changers of first century Jerusalem, there is no risk of punishment today for taking actions to minimize a fraudulent exchange rate mark-up. The church that charged Fred a 67 percent currency exchange mark-up in May 2013 did not face Roman soldiers ordered to impose Rome's monopoly on coinage. It only needed to accept credit cards.

Europe, the source of more wars generated by financial manipulation than any other area of the world, has a unified currency, and, as a result of the recent crisis, seems to be on a path to reforming its banking system. To date, however, it has taken few steps to create an open market for trading bonds or making financial information more readily available to the public. Such reforms would give Europe the type of credit-spread data that now allows the United States to track the impact of daily investor responses to financial policy changes that affect the cost of Adam Smith's great wheel of circulation.

At least for now, England trades in the unified economic area of the euro, but it continues to reject participation in the currency, generating the duplicity of Fred's recent exchange experience. Nobody has any idea if and when Europe will create a central governance structure that provides support for both the needs of individual sovereign states and the unified economic needs of Europe as a whole.

The United States has learned (and continues to learn) that errors in the features of market structuring are what trigger crises. Both the crash that led to the Great Depression and the crisis of 2008 were triggered by events that events that forced recognition of a massive and systemic accounting fraud—off-balance sheet liabilities.

Solutions for panics that the United Kingdom used long before the Great Depression failed in the United States after the 1929 crash because we did not pay attention to the state-by-state elements needed to prevent abuses of our financial system. Those failed structures are what led the U.S. Supreme Court to correctly declare that an imperfect pledge of collateral "imputes fraud conclusively."

Before such reforms as the Uniform Commercial Code, the U.S. Bankruptcy Code, and the Uniform Fraudulent Transfer Act, pledging collateral in the 1930s created a secret second measure of credit. As noted earlier, while the Supreme Court's ruling in 1925 was correct in principle given the laws of that day, the decision by Louis Brandeis in the *Benedict* case precluded the lender-of-last-resort application of Bagehot's dictum to prevent the Great Depression.

In response to the collapse of private credit creation in the late 1920s, we had to nationalize our financial system in 1933, but we imposed draconian rules that nearly strangled the global economy before we generated new laws that opened markets to both growth and crises. In the latest crisis, the Fed did a remarkable job managing and creating the necessary financial bridge that restored equilibrium. But Congress, in a natural political reaction, has placed new restraints on growth and credit creation that may constrain a full recovery for years to come. This time the United States must do a much better job implementing the features of new reforms that will allow the United States to unwind what the Fed created and restore effective private-sector bond trading markets.

When the authors speak to groups at home and abroad, the history of decades of U.S. financial market errors is quite helpful. It allows the U.S. mistakes of experience to generate humor that helps both our citizens and other nations gain wisdom that avoids similar folly. Unfortunately, folly is a universal human frailty and one that repeats itself with great regularity. The best advice of leaders rarely works.

The United States helped Japan create a corporate reorganization law in the early 1950s. As applied there, however, the law only worked during inflationary periods. It was not useful when Japan slipped into deflation for more than a decade after its real estate bubble burst in the late 1980s. Starting in 1998, U.S. experts offered Japan new reorganization techniques that allowed it to unwind mistakes of the 1980s that produced a lost decade in the 1990s. Within a few years, however, those lessons were too often ignored in both Japan and the United States.

Perhaps it is only extended life expectancy that can bring about financial stability. In different form, the problems that caused the Great Depression of the 1930s were the problems that caused the Great Recession of 2007–2009. The facts common to both financial crises are separated by more than 70 years— not a particularly long period of time. Yet it was enough time for several generations of Americans to forget the lessons learned by their parents in the years following the 1930s.

For financial stability and economic prosperity to be the rule rather than the rare exception, we need people with sufficient experience to avoid repetition of errors and to punish acts of fraud effectively. It is only recently that life expectancy has increased to a point where the world can hope to sustain financial stability. Perhaps that fact alone offers the world hope for success despite 4,000 years of experience to the contrary. And yet there have been few prosecutions for fraud resulting from the subprime financial crisis and subsequent recession.

Marty Robins argues that there are not sufficient laws in place to prosecute the frauds committed before the financial crisis (Robins 2014). But that is clearly not the case. Starting from the Brandeis decision in 1925 and moving forward, past generations of leaders in the United States have put in place more than sufficient legal tools to punish fraud and related misdeeds, and thereby give financial stability a real chance. What has been lacking is the political will to punish duplicity in the financial markets. Judge Jed S. Rakoff of the Southern District of New York notes in response to Robins,

> The reason cannot be, as Mr. Robins suggests, that there is no state or federal statute covering such behavior. On the contrary, at the federal level alone, there are numerous statutes that criminalize the intentional making of false statements regarding the creditworthiness of mortgage-backed securities, including the mail fraud statute (18 U.S.C. §1341), the wire fraud statute (18 U.S.C. §1343), the bank fraud statute (18 U.S.C. §1344), the securities fraud statute (15 U.S.C. §78ff), and many more. Thus, I respectfully disagree with Mr. Robins's ultimate suggestion that we need more laws "to deter this problematic behavior." So far as criminal prosecutions are concerned, the legal weapons are already there. The question is, who will use them?

Contrary to the popular view that the frauds committed prior to the subprime crisis could not be pursued because of a deficiency in the law, in fact the legal framework existed decades before 2008. When a financial institution is injured, the civil and criminal remedies under existing federal banking laws are quite effective when prosecuted correctly. As we learned in the 1930s, it takes judges and prosecutors time to recall old principles (and advise other officers of the court).

Take the case of the convicted defrauder Allen Stanford. Initial ineptness led to a near-wipeout of investors, largely because the offshore jurisdiction that housed most of his Ponzi scheme refused to prosecute the fraud. Once the Texas case got going, however, Stanford had all his directors' and officers' liability insurance cut off because the insurer convinced the U.S. court there was probable evidence of a crime. A receiver was appointed and Stanford is now rather permanently in jail. The case of the Madoff fraud is another illustration of how justice is served when resolute lawyers and prosecutors move with purpose to punish fraud using existing civil and criminal statutes.

But the trouble with the vast majority of fraudulent transactions committed prior to the subprime debacle is that they involve a universal class of assets—namely residential mortgages—which flowed through the largest financial institutions in the country. Many of the mortgage-backed securities issued between 1998 and 2008 were not created using true sales. They were secured borrowings instead. The duplicitous reporting of such transactions as sales "imputes fraud conclusively." Citigroup; Bear Stearns; Lehman Brothers; Countywide; and Washington Mutual—just to name a few cases—provide rich opportunities to research the issue of fraud using the guidelines in this volume.

But the fact is that the political will simply did not exist to pursue these frauds because doing so would have brought the system itself to its knees—this at the very time that the Fed and other agencies were attempting to save it. But that does not lessen the need to understand and recognize frauds committed in the future. That, at the end of the day, is why we have written this book.

Proofs of the Theory of Financial Stability

Mathematics: $(1 + i)^x > (E = mc^2)$

At a press conference when Albert Einstein retired, a journalist asked the great physicist to identify the most important mathematical formula in history. Einstein's theory of relativity led to the nuclear and thermonuclear bombs that Einstein warned against, as well as thousands of peaceful applications. Yet he smiled and said: "One plus i to the x." Einstein observed that the formula for compound interest had had more impact on humanity than any other equation.[1]

The theory of financial stability minimizes both i and x in the formula when applied to the assets and liabilities of financial intermediaries. That is how equilibrium in finance achieves the maximum level of equity and productivity growth for all sectors of an economy. Using that same formula,

---

[1] Islamic law prohibits the payment and collection of interest, but allows a nonobligatory return for risk. Therefore, r would replace i in the formula. Since r does not create liability, this makes the calculation of fixed financial asset values difficult (limiting the ability to trade debt and to enhance r using leverage), but eases the ability to discharge uncollectible obligations. Early Christian doctrine also prohibited the collection of interest. Since the Reformation, collection of reasonable i is allowed, leading to usury laws and the restraint and discharge of interest under bankruptcy laws. The United States defines the obligations of debt and its priority clearly. Fraud and theft laws (civil and criminal) protect creditors (and tax laws multiply liability) when money for debt is diverted to owners or managers, but the preference of one creditor over another is only cause for recovery if bankruptcy proves imminent. Under the Deep Rock doctrine, separation of liability using different entities is ignored when necessary to undo fraud or injustice. Recovery powers of U.S. bankruptcy trustees are sufficient that most (and perhaps all) losses of Bernard Madoff's investors will be recovered. If trustees' powers are inadequate, judges can add receivership powers to collect damages from participants in fraud. The U.S. Bankruptcy Code discharges nonfraudulent liabilities, with the now dubious exception that no modification is allowed for first mortgages on primary residences.

moreover, we can calculate the precise impact of changes in i on the investment value of any given level of cash flow that an economy produces. That result is illustrated in Table 9.1.

Financial stability minimizes the burden of finance on production and maximizes the efficiency of investments that generate productivity. It does so, however, by minimizing the margin that financial firms often use to fund compensation paid to financial managers.

It is easy to demonstrate the long-term growth benefits to financial institutions from minimizing margins that maximize the growth of their customers' wealth and thus their needs for financial intermediation—the business of banking. It is almost impossible, however, to get managers to accept that low margins are good.

This dichotomy between the self-interest of management and the broader interests of institutions and society is the foundation of all moral hazard frauds and deceptions (e.g., off-balance sheet liabilities and shadow banking) by which high-margin and highly leveraged financial schemes are justified and then hidden from investors and regulators. The desire to limit competition, to rig the game using two measures to hide speculations, is as old as humanity itself.

The formula for compound interest is the Rosetta stone of finance by which macroeconomic benefits of low-spread margins are demonstrated. Table 9.1 uses base rates and spreads to set valuation cap-rates that translate cash flow into values of debt and equity that conform theory to experienced results.

Over time, it is only the value of an entity's (or nation's) cash flow that can support an economic valuation of wealth. By a long-established rule of law known as absolute priority, debt must be paid before equity is entitled to the benefits of cash flow. Therefore, the cash flow needed to support debt must be subtracted before valuing what is left to equity. Though viewed as essential for economic preservation, the 2008–2009 assistance packages provided to AIG, Bear, Stearns & Co., and Citigroup violated this ancient rule of priority, but that political fact does not change the basic analysis and Dodd-Frank precludes such assistance in the future. To receive future assistance, an entity must first be placed in receivership, with FDIC as receiver.

The rate and spread assumptions used are set forth on Table 9.1. From there, *one plus* i *to the* x does everything. The available cash flow is calculated by reverse analysis of the assumed debt/wealth reflected in the top/middle box and then kept constant for the other calculations. When economic conditions cause available cash flow to rise, all else staying equal, the values in Table 9.1 will necessarily rise.

In a low-spread complete market, the total value of a constant cash flow shown in Table 9.1 rises 68.5 percent as the base rate falls from 5 percent to 0 percent, and falls 30 percent as the base rate rises from 5 percent to 10 percent. By 50 percent leverage, however, equity rises 137 percent as the base rate falls and falls 60 percent as the base rate rises.

In each assumed base rate scenario, spreads have a much greater impact. At a 0 percent base rate, the difference between a complete market spread and the Armageddon of 2008 is a 55 percent decline in total value (a 123.5 percent rise by reversing the Armageddon effect) and a 78.6 percent decline in equity (a 366.5 percent rise by reversing the Armageddon effect). At a 10 percent base rate, the comparable numbers are a 23.5 percent decline in total value (conversely, a 31 percent rise) and an 82.6 percent decline in equity (again, conversely, a 474.3 percent rise).

The difference between a normal market and the application of two applied theories for regenerating normal when Armageddon hits is also portrayed using the same table. During the crisis of 2008, the United States went from normal credit spreads to Armageddon with 0 percent base rates. In the Great Depression, the United States (whether forced by law to do so or not) applied a draconian version of the laws at that time and fell into Armageddon while raising base rates, creating a 93 percent reduction of equity values.

In effect, the leaders of that era went back to Bagehot's original dictum that high rates were necessary to pull liquidity back into the markets, but were blocked by law from recycling that liquidity to entities in need. After seven years of government intervention, the evidence suggests that having the Fed provide excess reserves is not by itself inflationary. We need to see an acceleration of growth (rising cash flows) to turn around the stifling postcrisis force of disinflation. Rising demand is needed to really declare victory over the specter of debt deflation.

On Table 9.1 the top center box represents the precrisis level and is used to establish the assumed fixed-cash flow. The bottom left box is the Armageddon situation of 2008 using the policy followed by the U.S. Fed (0 percent base rates). The bottom right box is Armageddon with a Depression-era liquidation solution. Using the solution the United States applied, total wealth is 41 percent higher (and equity is 625.7 percent higher) than using the liquidation solution.

The hurdle for recovery, moreover, favors the U.S. solution to recreate stability by an even higher proportion. To recover from a crisis after using a Depression-era liquidation solution requires a 1,328.6 percent increase in equity values. Using the U.S. solution of 2008, only a 98 percent recovery is necessary. That means it is 13.56 times as hard to recover from applying the liquidation model used during the Depression as from the theory of financial stability applied by the United States in 2008.

Of course, for those that short or simply hoard cash to await the effect of a crisis, a deflation scenario solution creates an opportunity to buy equity at 7 percent of precrisis levels (versus 50.8 percent using the Fed's approach). When Henry Ford accelerated the banking crisis of 1933, he believed that he could survive the contagion, a stunning act of indifference to the suffering that would follow for millions of Americans. That's also the same selfish opportunity J. Pierpont Morgan pursued when he convinced fellow bankers to support his private solution to the 1907 panic.

Is it possible that Morgan convinced those who drafted the 1913 Federal Reserve Act to preclude the new central bank from paying interest to attract free reserves because he wished to perpetuate that opportunity for control and generate still more wealth for himself in a later crisis? It is unlikely records will ever prove that intent, but history certainly supports the possibility. The ease with which the current Fed liquefied the U.S. economy (and profited, at least temporarily, by doing so) once it had the authority to pay interest on excess reserves amply demonstrates the benefit of removing that impediment.

The effect of rising credit spreads on enterprise value and default rates on loans is also evident from the table. Even the best policy for handling a crisis after it arises reduces total equity by roughly 50 percent when credit spreads rise from the equilibrium of a complete market to Armageddon levels. Without any change in base rates, equity falls by about 75 percent.

If those are averages, of course, many marginal borrowers will be in default at just a 50 percent decline in total market equity. If people who track corporate defaults compare any of the corporate credit spread graphs used with this book to their default data, they will see a near-perfect correlation. Defaults rise and fall in sync with rising and falling spreads, respectively.

That rising credit spreads drive some enterprises into default causes their impact to be greater than that of rising base rates. When base rates rise, over time (as new debts replace old) the winners and losers offset each other. Thus, the U.S. Fed sees little long-term impact on the overall economy when it changes short-term rates. These numbers do not consider that offsetting impact, however, because the offset disproportionately impacts firms based on when bonds mature. If considered, this would place even greater weight on the impact of changes in credit spreads compared to changes in base rates.

To show how rising credit spreads/defaults impact banks, let's compare a bank characterized by the 1960s-era Rule of 3-6-3 to one with a lot of bad assets, using the formula for compound interest to show changes over time. If a 3-6-3 bank has $1 billion of loans, $900 million of deposits, and operating costs that are 2 percent of assets, its equity will rise 13 percent per annum, producing a compound rise of 84.25 percent in value over 5 years and a 239.5 percent rise over 10 years.

If defaults rise to a level at which operating costs offset asset earnings, and rising credit spreads cause the cost of deposits to rise 200 basis points (a modest increase compared to the 2008 experience), the 3-6-3 bank will be insolvent in two years.

Thus, when leverage is good it is "very good indeed" for banks, but when it is bad, leverage is "horrid" for banks. Since banks are essential for the functioning of society, any and all steps required to stabilize finance must be taken during good times and especially as bad times approach. When bank liabilities are ultimately insured by taxpayers, it is ridiculous for any liability or speculation of a bank to be reported off-balance sheet.

It is market control that allows managers to control lending margins and it is high lending margins that convert good loans into bad ones. Open markets and enforcement of restrictions on fraud are the keys that support reduced margins/spreads. The theory of financial stability is, therefore, supported by the laws of mathematics that apply to financial markets.

CHAPTER 15

Law: Incomplete Sale ≡ Secured Borrowing

In any nation that honors the rule of law, it is the law that determines all rights and protections of debtors, creditors, and owners. By law, auditors must ignore generally accepted accounting standards when those rules result in financial statements that fail to fairly state the financial condition of an enterprise. To assure compliance, financial statements must report what an entity owns (assets) and what it owes (liabilities) in order to accurately determine its equity (net worth).

The laws of mathematics prove that the level of a financial institution's leverage is the primary determinant of that institution's ability to survive as market conditions change. It is axiomatic, therefore, that debt must be reported accurately.

Where in this is there room for creating an off-balance sheet liability? To state the premise is to state fraud. The very words "off-balance sheet" are themselves duplicitous.

If it's a liability it is obviously necessary that it be reported on-balance sheet. The two concepts—off-balance sheet and liability—cannot exist together. When an asset is sold, both the upside and downside of the asset must be sold for the sale to be complete. In the 1925 opinion by Louis Brandeis, the U.S. Supreme Court ruled that any incomplete sale or pledge of any asset "imputes fraud conclusively." Lack of completion creates ambiguity, allowing two measures of ownership—the essence of fraud.

Thus, unless dominion over the assets transferred is surrendered by a true sale or pledge, the Supreme Court decreed that receivers representing the seller or borrower, or its creditors, have an absolute right to recover at least the upside value of a sold or pledged asset from the lender or buyer. Under the UFTA, when an incomplete transfer occurs, the transferee is defined as a secured creditor for the amount paid. There is, therefore, no basis for duplicity when a sale is incomplete—it must be reported as a secured borrowing with a pledge of collateral.

It is, therefore, now settled U.S. law that any incomplete sale is a secured borrowing by the transferor. Without confirmation of a complete sale (by demonstration that no fraudulent transfer occurred and the absence of agreements restricting a full transfer of control), all financial asset transfers with continuing involvement of the seller must be reported as secured borrowings.

In a case in which an investor seeks to transfer financial assets (loans, bonds, etc.), there are two cash flows that result from either a sale or a pledge: (1) the money paid by the buyer to the seller, and (2) the money due from the underlying obligor on the asset transferred. All other factors (covenants, future recoveries, etc.) are matters of negotiation between buyer and seller or between pledgor and pledgee. External circumstances affecting the transactions are necessarily identical. All factors that determine economics for the transaction are, therefore, identical whether the transfer is a sale or a pledge.

It is *only* law that determines which of the two transactions (sale or secured borrowing) is accomplished. Therefore, only law decides whether parties create a loan or a sale by their transaction. According to both the U.S. Supreme Court and the UFTA, only when a true sale exists can an asset transfer be reported as a sale.

With respect to a pledge, every U.S. state has adopted Article 9 of the Uniform Commercial Code since it was first proposed in the 1950s. Under Article 9, pledges and sales of financial assets are accorded identical treatment. They both create senior rights over the transferor's creditors when specific steps are taken to overcome the concerns Justice Brandeis expressed as conditions to proving a complete pledge. Any transaction that conforms only to the UCC can only be a true sale if and when the transaction completely transfers dominion over any rise in the net (after debt) value of a transferred asset.

A pledge, whether written as a sale or otherwise, confers only secured creditor status to the transferee, with only the right to recover the rights of a lender.

Under the USBC and the UFTA, when steps to avoid creation of a fraudulent transfer are not fulfilled, any transferee that advances sums in good faith remains entitled only to a lien for the amount advanced. When the transferee is only entitled to the value established by its purchase price plus (perhaps) interest, the transferee is a pledgee, not a buyer. Such transferees are secured parties (creditors), not buyers.

By law today, therefore, any financial asset sale that is incomplete will "impute fraud conclusively" if it is reported as a sale. Therefore the transaction is, and must be recognized as, a secured borrowing. In the appendix we provide the tests by which a true sale of financial assets is distinguished from transactions that are, by law, secured borrowings.

Law, therefore, confirms the theory of financial stability by demanding transparency and reporting of all incomplete transfers as debt, eliminating all argument that a liability may ever be reported off-balance sheet.

The concept of off-balance sheet shadow banking is, therefore, inconsistent with the law and the theory of financial stability. Absent a complete or true sale (which demonstrably complies with all requirements of fraudulent transfer law), all financial asset transfers create debt for the transferor. A transferee who in good faith pays money for an incomplete transfer is a secured creditor; otherwise the transferee is at best an unsecured creditor and often subordinate to creditors.

CHAPTER 16

Economics: Savings = Investment

It is an axiom of economics that savings must equal investment. That is to say, the total capital goods of a nation (or the world) must necessarily equal the sum total of all public and private indebtedness and equity.

In 2005, capital goods in the United States totaled roughly $100 trillion. Total reported debt was about $50 trillion, and total equity was the remaining $50 trillion. For the world, each category was roughly double the U.S. total.

Where did the shadow banking market, off-balance sheet liabilities, fit into this axiom? In the United States, that category was said to total $30 trillion (for the world, $67 trillion).

The crisis began when some financial institutions reported in 2007 that they would not honor off-balance sheet liabilities. That's when the investors who had put cash into shadow banking funds began to flee the markets. It did not take long for all investors to question the value of equity by applying the axiom governing the relationship between capital goods and investment. If reported U.S. debt was in fact understated by $30 trillion—and world-wide debt by some $67 trillion—then equity had to be $20 trillion instead of $50 trillion in the United States and $33 trillion instead of $100 trillion worldwide. This realization that the assets and liabilities of the world economy were mismatched was the key catalyst for the financial crisis.

A massive *oops* occurred. This realization was equivalent to shooting a howitzer across the bow of the investment ship. Every investor with a model that produced the standard results shown in Table 9.1 would have noted the same relatively close correlation. If $30 trillion of shadow banking liabilities are added to reported debt, equity values must fall by $30 trillion, or some 60 percent. The experienced loss correlates directly to that assumption when base rates fell to 1 percent and spreads widened to Armageddon levels.

In that scenario, of course, the assets one would want to hold would be cash or Treasury debt that was, if still available, at a maturity that would allow the investor to ride out the storm obviously coming as more and more investors got it.

Smart investors knew equity was headed for a 60 percent drop in the United States and 67 percent worldwide. If one takes into account the time for a total collapse to occur, what investors saw in 2007 is exactly what had occurred by March 2009. The tragedy that began with Mr. Paulson's announcement of a Super SIV to rescue Citigroup and other TBTF banks took 13 months to reach the climactic credit-spread spike of September–November 2008. The precise predictions of Irving Fisher in his 1933 *Econometrica* article came true.

The world fell into debt-contraction deflation. It was saved from the debt deflation result by replacing unsustainable private-sector debt with public-sector debt at rates low enough to support greater equity values over time, which allows a later return to private sector debt.

Under the theory of financial stability, this means we can completely recover if market policies are adopted that allow private-sector participants to refund the Fed's public-sector bridge loans with private-sector substitutes that sustain a renewed period of economic expansion. The theory is, therefore, supported by the laws of economics.

CHAPTER 17

Accounting: Assets ≡ Liabilities + Capital

A ccounting uses the laws of mathematics to express economics in a manner consistent with the legal obligation of firms and individuals to fairly report their financial condition when they provide financial statements.

Accountants are supposed to safeguard against fraud by making firms apply one measure consistently. While it follows general principles to achieve consistent reporting, accountancy's only goal is to responsibly reflect conclusions from other sciences and fields. Failure to recognize this ancillary (though vitally important) function of accounting has contributed to abuses that create instability in finance.

The vitality of accounting lies in the power of the double-entry system that is the heart of this analytic tool. Every credit or debit must generate a corresponding entry in order to maintain the two essential balances expressed in financial statements: (1) assets must always equal the sum of liabilities and capital, and (2) revenues must always equal the sum of expenses and earnings. Finally, cash flows and inventories must accurately carry balance positions from one financial statement period to the next.

When transactions are reported in a manner that reflects accounting practice but fails to reflect the law, mathematics, and economics, then accounting practice must change to assure compliance. Since 1997, accounting standards have conformed transactions involving financial asset transfers to the law, mathematics, and economics by recording financial asset transfers as sales only when the transaction puts assets presumptively beyond the reach of the transferor and its creditors, even in the case of bankruptcy or other receivership. The tests that address that standard are set forth in the appendix of this book.

This standard, if universally and uniformly applied, conforms accounting to the legal standards found in U.S. Supreme Court decisions on complete (or true) sales and statutes. That aligns accounting with the theory of financial stability.

From 1983 (when doubt remained as to the legal impact of an incomplete sale, because the UFTA had not been written) until 1997, accounting rules depended on the form of the asset transfer transaction. Transfers in a form that purported to be a sale were recorded as sales, while those that purported to be secured borrowings were reported as debt. Under the UCC a transfer is effective, whether it purports to be a sale or a pledge. The UCC was written to address only the Supreme Court's 1925 concerns relating to pledges.

Whether a sale is complete matters in accountancy, because that is where one must distinguish sales from transactions that grant security interests (debt). To reopen markets for secured lending, the UCC gave pledgees and transferees that buy accounts identical rights: those of a secured creditor. In 1983 it was necessary to create a new accounting standard because standalone CMOs invalidated the assumption that one cannot add value merely by changing the form of a financial instrument. The 1983 standard was a big mistake.

Combined with economic circumstances of the 1980s and laws that allowed speculation by previously regulated thrifts, the 1983 standard led to duplicity. It was based on legal form, not legal result. Therefore, entities could choose a pledge form to avoid reporting a loss on a transfer and a sale form to report a gain.

This was a contributing factor to losses the federal government sustained in the S&L crisis (that, as we've noted, Bill Seidman labeled the biggest mistake in the history of government—a record that endured until the 2007–2009 crisis beat it by two orders of magnitude).

By requiring that *only* complete (or true) sales of financial assets be accounted for as sales, the accounting profession became aligned with the law in 1997. Had the new standard been applied uniformly, financial accounting would have had no role in the deceptions created by shadow banking and off-balance sheet liabilities. All such liabilities would have been reported on-balance sheet.

Before the 1997 standard became effective, the FDIC adopted it for banks, only to discover that the standard, applied literally, made it impossible for banks to sell financial assets. That's because the FDIC, as a bank's receiver, succeeds to the rights of innocent insured depositors and has power, by statute, to unwind any transaction.

This was pointed out to the FDIC soon after the 1997 effective date of the new accounting standard. Between then and the April 1, 2001, effective date of a revision to the 1997 standard, the FDIC was invited to reconsider its authority to unwind transactions. To preserve liquidity for solvent banks, in 2000 the FDIC adopted a safe harbor that, it later noted, gave banks a bye on legal compliance in allowing their transfers to be reflected as sales even in cases in which there was continuing involvement on the part of the bank that was inconsistent with the Supreme Court's true sale standard.

It is within that safe harbor that U.S. banks hid a great deal of the off-balance sheet shadow banking liabilities that fueled the 2007–2009 financial crisis. In 2010 the FDIC reconsidered and ended the safe-harbor rule, meaning that bank transfers after November 2010 must meet the high legal isolation standards applied to sales by other entities. That finally gave the United States a single measure for a sale. Any transfer of a financial asset that is not a true sale must be reflected as a borrowing. The appendix provides the standard and the opinions needed for compliance.

Accountants are liable (along with other parties affiliated with an institution) for frauds committed by financial institutions. To avoid this hazard, accountants must obtain legal opinions that support reporting a transfer as a sale. If any part of the standard is not met, the transfer is a secured borrowing. Anything less "imputes fraud conclusively."

Transfer terms must meet standards that preclude avoidance under requirements of the UFTA, the USBC, and various cases, which reject transfers that (1) violate the absolute priority of creditors over owners, (2) abuse corporate law to unfairly confer common shareholders priority over preferred security holders, or (3) give the compensation of owner-managers an unfair priority over creditors.

Properly applied, this accounting standard would eliminate shadow banking and all other off-balance sheet liabilities. All repurchase agreements should be reflected as grossed up on balance sheets and participations that do not involve complete transfers of underlying financial assets would be reported as secured loans (assuming the requirements for a valid pledge are met) and otherwise as subordinate borrowings by the lead bank from the participant. In cases in which derivative contracts obligate payment without regard to actual collection of related assets, the obligations and assets would be grossed up and not reported on a net basis.

In short, any transaction in which two measures are used "imputes fraud conclusively."

The resulting changes in reporting will, of course, require adjustment to various capital standards so that assets and liabilities are not double counted. This, however, is something with which regulators are familiar. For decades, interbank deposits have been reported on a gross basis for financial reporting purposes and netted when calculating reserve requirements, to avoid multicounting.

Applied correctly, accounting for assets and liabilities avoids the problem, discussed above, that unreported debt creates for the economic axiom that savings must equal investment. In 2007, $30 trillion of U.S. shadow banking (off-balance sheet liabilities) generated an equivalent hole in accounting. Since investors had no real idea as to which financial entities had what amount of unreported debts, the only safe thing to do was to sell every investment that was potentially affected.

By virtue of the resulting crash, accounting confirmed the theory of financial stability. To create stability, all netting and off-balance sheet reporting of liabilities must end. Once we accept that the term "off-balance sheet" implies fraud, the rest becomes easy.

CHAPTER 18

International Trade: Current Account Deficit ≡ Capital Investment – Domestic Savings

The international trade axiom that holds that a current account deficit is identical to capital investment minus domestic savings is the means by which Ben Bernanke convinced the world that the U.S. Fed knew how, with cooperation, to prevent a then-looming crisis in September 2007. After Mr. Bernanke's solution was bypassed and undermined for about a year (as the crisis built), it is by this axiom that the theory of financial stability, applied by the Fed and other monetary authorities, created a bridge to support new policies that have the ability to generate a worldwide recovery. There must be worldwide cooperation, however, to establish market policies that are consistent with this theory.

The implications of this equation explain not only the 2007–2009 crisis, but also each and every international financial bubble and bust that occurred since international trade began. As mercantilist exporters, every major nation in Europe (and Asia) has been surprised when excesses relating to investments made in the capital markets of importing nations (and real estate inflation at home) end up as banking or investment crises.

That is the price of all mercantilist folly, however. By refusing to spend imported currency (to maintain the mercantilist's desire for a current account surplus), the money received for its exports must be invested to inflate something. When growth of consumption is precluded by policy, the money must either inflate domestic prices of capital goods or the capital markets of importing nations—and in each case, the capital markets most easily inflated are those for real estate.

Consider Japan in the 1970s and 1980s. Products were exported at prices below the cost of production in Japan. Major exporters made up their losses by selling Japanese real estate at prices inflated by bank lending that absorbed imported dollars while keeping the yen at exchange rates that were lower than normal.

One widely read reorganization disclosure document revealed that a major Japanese lender had kept absorbing losses on defaulting loans by the expedient of refinancing to absorb unpaid interest. Rather than disclosing nonperformance, the lender simply assumed an equal increase in the value of Japanese real estate. As a result, the law of compound interest expanded loan balances while contracting rents, which had the opposite effect on the saleable value of Japanese real estate held as collateral.

By the time that firm filed for reorganization, unpaid interest had compounded the loan balances to $20 billion while the value of sustained cash flows from its real estate holdings justified a total collateral value (for assets with any discernible value) of only $800 million. This reality was recognized when more than 95 percent of creditors accepted a plan of reorganization giving them only the fair value of their collateral (4 percent of their loan balances).

Meanwhile, money Japan imported in exchange for exports to the United States was invested in U.S. real estate and then lost as accelerating inflation, and later constraints on lending (caused by inflation fighting and unnecessary investments), burst as part of the U.S. S&L bubble. As a result, investments in such U.S. assets as the Pebble Beach golf course and Rockefeller Center produced still further losses for Japan.

The consequence of the international accounting identities referred to by Mr. Bernanke in 2007 is that a mercantilist nation's desires to preserve exports by preventing currency adjustments (that otherwise translate into net export reductions) must be met by investing trade surpluses in the capital markets of importing nations. When productive uses for capital inflows do not exist (because manufacturing jobs are exported to the mercantilists), the balancing effect inherent in this axiom ends up creating a bubble in real estate. That was the ultimate driving force that generated the 2005–2006 housing bubble in the United States.

When a point was reached that good housing and mortgage investments were absorbed, some of the bankers who made money generating mortgages for sale overseas turned to lower and lower quality segments to keep their sell-side machines running. When poor quality led to nonperformance, however, and demands for recognition as debt of too-big-to-fail entities were denied, the accumulation of this excess liquidity burst and investors tried to reverse course.

To allow them to continue to avoid the need to change course (or to cushion the impact), mercantilist nations were then required to invest in U.S. obligations, at negative rates if necessary, to maintain their desired currency values. Thus, abiding by this trade axiom generated a liquidity trap wherein rates fell dramatically. It is also the reason rates are likely to stay low for an extended period of time.

Discontented mercantilist nations that continue to stay their course of supporting exports in the face of this folly will necessarily suffer by repression of return on investments (or other loss) for a correspondingly extended period. As the saying goes: it's axiomatic.

In the case of Europe, corrections within the eurozone seem, finally, to be sorting out in a rather civilized manner because of the TARGET2[1] process for adjusting interbank transfers under the treaty creating the euro. The effect, for example, of a Greek banking crisis is that Greek deposits flow within the eurozone to the strongest economy, Germany. When Greek banks cannot fund deposit transfers by cash transfers to German banks (because they cannot collect loans), the TARGET2 process gives the receiving German bank an asset that corresponds to (and offsets) the deposit liability booked in Germany. The asset received is a Greek bank liability guaranteed by the Greek government.

Thus, for all the insistence by Germany that Greece must do this or that, to the extent Greece is financially harmed by Germany's demands, the result is an increase in the exposure of German banks to Greek losses. Eventually, as is the case in the United States when one region engages in banking folly (e.g., Texas in the early 1980s), this TARGET2 process will generate a balance that preserves Greece.

Since Germany will not collect by force (i.e., through war, the prior remedy for mercantilist failures) because the advantages of a united Europe far outweigh the cost of unwinding Germany's mercantilist folly, TARGET2 will, it appears, compel an EU resolution that does not destroy Greece and other financially impaired nations. The approach applied in the eurozone uses regional adjustments rather than federal funds to put responsibility back on the EU's internal mercantilists.

Once the politics of this process had been worked out, it was easy to predict a financial stability solution for the euro crisis that will not result in hostilities. Recent data indicates positive economic trends in Greece, so it appears TARGET2 is working. It is more difficult to find solutions for situations in which there is no underlying treaty to uphold, but the logic of worldwide need will, we believe, lead others to find the means for correcting the $67 trillion of accumulated worldwide investment folly that created the 2007–2009 crisis.

Thus, fundamental principles of international trade confirm the theory of financial stability. Let's hope, moreover, that we have now learned how to smooth the recovery process.

---

[1] TARGET2 is the second generation of the TARGET, or Trans-European Automated Real-Time Gross Settlement Express Transfer, system.

CHAPTER 19

Philosophy: Benevolence >
Self Interest > Fraud

In Jerusalem, as the Common Era began, Hillel the Elder stated that Jewish law was to love your neighbor as yourself and that all the rest was explanation. Jesus saw no benevolence in the forced exchange of currency as a means for priestly profit and chased money changers out of the Temple a few decades later. Neither religious leader accepted fraud or unenlightened self-interest as the foundation of a faith that would bind and sustain humanity

The last edition of Adam Smith's treatise on moral philosophy, *The Theory of Moral Sentiments*, was written in 1790, the year he died. In that work, Smith substantially revised the last part to address different theories as the foundation of moral sentiments. Rejecting self-interest and other approaches from the Greek philosophers forward, Smith concluded that only benevolence can sustain a society as the foundation of morality. We learn the same lesson from recent economic studies and by a growing recognition of universal theology based on a duty to do good, not just avoid doing bad.

All humans share one world. It is only by acts that build the world's benevolent production and productivity, in the end, that we maximize the world's strained capacities to support humans. There is, of course, an overriding element of self-interest when one recognizes this unity.

Fraud is the ultimate expression of unenlightened self-interest in comparison to self-interest that is enlightened by benevolence. Just as the theory of financial stability cannot be fulfilled in the face of fraud, it cannot be maximized by self-interest alone. When risk is accommodated properly, the risk-free arbitrages that generate sustained financial stability naturally support productive innovation by sustaining equilibrium at rates that reward the most increase in equity to the most productive uses of leverage.

By sustaining stability, moreover, growth of value more readily accommodates inevitable losses on less productive investments. Adam Smith's treatise on moral philosophy is, therefore, a proof for the theory of financial stability. As one supports the philosophical foundation of benevolence, the other supports benevolent guidance of the invisible hand of economics to the goal of maximizing productivity and wealth.

The Future

Achieving Wisdom While Avoiding the Mistakes of Experience

Earth has existed for at least 4 billion years. The first humans appeared in Africa perhaps 4 million years ago. Climate changes affecting glaciers apparently caused a group of anatomically modern humans to walk out of Southeast Africa's environmentally unique cradle and begin populating the rest of the world about 40,000 years ago. We started this discussion with a definition of fraud that might be 4,000 years old. It's been about 400 years since dissatisfaction with royal rule began the process leading to England's current constitutional monarchy. The United States will soon be 240 years old—a very young nation by most historical measures, but still the world's oldest truly democratic republic.

The United States has only 40 years' experience (one-sixth of its lifespan) with pursuing a workable legal foundation for stable financial markets. The American model promises to replace the bank monopolies by which emperors, kings, priests, and other despots ruled by controlling money (and thereby all people who need and use it). In that tiny span of 40 years, the United States and world economies have sorted out trade and human population imbalances that are monumental.

Any reasonable look at economic and life expectancy data for the past 200 years shows strides toward health and wealth that are unsurpassed in world history. Much of the success in making the world healthier and wealthier occurred during just the past 40 years. There is also hope that the world may yet succeed at efforts that establish the climactic events of World Wars I and II as the end-all for the decimation of many millennia of wars.

Consider how many people live in some form of comfort today compared to the period at the end of World War II, when much of the world lay in ruins. The progress toward freedom and away from war and starvation began with the shocking difference between the assistance that the victors gave to former enemies after World War II and the retribution sought after every other major war in history. By 1973 those former enemies were selling the world superior products that eventually destroyed leading U.S. manufacturers, the same companies that made the machines that overcame the dictators who led those enemies into World War II.

Some may still debate whether George C. Marshall was right to convince the United States and its allies to forgive prewar debts, forego reparations, and aid former enemies. People that argue against what Marshall (and others) achieved by generosity are either stunningly ignorant or outrageously arrogant. In 1790, Adam Smith intellectually trounced all other bases for morality in favor of those based on benevolence. That is what guided the Marshall Plan and it worked far beyond anyone's wildest dream. It expanded the pie for us all.

You may argue that the United States has systematically blown 40 years of efforts to achieve financial stability by democratizing the control of money using deregulated free markets. But nobody ever tried to do this before. The efforts to date have failed, in part, because we failed to direct benevolence properly. That is a reason to learn from our mistakes and try again, not to give up or go back.

Greed is never good when it is a disguise for fraud, and surrendering to fraud risks the barbarity of letting bullies harm those who deserve benevolence. These are mistakes that will not set us free.

Done correctly, economics proves that sound debt is good. The world has no outside creditors. All debt, therefore, represents trust that some humans have bestowed upon other humans. As we noted earlier, the image of the depositors in Frank Capra's film *It's a Wonderful Life* is also a metaphor for all human interaction based upon trust.

Combined with equity, debt generates capital goods and capital goods raise productivity. Even the most ardent labor economists agree that maximizing productivity is the main long-term determinant of growth in real wages. Seeking productivity without balance leads to a reduction of the demand needed to sustain growth.

This book shows that secret leverage, hidden by a fog of international imbalances, trapped the world in a $67 trillion hole in the presumed 2006 worldwide balance between the debt and equity that support investment. That was a horrific error that could have led to the destruction of all previously generated wealth. It was an error of disclosure and pervasive corruption, however, not of the propriety of sound disclosed debt.

The lost money did not get shipped to Mars. Some people took it from some other people and hid that capital from productive uses. With hindsight, a lot of what occurred during the subprime boom was illegal, but a lot of the rest of it was innocent, though perhaps irrational, exuberance.

In 2006, the world was being told by accountants and businesses that there was $67 trillion more invested in stocks and other equities than there actually was. The difference consisted of an accumulation of $67 trillion in unaccounted debt—shadow banking that created off-balance sheet liabilities. When the bubble burst, this undisclosed debt became a $67 trillion hit to equity—knocking two-thirds of the value off worldwide equity. Panic naturally ensued when this reality was exposed.

For a while, the people of the world were once more on a debt contraction course to total insolvency. This process was explained by Irving Fisher in 1933. The course changed when markets learned that a few central bankers actually knew what was needed to fix the problem. For a year and more, many U.S. and world leaders refused to accept what Messrs. Bernanke and Kohn said in mid-September of 2007. As a result, we fell into a deep financial hole and the world economy nearly imploded.

More than six years later, by a combination of rising equity and nationalization cum monetization, the world has a central bank bridge over that $67 trillion hole. Before the bridge can be removed safely, the world must repair what went wrong with financial markets. That is what will allow a smooth transfer of monetized funding held in central banks back to the private sector as rising equity and disclosed debt refill the hole.

We need to speed up that process. Before the crash, the total value of capital goods in the world was something like $200 trillion. If predictions about the capital needs of the world are anything close to right, we may need $2–$4 quadrillion of debt and equity savings to support a like amount of investment in capital goods to meet challenges the world may need to overcome in the next 40 years.

The only real hurdle is confidence. Today's low U.S. bond credit spreads are supported by the continuing wisdom of the Fed's leadership that goes back to the earliest days of the central bank. Fed Chairman William McChesney Martin (1951–1970) is famous for saying that the role of the Fed is "to take away the punch bowl just when the party gets going." But the real role of the central bank was demonstrated by Chairman Bernanke and his colleagues on the Federal Open Market Committee. It is to lend wisely in times of crisis to prevent the type of debt deflation America and the world experienced in the 1930s.

Looking at the graphs in this book, compare the nearly $4 trillion debacle of 2011 (when a minority within the U.S. House of Representatives created anarchy and cost the United States its AAA rating at one rating agency) to what appears to be a less than $300 billion hiccup when that same group threatened to intentionally force a default on U.S. obligations in 2013. Fed Chairman Janet Yellen, Ben Bernanke's replacement, will determine not what must be done, but only how easily it will be accomplished. She is certain to be tested in that regard.

The United States has solved the ancient mysteries of financial stability, but we have not implemented the reforms needed to sustain stability. *All* that is required is transparency plus freedom over exchange without fraud. Experts have affirmed this solution for two millennia, but the rule of dictators, priests, and monopolists and the role of folly and inertia in human nature have prevented implementation. As a result, we recently faced the worst financial crisis in modern history.

From that, however, we may finally understand how to perpetually (1) reconcile imbalances that have historically caused crises leading to starvation and war, (2) prosper with balanced markets by countering procyclical tendencies before they trigger new crises, and (3) confer on the world the ability to generate the capital needed to preserve human life as we know it in the face of dwindling fossil fuel energy and climate-changing pollution.

The problem is doing it.

Chinese is both an ancient and a modern language. Experts challenge those who say that the Chinese characters on the inside cover, translated as crisis in English, also mean opportunity. They say the characters mean a dangerous, critical moment—in other words, a crisis. In the United States, when fraud is exposed, people who fear prosecution react indignantly in denying fraud, even after the existence of duplicity is made certain by exposure. The issue is a matter of semantics.

Fraud can be intentional or innocent. In a crisis, that difference is immaterial, because rescission of an exchange made before the crisis is, in crises, a full remedy for the harmed party. Rescission is available for both types of fraud. If the defrauder is solvent, therefore, crisis creates an opportunity for the victim to redeem loss without proving intent.

Without a crisis, persons associated with fraud deny knowing the duplicity that was perpetrated because in that case, only intentional fraud is significant. Only a knowing fraud creates a private right to damages beyond rescission.

In rising markets, moreover, rescission (by which the defrauded party must give back the original asset) is an ineffective remedy. A fraud victim rarely wants to recover a less valuable asset. So, crisis is a dangerous critical moment for defrauders and, when the defrauder survives the crisis, an opportunity for the victims of fraud.

Fraud, however, creates crises. That is why governments must demand transparency and regulate fraud in good times. Governments must enforce these requirements vigorously—because restraining fraud supports preservation of free market exchanges that preserve financial stability. In good times, moreover, private parties lack remedies to pursue fraud, thereby generating procyclical behavior that increases the severity of crises in the absence of vigorous regulatory enforcement.

Smart investors who are guided by self-interest but lack benevolence pose the greatest risk of harm because they inevitably support the folly that guides most fraud—a far greater danger to society than evil. Evil can be exposed by logic and fighting evil is understood (and broadly supported) as a necessary role of government. Folly, however, is illogical—and therefore difficult to expose.

Generating support to fight folly is far more difficult than creating support to fight evil. Too few understand the need to fight folly because self-interest is observed as good by its perpetrators. Folly is seen as benefiting the individual's self-interest. So, how can it be bad?

Perhaps worst of all, for people who learn about folly before others, fraud creates opportunity. Before 1907, J. Pierpont Morgan certainly understood that the prevalent abuse of creating leverage in subsidiaries and reporting the subsidiary's value on a net basis (before consolidation of subsidiaries was required in the 1930s) was a form of fraud. The practice duplicitously hid the leverage in undercapitalized trust companies that blew up in that crisis more than a century ago.

The practice of hiding leverage in subsidiaries was created by the innocence of folly built on the moral hazard of self-interest by managers who benefited as hidden leverage accelerated a rising tide of equity values by the pyramids they built in good times. When things turned bad, of course, that hidden leverage turned "horrid."

A very smart man, Morgan surely understood that when the pyramids of leverage fell, that the bigger the fraud, the bigger the crisis, and the bigger the opportunity for those able to create new leverage while others were cut off. In 1907, creditors trampled each other as they sought to retreat from leverage by accepting whatever price they could get. That let Morgan's friends buy just about anything—*because new leverage was available to him that was unavailable elsewhere.*

It is equally logical that Morgan, following the experience of 1907, would help the United States create its Federal Reserve System in 1913 to serve as a substitute lender of last resort. Even the House of Morgan could no longer play that role. That way he would not need to press friends for funds when the next crisis occurred. It is hard to count on a "fool me twice" strategy. By the time of the next opportunity, his friends would likely understand how they had helped to fund Morgan's profitable exploitation of the 1907 crisis.

Unfortunately, it appears that Morgan got greedy and may have helped to cause the next crisis, which became the ultimate U.S. economic folly: the Great Depression. He helped structure a Fed that could not pay interest on free reserves. Moreover, Justice Brandeis certainly understood how Morgan and other lenders could use secret common-law pledges to keep the fruits of their last-resort lending while at the same time decimating unsuspecting depositors and unsecured creditors.

Consequently, as the next crisis hit in 1929, Morgan's folly backfired. His substitute lender of last resort, the Fed, lacked the ability to pay interest, so it could not buy up the unsecured free reserve funds it needed to take up Morgan's 1907 role. Moreover, both the Fed and Morgan's intended beneficiaries—the major money center banks—could not demand secret transfers of collateral that let them decimate unsuspecting unsecured creditors (including depositors) of firms that did not prepare for the crisis.

Morgan created a constrained Fed and the U.S. Supreme Court justifiably and correctly demanded transparency in secured lending that precluded Morgan's bank and others from enjoying the benefits of Bagehot's dictum—an ability to extract huge profits from a crisis. That forced the United States to follow a very long path of debt deflation out of the Great Depression and into World War II. Indeed, mistakes made during that recovery period contributed to the recent crisis.

It took the United States more than 60 years of state and federal law reform to force sufficient transparency into the practices of pledging collateral to overcome the deceit of retained dominion practiced by J. P. Morgan that "imputes fraud conclusively." By so doing, however, the United States now forces fair financial statement transparency standards on accountants and precludes off-balance sheet liability and shadow banking deceptions.

As a result, the end of reforms in the United States will be observed when credit spreads stabilize within the complete-market ranges near the bottom of Charts 9.1, 9.2, and 9.3 that track failure and recovery through the recent crisis. By achieving and sustaining that equilibrium, the world will have the resource of U.S. markets and expertise on which to build a worldwide economy that supports debt reconciliation, wealth accumulation, and the sustained living standards of which humanity is capable.

The conditions that fulfill the theory of financial stability are, therefore, as attainable as they are essential for the future.

CHAPTER 21

Capital Needs

The world faces dwindling resources of everything from oxygen to the fuel that consumes it. As one lists the squandering follies of mankind's history, it becomes increasingly difficult to see a future for humanity as we know it. Efficiency, whether measured by increased productivity or elimination of adverse environmental impact, requires capital investment.

What amount of investment will it take to reduce worldwide temperatures that are already stressing the limits of earth's capacity to sustain life as we know it? That is impossible to calculate, of course, but it is equally impossible to imagine a world without the capacity to sustain life. Like the central bankers who solved the financial crisis of 2007–2009 by announcing that they would do whatever it takes to overcome the crisis, that is what we must do to solve world preservation.

We may not like particular aspects of the process to overcome problems, but we *must* overcome the problems. Therefore, readers can substitute whatever number they want for the estimates provided here.

Let's postulate that solving the problems that threaten humanity with extinction will require $4 quadrillion of capital investment over the next 40 years or so. If worldwide capital investment was $200 trillion in 2006, the crisis and private-sector debt contraction since then (offset by a recovery of equities and expansion of public-sector debt of central banks) suggests we have made little progress in capital investment over the past seven years.

It has been reported that total world wealth recently reached $240 trillion, of which $110 trillion is represented by the United States. To achieve a nearly twentyfold increase in capital investment over the next 40 years will only require a 7.75 percent per annum increase in debt and equity values. If debt is stable, however, that requires growth of more than 15 percent per annum in equities (and vice versa if there is no growth in equity). If there are any future crises, the greater the crisis, the higher the necessary recovery rate thereafter. For example, a 50 percent decline in equity value necessitates a 100 percent recovery just to regain the precrisis level.

As the Dutch learned when they began the very long process of turning the bottom of the ocean into farms by building dikes, capital growth requires stability and stability requires confidence. The Dutch also created one of the world's first speculative blunders (with the tulips they acquired to beautify the fields they created). The Dutch recovered from that crisis, and we can achieve the growth needed to save the world, but only if we solve the problem of financial stability.

CHAPTER 22

Sources of Capital

As discussed in Chapter 18, worldwide capital investment relates to worldwide savings (debt and equity) by a mathematical identity. Increasing debt and equity relates, identically, to increasing capital investment, as long as the increases are sustained without decimation by future crises.

To achieve an 8 percent per annum growth in capital, fear of crises must be eliminated. As long as we overcome fear, there is no limit on the ability of humans to increase capital—the process is a simple function of trust and efficiency.

Transparency allows trust by open disclosure. Protection from fraud sustains trust by precluding the risk of crisis. Freedom of exchange combines trust with resources to generate capital.

Since all forms of capital are generated by combining capital needs with the trust that some humans have in other humans (we are neither creditors of, nor owned by, extraterrestrials), the fruits of reconciliation, prosperity, and life are the ability to further provide reconciliation, prosperity, and life. As with the formula for compound interest, the more reconciliation and prosperity, the more abundant life becomes. The more abundant we make life, the greater the chance for reconciliation and prosperity. The greater prosperity becomes, the greater the possibility for life and reconciliation. These are all exponentially related and all are summed up as benevolence.

The theology of the golden and silver rules is, therefore, the psychology of financial stability. The secular economics of forcing transparency on money changers is the mechanism for preventing fraud and the crises that follow. Temple leaders who could not change for fear of losing profits under Roman scrutiny lost the Temple to Roman anger a mere 40 years later.

Financial stability is the process that can generate whatever is needed to preserve reconciliation, prosperity, and life. Unless achieved, the consequence of the next 40 years just might be the end of everything.

CHAPTER 23

Managing the Water Balloon

The world of finance is the sum total of Earth's capital resources and can be both measured and observed as liquidity inside an earthly balloon.

Within a water balloon, each and every push on the balloon has consequences that generate an equal and opposite reaction somewhere else on the balloon's surface. When consequences fail to appear, or appear unequally, there is a need to dig deeper.

Prior to every financial crisis in world history, investors became convinced (through ignorance or deceit) that vast sums of new liquidity had somehow burst into existence without negative consequence (or as irrational exuberance with indefinite consequence). During the years leading up to the crisis of 2007–2009, people with great financial expertise (e.g., Alan Greenspan) were lulled into complacency as the world expanded a $67 trillion bubble through fraudulent off-balance sheet liabilities and shadow banking until that bubble burst with horrific consequences that may continue to restrain essential growth for a sustained period into the future.

It is safe to assume that any period during which spreads are sustained at a level of equilibrium that is near or below the complete-market range requires further examination (see, again, Charts 9.1, 9.2, and 9.3). When no logical explanation exists for this phenomenon (for example, a level playing field on which entities with no government support actively and transparently maintain equilibrium by trading risk-free financial arbitrage securities), it is safe to assume systemic fraud of some sort exists, which must be contained or a crisis will follow.

Responding to spread changes that are tracked daily and correlated with the events of each day will, eventually, provide the means for fixing just about every policy mistake that creates a crisis.

Successfully managing Earth's water balloon of financial liquidity can be achieved by the same process of daily correction that statistical analysis brings to every successful productive business enterprise. Folly, created by an incapacity for empathy and common woodenheadedness (whereby change is a four letter word), is the demon that precludes the adjustments necessary for sustained financial stability.

We should acclaim those who, in 2005, gave U.S. investors the means to follow the daily race among holders of bonds—either toward or from risk. Unfortunately, it was only after investors' near-total abandonment of U.S. risk in 2008 that our leaders finally found the necessary empathy and listened to minds unhampered by an excess amount of wood (most notably, Messrs. Bernanke and Kohn).

On the other hand, the U.S. experience in 2008 also establishes that it is *never* too late to change course. While the law of compound interest means that there is always a cost of delay, ending folly is what always leads to recovery.

In 2008, U.S. electors dumped a group of leaders that had converted an economy expanding wealth at a pace of more than $4 trillion per year to one that shrank wealth at the rate of more than $17 trillion per year. In the end, even those that had decimated worldwide economic health by their stubborn lethargy changed course. By the time they'd changed course, however, about $14 trillion of the $21 trillion per annum damage had occurred and the path to a worldwide potential loss of $67 trillion was set. The risk factors that led to the rest of the loss had been put in play.

The cost of knocking wood out of the heads of democratically elected leaders should never be that great, but history offers little consolation to those who wish for improvement. In her award-winning histories of woodenheaded folly (*The March of Folly: From Troy to Vietnam*), Barbara Tuchman notes that the scales of history are far more heavily weighted toward inertia than change.

Fear that the crisis of 2008 will recur (or that proposed reforms, such as risk retention, will only generate a new form of the same disease) continues to inhibit growth in the United States and around the world. Never in history, however, has a return to growth been achieved so quickly after experiencing an episode of systemic debt-contraction deflation. The Dutch tulip mania did not impact the banking system directly, but it still took seven years and debt forgiveness to finally regain substantive growth as affected groups ventured back into private-sector risk investments.

What's left in the United States today is largely up to Congress, under the terms of the U.S. Constitution. We need mortgage forgiveness and document reconciliation, but only Congress can achieve that. We need new infrastructure development, improved health care, reform of income tax policies and the financial system, enlightened immigration policies, and human rights advances—and all must be accomplished with responsible long-term limits on unproductive speculation (there should be no limit on productive borrowing and spending; it generates more revenue than it costs).

All of these are within the exclusive legislative powers granted to Congress by the U.S. Constitution. Unlike in seventeenth-century Holland, our Constitution does not allow for a king who can decree debt forgiveness. In the United States, debt forgiveness can only be permitted through Congress enacting changes to uniform bankruptcy laws.

Managed properly, the world's capital-sustaining water balloon has no size limit. We can, therefore, achieve whatever productive investment needs mankind wants. Proper management, however, assumes the capacity to overcome evil and folly. The path to sustained financial stability is clear, but can mankind follow the path?

CHAPTER 24

Balancing the Bubbles

U.S. financial asset markets recovered from the Armageddon of 2008 more rapidly than other financial markets around the world. As can be seen in Charts 9.1, 9.2, and 9.3, since the beginning of 2013 financial assets have traded in the United States at spreads that are near (or even below) the complete market bands near the bottom of each graph.

Trading in this range represents attainment of the financial market equilibrium Adam Smith envisioned in 1776. As a consequence, the response of U.S. capital markets has been in line with the projections shown in the complete market row (top row) in Table 9.1. Complete market conditions mean that the cost of operating Smith's great wheel of circulation is sustained at the minimum price necessary to keep it functioning—ideal conditions for growth of productive sector capital and wealth generally.

It is in these conditions that bubbles are most likely to develop and spawn the fear that creates new crises. Bubbles pose, therefore, a long-term challenge to the theory of financial stability. As credit spreads rise above equilibrium, it is clear that the ability of an economy to grow is impaired. As that rise becomes more rapid and significant, moreover, a financial crisis occurs. By observations made between 2005 and 2014, the United States now has sufficient experience with policies that benefit and harm markets to handle future crises of fear caused by high and rising risk spreads.

A final question we should address, therefore, is: *Can the world sustain equilibrium in finance without generating future crises?*

To answer affirmatively requires a commitment to continuous improvement that has proven elusive in the past, and an understanding of how the mathematics that drives financial market values changes at equilibrium. The first part is a moral, legal, and social issue. The second part is a difficult intellectual challenge for investors who see mathematics as the ultimate unchanging certainty of science.

Thus, the hardest part of explaining financial stability is to (1) show that the same laws of mathematics that assure the world's capacity to regain stability during a crisis guarantee instability at equilibrium, and (2) convince investors that this is just fine.

At equilibrium, we must sustain financial stability by balancing mathematically assured instability. That is why we must end too-big-to-fail and pursue the elimination of fraud. We must burst bubbles while they are small (knowing that others will grow), and take steps to ensure no bubble becomes too big to burst on its own. That is how long-term financial market stability is assured.

Let's start the discussion of this apparent contradiction with an English nursery rhyme

> *Oh, the grand old Duke of York,*
> *He had ten thousand men;*
> *He marched them up to the top of the hill,*
> *And he marched them down again.*
> *And when they were up, they were up,*
> *And when they were down, they were down,*
> *And when they were only halfway up,*
> *They were neither up nor down.*
>   ("The Grand Old Duke of York," *traditional nursery rhyme*)

and a story.

Before he headed AIG Financial Products, Tom Savage, the PhD mathematician who built that business and ran it until 2001, worked at a New York investment banking firm. In the early 1980s, he provided the mathematical foundations for stand-alone CMOs. But his work also showed that despite the mathematical precision of cash flows and prepayments involved in a CMO, there is also a great deal of uncertainty.

While writing the prospectus for the first stand-alone CMO, drafters encountered a problem calculating the rate of return for holders of the equity tranche. Owners of that class are sometimes required to pay taxes in addition to their initial investments, while at the same time receiving distributions that often (but not always) offset future payments. As a result, they are investing and receiving returns at different times throughout the 30-year life of the structure.

A prospectus writer's calculator kept showing different rates of return on the owners' investments even though he was using identical data inputs for each calculation.

When Savage was consulted he told the stunned writer, "all your answers are correct." He explained that whenever an investment turns from inflow to outflow more than once, return on investment has more than one solution.

Savage offered an example of a leveraged lease with multiple investments. Bankers had sold it as an investment providing a 30 percent rate of return. A disappointed buyer showed them that it was yielding only a 6 percent rate of return (using the bankers' stated assumptions) and demanded rescission for fraud (recall that rescission does not require a showing of intent to defraud, only a misrepresentation that is, in hindsight, material). The mathematician proved both answers were correct.

Now, let's go back to the nursery rhyme. The duke's army knew what was up and what was down but "when they were only halfway up they were neither up nor down."

So it is with financial stability. Under the law of compound interest, when spreads are heading up we know that's bad and when they are heading down we know that's good. But when credit spreads are at equilibrium near their minimum sustainable levels, they go neither up nor down to any appreciable degree.

In these circumstances, investors move money in and out of investments all the time. When they do both more than once, the ability to say, with certainty, how their investment fared terminates by the same laws of mathematics that give absolute certainty to returns when money is only (1) invested and (2) returned.

When spreads are narrow, moreover, investment brokers face an ever-increasing incentive to create more and more transactions. For investors, each new transaction has an ever-increasing risk of being one that suffers because expectations of gain eventually prove to be exaggerated. Thus, very few periods of sustained low credit spreads have ever ended well.

Under the laws of mathematics, that's axiomatic. The science of physics also teaches us that a stable state is not a usual condition. So how do we sustain financial stability when we know stability is unstable?

The first sustainer is diversification. The second comes by a recognition that instability and fraud increase in tandem. Therefore, there must be an ever-stronger commitment to overcome fraud when times are good. At low spreads, more and more investments are made that create ever-changing risks. That means more and more fraud will be committed because more and more investments require multiple cash inputs and create multiple rates of return. That assures an increase of investments that use two (or more) measures, the fundamental duplicity that for 4,000 years has defined fraud.

In the leveraged lease example, the way to have avoided fraud would have been a disclosure that the rate of return would be both 6 percent and 30 percent, depending on the buyer's perspective. That's a much harder sell than advertising a 30 percent return, but it's the only sell that will prevail when events make it profitable for the investor to seek rescission.

Too-big-to-fail also comes into play when spreads are low. When fraud increases, brokers want the government to guarantee any returns that could later become the basis for rescission by investors.

So, mathematics assures an ever-increasing amount of fraud and ever-rising pressure for government support as policymakers achieve financial market equilibrium. Consequently, the world can sustain financial market stability by eliminating too-big-to-fail and maximizing pressure to avoid fraud.

The result is a balance between inflating and bursting tiny bubbles—ones that do not create systemic risk—rather than permitting enormous crisis-generating bubbles. That is what distinguished the dot-com bubble of 2000–2001 from the crisis of 2007–2009. Investors lost a lot of money when the Internet bubble burst, but there was no systemic risk of 1930s-style debt deflation necessitating the application of nationalization cum monetization to restart the system.

The source of too-big-to-fail is the linkage of fraud to entities with government guaranteed liabilities (banks, brokers, and pension funds, to name a few). By guaranteeing liabilities, government enhances stability in normal times by assuring investors that it has an interest in avoiding crises in which guarantees become forced expenditures. The process, however, is easily contaminated.

Politicians quickly learned that cash invested by the high-risk S&Ls of the early 1980s created just as many new jobs as an equivalent amount of government expenditures, but without the need to budget the costs. In short, investments by artificially inflated S&Ls quickly generated an off-balance sheet Ponzi scheme sponsored by the U.S. government. That led to a political crisis in 1988–1989 as the insured deposits came due and speculating S&Ls went broke.

That process was repeated in the late 1990s and early 2000s using fraudulent SIVs and financial-asset sales that were allowed by the FDIC even though they were not true sales. Both created off-balance sheet liabilities of numerous types of United States–guaranteed entities. This invisible added leverage boosted short-term economic growth but also embedded instability into the system. The Great Recession, moreover, involved uninsured entities (e.g., AIGFP) that became so intertwined in the financial affairs of insured entities, such as Citigroup, that they created systemic failure risks because of the number of insured and guaranteed entities that relied on them for solvency.

The fraudulent use of SIVs largely ended with the recognition that the liabilities of an entity managed by another entity that also supports an SIV's unexpected loss are debts of the manager. Fraudulent sales will end when the accounting and legal professions universally and uniformly accept and apply the very high true-sale standard that the U.S. Financial Accounting

Standards Board adopted in 1997, and that the FDIC accepted in 2010. The appendix to this book includes (1) a worksheet for auditors to monitor the six circumstances that must be addressed to create a true sale (within and between enterprises), and (2) the form of legal opinion that demonstrates that a transferor has achieved that standard.

Sustained financial stability can, therefore, be attained. The process to do so, however, cannot be assured without achieving worldwide cooperation among financial professionals, regulators, and investors. Only when these three constituencies agree to do the right thing can we hope to achieve some semblance of long-term financial stability.

Epilogue

Truth and Consequences

This book traces fraud from its first definition, the use of two measures (outlawed in Deuteronomy 25:13–19), through recognition that only the universal application of the standards laid out in this book's appendix (that force the exposure of frauds) can perpetuate financial market stability.

The underlying cause of all financial crises is a collision between fraud and truth. Fraud hides leverage, whether by misrepresentation, theft, or manipulation (including corruption and monopoly). Truth exposes the leverage, and debt is senior to equity. Thus, the necessary consequence of a collision between truth and fraud is a sudden reduction of equity values—a financial crisis caused by exposure of theretofore hidden liabilities.

Ben Bernanke explained the collision of hidden international trade imbalances that caused the 2008 financial crisis, by undeniable logic, to an assembly of the world's monetary policy leaders in Berlin in September 2007. He revealed a world in which equity value was exposed to $67 trillion of hidden trade imbalances. Liability for that imbalance had been hidden from investors by the application of a second measure of debt (off-balance sheet liabilities) that attorneys, auditors, regulators, legislators, business and political executives, and investors somehow became convinced they could ignore. Now these same leaders talk about capital, rather than fraud, as the cause of the crisis.

In the clarity of hindsight, the investment community was deluded. Whether reported or not, *all* hidden debt is somebody's obligation; and for the economy of the world to function, debt *must* have priority over equity. To prevent crises, therefore, all debt must be exposed. The problem is not insufficient capital, but inadequate disclosure.

For more than six years now, deluders and the deluded have stumbled together into a $67 trillion hole of debt contraction that government had no choice but to fill. America's greatest economist, Irving Fisher, proved that beyond anyone's doubt in 1933.

Investors were rescued *only* because the financial system *must* survive or the world will return to the Stone Age as humanity is devoured by environmental forces that must, somehow, be contained to avoid human extinction. We've known how to cure a debt-contraction deflation or depression since 1933, and Ben Bernanke was the world's economic conductor to orchestrate its recovery from the Armageddon of 2008.

We now therefore know that the world, acting together, can resolve any financial crisis. What we cannot do, however, is eliminate the consequences of exposed truth. We can provide liquidity to markets and absorb undisclosed obligations that can be funded as exposed debt, and we can forgive debt that will never be collected.

Even debt forgiveness, however, does not end income tax liability. Exposure of hidden debt (created by theft, fraud, or plain stupidity) creates income to the extent it is not repaid. Uncollected debt exposes obligors to taxation. When a business fraud is exposed, repayment and taxation reduce liquidity and earnings. When public corruption is exposed, elected officials go to jail and dictators generally flee or die.

In the case of innocent loss and particular hardship, bankruptcy discharges tax liabilities, but no nation of free peoples can long tolerate any other program of tax forgiveness. To do so rewards cheats while burdening honest taxpayers. It is, therefore, rare that an amnesty program for tax collection in a democracy will forgive taxes that are hidden from collection by even the most innocent errors. In the United States, one measure among its 2008–2010 crisis-resolving tax stimulus programs allowed long-term deferral of debt forgiveness income. It led to abuses and soon ended. But even if abuse can be resolved so that program can be reinstated, it only defers taxation.

Recent events in Ukraine exemplify the ages-old problem of a corrupt regime ending when it comes in conflict with the success of economic freedom (there represented by the euro). The president of Ukraine fled and Russia may protect him because Russian leaders find it difficult to fully embrace freedom. But even Russia has found free markets difficult to oppose. Russia's leaders have acknowledged that investors fled Russian stock and bond markets in response to their actions in Ukraine.

To date, U.S. markets have shown little, if any, harm (and may have benefited) from Russia's difficulties. Charts 9.1, 9.2, and 9.3 show remarkably low and stable U.S. credit spreads throughout March, April, and May of 2014, while credit spreads for Russia and its businesses rose dramatically. The problem is the impact of holding Ukraine hostage on the success of the euro.

The 1979–1981 U.S. experience with Iran is instructive for Western Europe. Like Iran's seizure of the U.S. embassy and employees, Russia has created an immediate and significant threat to peace and prosperity in Europe. Within a month after the U.S. embassy was seized in Tehran, the Carter administration adopted regulations for resolution of Iranian financial assets it had frozen in U.S. institutions. Face-saving prevented Iran's religious dictators from acquiescing to the demands of those regulations while Mr. Carter was president, but they complied immediately after Mr. Reagan was elected and inaugurated.

In *Tower of Basel*, Adam Lebor persuasively asserts that allowing the central bank of Nazi Germany to participate in the Bank for International Settlements was critical to Hitler's capacity to finance aggression and murder (Lebor 2013). If the BIS and the ECB construct appropriate financial restraints on Russia's actions, there is little doubt that Russia will ultimately comply. Care must be taken to take measured actions so egos do not interfere with wisdom, but no nation as substantial as Russia can prevail without the fund flows needed for trade. Western Europe controls those flows. Since the Fuggers' bank funded the Habsburg empire, history has been consistent on what happens if Europe acts wisely.

By comparison, the much larger issue of unpaid tax deferral overtook U.S. markets in 2014. News about a major litigation finally posed the following question: if the world had $67 trillion of international imbalances in 2007, how much of the income generated by that accumulation of transferred wealth was secreted away in phony off-balance sheet liabilities shifted to tax-haven entities?

The lawsuit was brought by a bankrupt U.S. firm against its tax advisor. It disclosed that standards for sale of financial assets set forth in the appendix are, by law, the tests used by the U.S. Securities and Exchange Commission and Internal Revenue Service. Thus, tax obligations that the bankrupt firm thought it deferred by transferring accounts to offshore entities were, in hindsight, due when the incomplete sales (secured debt transactions) occurred. That forced restatement of the debtor's income and the incurrence of unpayable income tax liabilities.

The advisor may not be liable for its client's bankruptcy (after all, the advisor's opinion only deferred reality—it did not change U.S. tax or securities laws for which the client was responsible). Doctors regularly make mistakes, but not all mistakes are malpractice.

The problem is that a significant number of firms may have structured their tax plans by ignoring the sale standards presented in the appendix. A $67 trillion trade imbalance may create $10 trillion or more of undisclosed tax liability. And we wonder why U.S. equity markets began to fall when word of that lawsuit was widely disseminated in January 2014?

What can be done to avert a crisis from this new collision of truth and fraud?

Collecting taxes without regard to consequences reintroduces the bad logic of the Treaty of Versailles after World War I that led to the Great Depression and World War II. Eliminating tax obligations unfairly shifts the burden of government from cheaters to honest taxpayers.

The solution is a combination of recognition, deferral, and policies that responsibly provide liquidity to the economies of the world to accommodate the errors that were made, and moving on.

That is the theory of financial stability. As investors have realized the capacity of free markets to resolve this matter, U.S. credit spreads have narrowed and equity markets have recovered.

Six Legal Isolation Requirements

A failure of compliance with any of the six tests included in Table A.1 requires that a financial asset transfer be reported as a secured borrowing with pledge of collateral—otherwise the transfer "imputes fraud conclusively."

Six "Legal Isolation" Requirements that Must be Overcome for "Sale" Treatment
Failure of compliance with any of the six tests below requires that a financial asset transfer be reported as ("a secured borrowing with pledge of collateral" or it "imputes fraud conclusively.")
"Legal isolation" means: "[B]eyond the reach of the transferor and its creditors, even in bankruptcy or other receivership."

Isolation "IN" / Isolation "FROM"	Normal court proceedings:	Bankruptcy:	Other Receivership:
	UCC for personal property (notes and other financial assets) and real estate law if and where applied to mortgage transfers (other jurisdictions may apply).	US Bankruptcy Code and proceedings in other jurisdictions (relating to transferors) where the powers of trustees are consistent with those of US bankruptcy trustees.	Federal and state receivers with the rights of innocent creditors (e.g., FDIC and receivers under the UFTA and in fraud cases) and by other applicable law.
Transferor: Includes rights of equitable rescission and powers of avoidance that a trustee in bankruptcy can exercise as successor to a transferor under US, state and other laws (e.g., *UFTA*; see Madoff case for limits).	1.	3.	5.
Creditors of Transferor: Includes special powers of receiversfor harmed creditors (e.g., FDIC's D'Oenchand Benedict powers) as well as all powers of transferors and trustees.	2.	4.	6.

TABLE A.1   Six Legal Isolation Requirements That Must Be Overcome for Sale Treatment

TRUE SALE OPINION AND NON-CONSOLIDATION OPINION

1. An example of the conclusions in an attorney's opinion for a U.S.-based transferor that provides persuasive evidence, in the absence of contradictory evidence, to support management's assertion that transferred financial assets are presumptively beyond the reach of the transferor and its creditors, even in bankruptcy or other receivership, is as follows:

> *"We believe (or it is our opinion) that in a properly presented and argued case, under all principles of law and equity which may have material application to the parties or the transactions described herein, the transfer of financial assets ("Financial Assets") would be considered to be a sale (or a true sale) of the Financial Assets and not a transfer thereof for security in respect of a loan and, accordingly:*

> *"(a) The Financial Assets and the proceeds thereof transferred to the Purchaser by the Seller in accordance with the Purchase Agreement would not be deemed to be property of (or be recoverable by) the Seller, any member of the Selling Group[1] or their creditors for purposes of all applicable bankruptcy, insolvency, conservatorship, receivership or other similar proceedings which may generally affect the rights of creditors, or otherwise by proceedings in law or equity,[2] and*

---

[1] The Selling Group includes the Seller and entities included in the Seller's consolidated financial statements (without regard to whether such affiliates are, or were, subject of any bankruptcy, receivership or other proceedings at law or in equity for the resolution of creditors' rights) and which (a) have any involvement in the transaction or are investors in (or provide support to) any securities issued by the Purchaser or (b) are supported, directly or indirectly, by the Financial Assets, except, in both cases, affiliates designed to make remote the possibility of bankruptcy or other insolvency proceedings. In the stand-alone financial statements of the transferor, the Selling Group would only include entities included in the transferor's stand-alone consolidated financial statements and would not include other entities such as those included in the consolidated financial statements of the transferor's parent.

[2] Any contractual right of the Seller (or other member of the Selling Group) to re-acquire the Financial Assets, or rights thereto, from the Purchaser should be recited in the description of the transfer documents and should be evaluated for compliance with ASC 860-10-40-5's other applicable requirements. Any contractual obligation of the Seller (or other member of the Selling Group) to re-acquire or absorb loss with

"(b) No person or entity that subsequently purchases or otherwise acquires from the Seller an interest in the Financial Assets, for value and without notice of the Purchaser's interest therein, would thereby obtain rights in or to the Financial Assets which are senior to (or would otherwise defeat) the rights obtained by the Purchaser under the Purchase Agreement.[3]"

---

respect to the Financial Assets (*e.g.*, recourse, subordination, and any obligation to repurchase Financial Assets that fails to conform to contractual representations and warranties or by virtue of servicing defaults) should be evaluated by the attorney when opining on whether a "sale" has occurred. For example, representations and warranties that are consistent with a "sale" when believed by the Seller to have been true when made, may constitute unacceptable recourse if known by the Seller to be false when made. See, Pantaleo, *et al,* "*Rethinking the Role of Recourse in the Sale of Financial Assets,*" 52 Business Lawyer 159, *et seq.* (1996).

[3] To qualify for ASC 860-10-40-5 "sale" treatment, the transferred Financial Assets must be established as "presumptively beyond the reach of the *transferor and* its creditors, *even in* bankruptcy or other receivership" (emphasis added). Therefore, the attorney opinion must address other laws that could impact the rights of the Purchaser, not *just* applicable bankruptcy and insolvency laws. Under U.S. law, for example, it is not appropriate to consider an asset "sold" when the Seller reserves "dominion that is inconsistent with effective disposition. . . ." *Benedict v. Ratner,* 268 U.S. 353, 363 (1925). Retention by the Seller of the ability (even though the exercise of that ability may be restricted by the Purchase Agreement) to unilaterally create rights in or to the Financial Assets for the benefit of third parties that would be superior, as a matter of law or equity, to those of the Purchaser is not consistent with this requirement. In general, where Financial Assets are represented by negotiable promissory notes and the transfer procedures include proper endorsement thereof to a third party that holds the notes for the exclusive benefit of the Purchaser and parties claiming through the Purchaser (to the extent of their respective interests therein), the involvement of parties other than the Seller would be required for any third party to obtain rights in and to the Financial Assets superior to the rights of the Purchaser. Moreover, when accounts are so effectively transferred to the Purchaser that it is only by actual collection thereof by a third party (before notice of transfer is provided to the account obligor by the Purchaser), action by the account obligor and the Seller are required to defeat the Purchaser's rights. Similarly, dominion over the Financial Assets that is inconsistent with effective disposition may not be held by any affiliate of the Seller that is included in the Seller's consolidated financial statements, except if the Purchaser is designed to make remote the possibility of its bankruptcy or other receivership. Where a Purchaser is consolidated by the Seller and meets this requirement, at least one independent director will have been appointed to represent investors not affiliated with the Seller, thereby precluding unilateral actions by the Seller which could defeat rights to the Financial Assets.

2. The legal isolation condition may be satisfied either by a single trans-action (that is, a "one-step" transfer of financial assets, whereby the transferor sells assets directly to a non-consolidated, unaffiliated transferee) or by a se-ries of transactions ("two-step" transfers) considered as a whole. In a one-step or a two-step transfer of financial assets, a true sale opinion could be obtained on the first step of the transfer, and in addition, for a two-step transfer, a true sale opinion could be obtained on the second step of the transfer.

3. A two-step securitization structure taken as a whole may satisfy the legal isolation criterion because the design of the structure achieves isolation. Typical two-step structures involve the following: first, the transferor transfers a group of financial assets to a securitization entity that, although wholly owned, is designed so that the possibility is remote that the transferor, its consolidated affiliates included in the financial statements being presented, or its creditors could reclaim the financial assets (that is, a bankruptcy-remote entity); second, the bankruptcy-remote entity transfers the group of financial assets to a securitization entity, often providing credit or yield protection to the holders of the beneficial interests in the securitization entity. To support management's assertion that the transferred financial assets are legally isolated, although a true sale opinion could be obtained on either or both steps, it is usually obtained for the first step in the transaction. The subsequent transfer to the securitization entity is often not a true sale at law, because of the credit enhancement provided by the transferor. Despite the fact that legal isolation may not be achieved in the second step, the consolidated entity would derecognize the financial assets when the transferor has obtained a true sale opinion and nonconsolidation opinion for the first step in the transfer, and neither the transferor nor its consolidated bankruptcy remote entity is required to consolidate the securitization entity.

4. Although a true sale opinion (as described in paragraph 1 of this interpretation) provides support for management's assertion on legal isola-tion, a true-sale opinion does not address the risk that a court could order the "substantive consolidation" of the transferee into the bankruptcy estate of the transferor. If the transferee can be substantively consolidated into the bankruptcy estate of the transferor, then the legal isolation criterion would not be met. Accordingly, an attorney's nonconsolidation opinion may also be required to support management's assertion that the transferee (including any bankruptcy-remote affiliates of the transferor) would not be substan-tively consolidated into the bankruptcy estate of the transferor.

5. A nonconsolidation opinion which addresses substantive consolida-tion applies when the entity to which the assets are transferred is an "affiliate"[4]

---

[4] As defined in applicable laws relating to the transfer and all parties thereto that have continuing involvement with the transferred assets.

of the selling entity (the transferor) and may also apply in other situations as noted by the attorney. For example, if a two-step transfer structure is used to achieve legal isolation, a nonconsolidation opinion usually is required with respect to the transferee in the first step of the structure. When the transferor enters into transactions with an affiliate that could affect substantive consolidation, the opinion should address the effect of that involvement. An example of a nonconsolidation opinion is as follows:

> *"Based upon the assumptions of fact and the discussion set forth previously, and on a reasoned analysis of analogous case law, we are of the opinion that in a properly presented and argued case, as a legal matter, in any reorganization, receivership, conservatorship or liquidation proceeding which, by law, order or determination of appropriate authorities, would be applicable in respect of the Seller, the trustee, receiver, conservator or liquidator would not have authority to order (and a court would not order or confirm an order of the trustee, receiver, conservator or liquidator) consolidating the assets and liabilities of the Purchaser with those of the Seller or any member of the Selling Group without obtaining consent of the Purchaser subsequent to the commencement of any such proceeding."*

Examples of Inadequate Opinion Language That Would Not Provide Sufficient Appropriate Audit Evidence

6. An attorney's opinion that includes inadequate opinion language does not provide sufficient appropriate audit evidence to support management's assertion that the transferred financial assets have been put presumptively beyond the reach of the transferor (including its consolidated affiliates) and its creditors, even in bankruptcy or other receivership. A legal letter that includes conclusions expressed using any of the following language should be considered inadequate because the opinion provides other than **"would level"** assurance. Accordingly, such a letter would not provide persuasive evidence that a transfer of financial assets has met the isolation criterion of ASC 860-10-40-5(a):

- "We are unable to express an opinion . . ."
- "It is our opinion, based upon limited facts . . ."
- "We are of the view . . ." or "it appears . . ."
- "There is a reasonable basis to conclude that . . ."

■ "In our opinion, the transfer would *either* be a sale *or* a grant of a perfected security interest . . ."[5]

■ "In our opinion, there is a reasonable possibility . . ."

■ "In our opinion, the transfer *should* be considered a sale . . ."

■ "It is our opinion that the company will be able to assert meritorious arguments . . ."

■ "In our opinion, it is more likely than not . . ."

■ "In our opinion, the transfer would *presumptively* be . . ."

■ "In our opinion, it is probable that . . ."

QUALIFICATIONS, LIMITATIONS, OR DISCLAIMERS INCLUDED IN AN ATTORNEY'S OPINION

7. An attorney's opinion that includes inappropriate qualifications, limitations, or a disclaimer of opinion, or that effectively limits the scope of the opinion to facts and circumstances that are not applicable to the transaction, does not provide sufficient appropriate audit evidence to support management's assertion that the transferred financial assets have been put presumptively beyond the reach of the transferor (including its consolidated affiliates) and its creditors, even in bankruptcy or other receivership.

8. Limitations in the legal opinion may negate the opinion by instructing the reader to consider performing additional legal analysis, thereby implying those factors have not been considered by the attorney. For example, the following limitation generally precludes reliance on the attorney's opinion:

"We note that legal opinions on bankruptcy law matters unavoidably have inherent limitations that generally do not exist in respect

---

[5] Certain transferors are subject only to receivership (and not to proceedings under the U.S. Bankruptcy Code or the Federal Deposit Insurance Act) under laws that do not allow a receiver to reach assets in which a security interest has been granted and is not subject to avoidance or a stay of collection proceedings. In such circumstances, an opinion that concludes that the transfer would either be a sale or a grant of a security interest that puts the transferred assets beyond the reach of such receiver and other creditors would provide persuasive evidence in the absence of contradictory evidence that the isolation criterion is met.

In certain circumstances, an attorney may provide an opinion on both steps of a two-step structure. Such language would also be acceptable in an opinion for a transfer of assets in the second step of a two-step structure as described in ASC 860-10-55-22 and 55-23 provided that the opinion on the transfer in the first step is sufficient to evidence legal isolation.

of other legal issues on which opinions to third parties are typically given. These inherent limitations exist primarily because of the pervasive powers of bankruptcy courts and other factors. The recipients of this opinion should take these limitations into account in analyzing the bankruptcy risk associated with the transactions as contemplated by the agreements."

9. Qualifying language in some attorney's opinions discusses how a court would view the level of recourse, with the attorney not providing an opinion with respect to this aspect of the transaction. For example, when recourse provisions are included in the transaction, the transferor's legal isolation analysis should consider whether the attorney's opinion conclusively considers the nature and significance of any recourse provided for in the transaction. Limited historical information, heterogeneous assets or significant changes in underwriting are a few factors that may cause the attorney's analysis to be more difficult. The auditor should consider whether these analyses of any recourse provisions are consistent or inconsistent with other information used by management to make any related estimates.

10. Furthermore, conclusions about hypothetical transactions may not be relevant to the transaction that is the subject of management's assertions. Conclusions about hypothetical transactions may not contemplate all of the facts and circumstances or the provisions in the agreements of the transaction that is the subject of management's assertions, and generally would not provide persuasive evidence. For example, a memorandum of law from an attorney usually analyzes (and may make conclusions about) a transaction that may be completed subsequently. Such memorandum generally would not provide persuasive evidence unless the conclusions conform with this interpretation and an attorney opines that such conclusions apply to a completed transaction that is the subject of management's assertion.

References

Bernanke, Ben S. 2007. "Global Imbalances: Recent Developments and Prospects," www.federalreserve.gov/newsevents/speech/bernanke20070911 a.htm.

Borden, Bradley T., and David J. Reiss. 2013. "Dirt Lawyers, Dirty REMICs." *Probate & Property* 27 (3, May/June). Available at www.ssrn.com/abstract = 2209863.

Dübel, Hans-Joachim. 2012. "Transatlantic Mortgage Credit Crisis—the Role of Financial Structure and Regulation." Presentation at the SUERF/Nykredit Conference, Copenhagen, November 15, www.finpolconsult.de/mortgage-sector.html.

Dyson, Freeman. 2014. "The Case for Blunders." *New York Review of Books*, March 6, www.nybooks.com/articles/archives/2014/mar/06/darwin-einstein-case-for-blunders.

Feldkamp, Fred, Patricia Lane, and Bryan T.D. Jung. 2005. *The Law and Economics of Financial Markets: Lessons of History That Assure Success in the Future.* Boston: Aspatore.

Geithner, Timothy F. 2014. "Stress Test—Reflections on Financial Crises," New York.

Hetzel, Robert L. 2009. "Should Increased Regulation of Bank Risk-Taking Come from Regulators or from the Market?" *FRB of Richmond Economic Quarterly* 95 (2, Spring): 161–200. Available at www.ssrn.com/abstract = 2188487.

Joo, Thomas Wuil. 1999. "Who Watches the Watchers? The Securities Investor Protection Act, Investor Confidence, and the Subsidization of Failure." *Southern California Law Review* 72 (May). Available at www.ssrn.com/abstract= 169208.

Kasper, Thomas A., and Les Parker. 1987. "Understanding Collateralized Mortgage Obligations," *Columbia Business Law Review* 139 (1).

Keynes, John Maynard. 1933. "National Self-Sufficiency," *Yale Review* 22 (4, June): 755–769.

Lebor, Adam. 2013. "Tower of Basel," New York: PublicAffairs.

Markham, Jerry W. 2002. *A Financial History of the United States.* 3 vols. Armonk, NY: M. E. Sharpe.

Merriman, John. 2009. *A History of Modern Europe: From the Renaissance to the Present.* New York: W.W. Norton.

Mitchell, Lawrence E. 2007. *The Speculation Economy: How Finance Triumphed Over Industry.* San Francisco, CA: Berrett-Koehler. Abstract available at http://ssrn.com/abstract = 1017923.

Pantaleo, Peter V., et al. 1996. "Rethinking the Role of Recourse in the Sale of Financial Assets." *Business Lawyer* 52 (1): 159–198.

Pethokoukis, James. 2008. "The 11 Blunders of Hank Paulson." *US News & World Report*, November 17.

Robins, Marty. 2014. "Why Have Top Executives Escaped Prosecution?" *New York Review of Books*, April 3.

Sanders, Sol. 2014. "The Test We Musn't Fail." American Center for Democracy, February 17.

Sparling, Earl. 1930. *The Mystery Men of Wall Street*. New York: Blue Ribbon Books.

Villani, Kevin. 2013. "Occupy Pennsylvania Avenue: How Politicians Caused the Financial Crisis and Why Their Reforms Failed." Summary policy analysis, November 25. Available at www.ssrn.com/abstract = 2359584 or www.dx.doi.org/10.2139/ssrn.2359584.

Von Mises, Ludwig. 1949. *Human Action: A Treatise on Economics*. New Haven, CT: Yale University Press. Available at www.mises.org/Books/humanaction.pdf.

Wojnilower, Albert M. 2014. "Calm on the Surface." Craig Drill Capital, March 14.

Whalen, Christopher. 2014. "Dodd-Frank and the Great Debate: Regulation vs. Growth," Networks Financial Institute Policy Brief No. 2014-PB-01 (February 21). Available at http://ssrn.com/abstract = 2399614.

About the Companion Website

This book includes a companion website, which can be found at www
.wiley.com/go/financialstability. The companion website contains contains articles for additional reading, including:

7/17/13: Can the Wisdom of Today Prevent the Next Financial Crisis?
7/24/13: Never, Never, Never, Never Give Up!
7/29/13: Attainable and Sustainable Financial Stability
7/30/13: When Failed Genius Rises
10/10/13: Stability Attracts Investment
10/14/13: T-, T-, Today Junior!
11/21/13: Four Score and Eight Years Ago
1/9/14: Happy New Year
2/25/14: The Beat Goes On and On and On
4/14/14: Marco Polo
6/23/14: Will 2014 be a Year of Jubilee?
7/24/14: Will the Putin Crisis End and Trigger a Rally?

To access the site, go to www.wiley.com/go/financialstability (password:
feldkamp02).

About the Authors

FREDERICK L. FELDKAMP

Mr. Feldkamp is a retired partner of the law firm Foley & Lardner, LLP. He was a member of Foley's Finance & Financial Institutions Practice, and its Automotive and Energy Industry Teams. He has worked in the firm's Milwaukee, Chicago, and Detroit offices and has advised clients on business, tax, regulatory, and financial law for the past four decades.

In 1973, Mr. Feldkamp provided the legal basis for Foley's pioneering bankruptcy opinion that permitted issuance of America's first rated private mortgage-backed security in the post-Depression era. Throughout the years, he has provided creative legal advice to support numerous securitization innovations that include:

- Several structures used to fund the retail and wholesale sale, and lease, of automobiles
- Creation of the largest foreign-owned Japanese mortgage service firm, through sponsorship of the largest nonbank financial-institution reorganization in Japan (2000)
- Utility transition securities, including the largest ABS offering of 1998
- The first stand-alone collateralized mortgage obligation (1983)
- Exemptive proceedings permitting several firsts, including grandfathering under Rule 2a-7, home loan conduit, and partial pool CMOs

His practice has included counseling U.S. and multinational corporations, international financial organizations, domestic and foreign regulatory agencies, and self-regulatory organizations on a variety of financial services matters. Mr. Feldkamp has consulted on projects to enhance legal, regulatory, and accounting rules to facilitate securitization in countries throughout the world.

Other areas of Mr. Feldkamp's practice include representation of financial service companies on all aspects of business, including corporate law, mergers and acquisitions, regulatory and operational matters, workouts, reorganizations, and bankruptcy matters. In addition, he has been involved in numerous bank, thrift, and finance company restructurings. He has advised on highly leveraged bond transactions, including procedures to assure legal compliance, and as counsel in proceedings to unwind and reorganize highly leveraged issuers.

In addition to his numerous publications (listed below), he was the contributing author for legal issues affecting AU Section 9336 published in October 2001 by the Auditing Standards Board of the American Institute of Certified Public Accountants. The audit guidance applies to any legal opinion that may be required to support accounting sale treatment for the transfer of financial assets by U.S. firms. Mr. Feldkamp has also given numerous speeches on U.S. securitization issues for the American Law Institute, the World Bank, the People's Republic of China, and for banks, investment banks, and banking and other regulatory groups in the United States and in countries throughout Asia.

Mr. Feldkamp was peer review rated as AV Preeminent, the highest performance rating in Martindale-Hubbell's peer review rating system, and was named one of the leading lawyers in Illinois by the *Leading Lawyers Network*. He was also included on the list of 2006 Michigan super lawyers by Law & Politics Media for his work in banking and on worldwide lists of leading financial lawyers.

Mr. Feldkamp graduated from the University of Michigan (JD, magna cum laude, Order of the Coif, 1971; AB, economics, with distinction, 1968) and was a student fellow with the Research Seminar in Quantitative Economics. He was the legal profession representative invited to serve on the FASB 140 Audit Issues Task Force of the American Institute of Certified Public Accountants.

Publications

Author

- "The US Markets Today: A Moment for Celebration and Reflection," *2006 Global Securitization Guide* (supplement to *Securitization News*), June 2006
- "The March 2005 Market Crisis: A Re-pricing Event, a Reaction to Rising Rates or Re-emerging Volatility of an Accounting Debacle?" *Global Securitisation and Structured Finance Guide 2005*, Globe White Page Ltd., sponsored by Deutsche Bank, April 2005
- "Credit Monopolies Harm Lenders and Borrowers," *2004 Guide to Structured Finance* (supplement to *International Financial Law Review*), July 2004
- "Ending Monopoly," *ISR Legal Guide to Securitisation, International Securitisation Report*, July 2004
- "Removing the 'D' from off-balance sheet—FIN 46 and Statement 140," *Structured Finance Yearbook 2003* (supplement to *International Financial Law Review*), October 2003

- "Who Let the Bears Kill Goldilocks?" *Futures & Derivatives Law Report* 23, no. 5 (July/August 2003)
- "The New 2003 American Securitization Model: Isolation and Risk Diversification," *Structured Finance Yearbook 2002* (supplement to *International Financial Law Review*), October 2002
- "From Depression to Prosperity, but Not Back: U.S. Debt Trading Market Reform," *ISR Legal Guide to Securitisation, International Securitisation Report*, July 2002
- "Saving Private Intermediation," *Structured Finance Yearbook 2001* (supplement to *International Financial Law Review*), October 2001
- "U.S. Developments: Protecting Goldilocks from the Bears," *ISR Legal Guide to Securitisation, International Securitisation Report*, July 2001
- "Asset Securitization: The Alchemist's Dream," *Securitization Yearbook 2000* (supplement to *International Financial Law Review*), September 2000
- "U.S. Developments: What Is Menacing the Virtuous Economy?" *The ISR Legal Guide to Securitisation, International Securitisation Report*, July 2000
- "Securitization Developments: United States—It's Moving the Cash Flow—Stupid," *Securitization Yearbook 1999* (supplement to *International Financial Law Review*), September 1999

Coauthor

- *The Law and Economics of Financial Markets: Lessons of History That Assure Success in the Future* (Boston: Aspatore, 2005)
- "Rethinking the Role of Recourse in the Sale of Financial Assets," *Business Lawyer* 52, no. 1 (November 1996)

RICHARD CHRISTOPHER WHALEN

Christopher is an investment banker and author who lives in New York. He is Senior Managing Director and Head of Research at Kroll Bond Rating Agency (www.kbra.com), where he is responsible for financial institution and corporate credit ratings. Over the past three decades, he has worked for financial firms such as Bear, Stearns & Co., Prudential Securities, Tangent Capital Partners, and Carrington. He was a cofounder of Institutional Risk Analytics and was a principal there from 2003 through 2013, when the firm was acquired by Total Bank Solutions.

Christopher is the author of *Inflated: How Money and Debt Built the American Dream* (Hoboken, NJ: John Wiley & Sons, 2010), now in its second printing.

Christopher is a member of the advisory board of Weiss Residential Research in Natick, Massachusetts (www.weissres.com). He is a fellow of the Networks Financial Institute at Indiana State University. Christopher is a member of the Finance Department Advisory Council at the Villanova School of Business and a member of the Economic Advisory Committee of the Financial Industry Regulatory Authority (FINRA).

Christopher is a member of the National Association of Business Economists. He is a member of Professional Risk Managers International Association (www.prmia.org) and was regional director of PRMIA's Washington, DC, chapter from 2006 through January 2010.

Christopher contributes articles to publications such as *Zero Hedge, American Banker, Housing Wire*, and the *National Interest*. Christopher has testified before Congress, the Securities and Exchange Commission, and the Federal Deposit Insurance Corporation on a range of financial, economic, and political issues. He appears regularly on such media outlets as CNBC, Bloomberg Television, Fox News, and Business News Network. He is active in social media under the Twitter handle @rcwhalen.

A partial listing of his speeches, articles, and interviews is available online at www.rcwhalen.com.

Index